Emerging
Land and Housing Markets
in China

Emerging Land and Housing Markets in China

Edited by

Chengri Ding and Yan Song

Lincoln Institute of Land Policy
Cambridge, Massachusetts

Library of Congress Cataloging-in-Publication Data

Emerging land and housing markets in China / edited by Chengri Ding
and Yan Song.
    p. cm.
  Includes bibliographical references and index.
ISBN 1–55844–156–5 (alk. paper)
1. Land reform—China. 2. Housing policy—China. 3. China—
Economic conditions. I. Ding, Chengri. II. Song, Yan, 1973–
HD1333.C6E44 2005
333.3'151—dc22   2004025928

Project management: Ann LeRoyer, Lincoln Institute of Land Policy
Copyediting: Debra Simes, wordslinger.net
Design and production: David Gerratt and Amanda Wait, NonprofitDesign.com
Cover photo: Getty Images
Printing: Webcom Ltd., Toronto, Ontario, Canada. Printed on 100% recycled paper.

Contents

Housing Policy Reform

Foreword

The very title of this book — *Emerging Land and Housing Markets in China* — reflects an important strategic change in China's recent history. Since 1949 China has pursued a centrally planned economy and for many years was reluctant to inject market mechanisms into its policy framework because of debates over socialist orthodoxy or other political issues. Today much has changed. The program of economic reforms announced in 1978 initiated a new, market-oriented campaign, and in the early 1980s the Chinese government launched sweeping changes in the institutional structures that govern land and housing allocation. While maintaining the fundamental features of a socialist society, including state or collective ownership of land, China has moved toward a system in which market forces shape the process of urbanization and individuals have greater choice about where they work and live. As an overlay to these efforts, China has had successes on several fronts, including the establishment of land and housing markets, but also faces an array of emerging issues. This volume reflects on the achievements of China's land and housing policy reforms and rededicates our efforts to addressing new challenges.

The Lincoln Institute of Land Policy is committed to supporting and disseminating new research on China's land and housing policy. As early as July 2001, the Institute sponsored sessions on China's land and housing reforms at the World Planning Congress in Shanghai, inviting speakers from both academia and the policy community to participate in the discourse. In 2003 the Institute established its new Program on the People's Republic of China in its Department of International Studies. Led by Dr. Chengri Ding, this program contributes to the implementation of China's land and housing policy by sponsoring educational and training programs for Chinese public officials and practitioners, and by supporting research and publications by both international and Chinese scholars.

This book represents our efforts to uncover and examine the economic, social and political impacts of recent changes in China's land and housing policies. The chapters — by leading urban scholars, economists, sociologists and consultants in regional development and municipal administrative reform — constitute an historical review of land and housing reforms and an evaluation of their accomplishments and flaws. These analyses identify profound changes, provoke our thinking about their meaning and provide context for understanding a nation that is breaking new ground on many fronts.

I am very pleased that the Lincoln Institute has been able to support the editors and authors of this important work. This volume will contribute to engagement and dialogue with policy makers and scholars interested in Chinese land and housing studies. It is difficult to imagine a place and time in which the resources of the Lincoln Institute could be more influential and help more people than in this realm — the evolution of China's land and housing markets and management at the beginning of the twenty-first century.

H. James Brown
President and Chief Executive Officer
Lincoln Institute of Land Policy

Preface

The magnitude of change in China provides a broad platform from which to conduct policy studies and offers a unique opportunity to examine various policy instruments. Knowing that China would hold the first World Planning Congress in Shanghai in July 2001, Gerrit Knaap and Chengri Ding, both then at the University of Illinois at Urbana-Champaign, proposed to Rosalind Greenstein, senior fellow at the Lincoln Institute, that they organize sessions at the Congress to explore the possibility of conducting research in China. Knaap and Ding received funding in 1999 to organize two conference sessions at the 2001 Congress: one on land policy and the other on housing studies. In Hong Kong in 2000 they met with Anthony Yeh, who provided valuable advice on how to proceed with this work. That fall, Knaap and Ding solicited participants to contribute papers for the two sessions at the Congress; most of those papers are included in this volume.

The development of *Emerging Land and Housing Markets in China* could not have been accomplished without the indispensable support of the Lincoln Institute in its sponsorship of the 2001 Shanghai conference sessions on China's land and housing policy reform. We would like to thank all of the participants in this project for their rich contributions and enthusiastic participation, and are especially grateful for comments made by Michael Leaf and John Logan at that conference. We have been most fortunate to have extensive support from H. James Brown, president and CEO of the Lincoln Institute. We owe a great debt, of course, to our mentor, Dr. Gerrit Knaap, now executive director of the National Center for Smart Growth Research and Education at the University of Maryland. The crafting of this volume would not have been possible without his help. Finally, we wish to thank editors Ann LeRoyer and Debra Simes for helping us communicate our ideas more effectively.

Contributors

Nelson Chan
School of Construction,
    Property and Planning
College of Law and Business
University of Western Sydney
Penrith South DC
New South Wales, Australia
n.chan@uws.edu.au

Chengri Ding
Chinese Land Policy Program
National Center for Smart Growth
University of Maryland
College Park, Maryland
cding@umd.edu

Samuel P. S. Ho
Centre for Chinese Research
Institute of Asian Research
University of British Columbia
Vancouver, Canada
paosan@interchange.ubc.ca

Gerrit Knaap
National Center for Smart Growth
University of Maryland
College Park, Maryland
gknaap@ursp.umd.edu

Yanru Li
Urban and Environmental
    Science Department
Peking University
Beijing
lee_yanru@sina.com

George C. S. Lin
Department of Geography
University of Hong Kong
Hong Kong
gcslin@hkucc.hku.hk

Sing-cheong Liu
Pearl River-Hang Cheong
    Real Estate Consultants, Ltd.
Guangzhou World Trade Center
Guangzhou
scliu@prhc.com.cn

John R. Logan
Department of Sociology
Brown University
Providence, Rhode Island
John_Logan@Brown.edu

Xiaochen Meng
Urban and Environmental
    Science Department
Peking University
Beijing
xcm@urban.pku.edu.cn

Yan Song
Department of City and
    Regional Planning
College of Arts and Sciences
University of North Carolina
    at Chapel Hill
Chapel Hill, North Carolina
ys@email.unc.edu

Bo-sin Tang
Department of Building and
    Real Estate
Faculty of Construction and
    Land Use
Hong Kong Polytechnic University
Hong Kong
bsbstang@polyu.edu.hk

William Valletta
Somerville, Massachusetts
wvalletta@aol.com

Anthony Gar-on Yeh
Centre of Urban Planning and
    Environmental Management
University of Hong Kong
Hong Kong
hdxugoy@hkucc.hku.hk

Xing Quan Zhang
School of Design & Environment
National University of Singapore
Singapore
rstzxq@nus.edu.sg

Introduction

CHENGRI DING AND YAN SONG

The "open-door" policy adopted by China's central government in 1978 marked the beginning of a series of economic reforms that have sparked profound socioeconomic transformations — including land and housing policy reforms that are altering urban and rural landscapes throughout the country.

Land and housing policies are of fundamental importance to sustainable economic growth and the well-being of the population. Therefore, research on land and housing policy reform has long been of interest to many academic institutions around the world. China's reform efforts have been considered a successful example of addressing land and housing policy issues, and a careful analysis of these reform mechanisms may pertain to other countries. The results of research on China's reforms have not yet been documented comprehensively, but it is possible to address the following areas: an examination of the impacts of reforms on urban development, resource management and quality of life; an historical policy review to support understanding of both accomplishments and flaws in the reforms; and proposals of innovative measures to address problems and issues that remain.

This book organizes the results of current research on China's land and housing policy reforms in a way that is accessible to a wide audience of decision makers, nongovernmental organizations and academics around the world; it is one of the few records of this kind available in English. Most of the chapters are based on the proceedings of sessions sponsored by the Lincoln Institute of Land Policy at the World Planning Congress held in Shanghai, China in July 2001. The chapters have been edited and updated to incorporate a review of the history of China's reforms, evaluations of the present situation and outlooks on the future.

Land Policy Reform

Chapter 1. Chengri Ding and Gerrit Knaap offer an historical context for understanding China's land policy reforms. They investigate the impacts of Chinese land use policies on urban development; summarize issues and challenges arising from the reforms; lay out challenges to future reform efforts; and encourage more studies, especially empirical analyses, to address those challenges.

Chapter 2. Anthony Yeh examines the new land development process known as the dual land market, caused by the overlay of the new land allocation system on the old. Yeh argues that, although the new land leasing system holds the promise of more efficient land use and a badly needed revenue stream for governments, in practice it has created a black market and led to unregulated land use changes. Further, he identifies how the land leasing system has spawned a new urban form, and endorses three goals in remedying the problems of the dual land market.

Chapter 3. William Valletta assesses the impacts of the 1998 Land Administration Law on land use, land allocation and urban development. He begins with a review of pre-1998 land laws, identifying some issues that previous laws have failed to deal with and the mechanisms the 1998 law uses to address them. In evaluating the impacts of that law, Valletta finds some evidence of strengthened farmland protection and improved planning and enforcement, but argues that the legislation failed to solve many of the intrinsic problems of the dual land market system. He concludes that a more attentive land use planning law — one that requires public scrutiny in land use decisions — is critical to the effort to balance economic growth with environmental protection and farmland preservation.

Chapter 4. George Lin and Samuel Ho analyze land use changes since 1949 by examining data from the 1996 national land survey. They highlight the importance of efficient use of limited land resources, given the current trajectory of growth and urbanization. The authors question the efficacy of China's current approach to maintaining a "dynamic equilibrium of farmland," and express skepticism about the impacts of this approach on land productivity, food grain production and the environment. Asserting that further reduction of China's cultivated land is an inevitable trend, they challenge the conventional wisdom that food security can be safeguarded only by the preservation of a fixed amount of farmland and propose a new approach that considers other important factors.

Chapter 5. Xiaochen Meng and Yanru Li focus on land acquisition and associated issues, such as property rights, income distribution effects, social structure and urban development, through two representative case studies: the Shangdi Information Technology (IT) industrial zone of Beijing and the Special Economic Development Zone (SEDZ) of Shenzhen. They identify two key problems with the land acquisi- tion approach in Shangdi: proliferation of illegal settlements in the urban fringe and increasing resistance from farmers. They describe the Shenzhen problems as the emergence of uncoordinated village sprawl, confusion among farmers about the implications of land ownership versus land use rights, and farmers' reluctance to accept assigned jobs from the government. As a remedy, Meng and Li propose an innovative land acquisition strategy that would "change peasants into shareholders."

Chapter 6. Nelson Chan explores the practice of increasing land supply for urban development through compulsory land acquisition, and notes his concerns about that approach: the high cost of development through land acquisition and the lack of transparency in the determination of compensation. His proposed solution to the problem of balancing the demand for land for urbanization and the considerable pressure to preserve farmland is to redevelop China's considerable brownfields acreage. Chan concludes that contaminated sites can be remediated for different land uses (and at varying costs), depending on location, site characteristics, underlying market conditions and seriousness of contamination.

Housing Policy Reform

Chapter 7. Yan Song, Gerrit Knaap and Chengri Ding provide a review of urban housing policy during four periods in China's recent history: 1949–1956, marked by a central government-controlled market from which private ownership and speculative building were eliminated; 1957–1976, during which an urban housing system was conceived as a fundamental element of socialist welfare and ideology; 1978–1989, characterized by a market favoring private ownership and relaxed government control; and the period since 1990, distinguished by a full commodification of the urban housing market. They point out that significant progress has been made in the expansion of the housing supply since China's determination that the long-term objective of housing reform would be the introduction of a market system through privatization. The authors describe that privatization process as incomplete, slow and fitful, however, and identify its attendant problems. They conclude that, as one integral part of a more comprehensive economic reform in a social context, housing market privatization inevitably faces many challenges.

Chapter 8. Xing Quan Zhang focuses on housing market development after the mid-1990s, citing several of its characteristics: increased local (rather than central) government control; greater autonomy of work units; rapid expansion of the commercial development sector and of financing institutions; and extensive suburbanization. His evaluation of the most recent challenges in the Chinese housing market notes an intensified problem of housing affordability; inappropriate housing subsidies that distort the housing market; an increased vacancy rate for newly developed properties; and inflated housing prices and housing standards. Zhang argues that the extensive involvement of work units in the housing market has distorted the price mechanism; speculation and unreasonable taxes and charges on commercial housing development have contributed to high housing prices; and the irrational behavior of many state-owned real estate developers has worsened the imbalance between producers and consumers.

Chapter 9. Bo-sin Tang and Sing-cheong Liu examine the behavior and performance of property developers in China. Specifically, they explore the strategies of three categories of developers — state-owned developers, Hong Kong-based developers and local private developers — to examine their operational constraints and explain their behavioral outcomes. The authors review the roles of four key forces that have emerged: land leasing, commercialization of housing units, enterprise reforms and municipality-based, comprehensive urban development. They then explain the relative successes and shortcomings of the different kinds of property developers through their respective business strategies and cultures.

Chapter 10. John Logan examines the performance of housing markets in China from a different perspective: that of equity. He argues that, although market reforms have markedly improved the standard of living for many Chinese, there is also evidence of growing inequality in many dimensions of urban life. Through an empirical analysis based on the city of Tianjin, he reviews features of both spatial inequality and income inequity. Logan expresses his concern about the impacts on social justice of two powerful trends — suburbanization and the urban renewal and redevelopment of inner-city areas — arguing that these trends will accentuate uneven development in the near future.

Conclusion

In offering extensive insight into the complexities of China's land and housing markets, these chapters reveal the presence of multiple markets and institutional imperfections in the Chinese system. These complexities affect the implementation of land and housing policy reforms through the interplay of supply and demand in a given market and, perhaps more significantly, through irrational bureaucratic behaviors, capricious political interference and other noneconomic constraints. Policy makers, therefore, need to take these imperfections and the presence of self-interested actors into account when making policy recommendations. As the government honors its commitment to carry out a range of thorough socioeconomic reforms, this book makes its contribution by providing an historic review of land

and housing reform policies; a comprehensive examination of the impacts of those policies on urban development, resource management and quality of life; and examples of innovative approaches to remedying the problems associated with current land and housing policies. This volume is intended to stimulate discussion, thereby eliciting a more vigorous exchange of ideas and policy recommendations among those engaged in research or practice in China's land and housing markets.

Land Policy Reform

Urban Land Policy Reform in China's Transitional Economy

CHENGRI DING AND GERRIT KNAAP

The People's Republic of China has achieved remarkable progress in socioeconomic advancement and in political and administrative reforms during the quarter century since 1978. The twin engines of policy reform and unprecedented economic growth have spurred dramatic changes in land development. Alongside fundamental economic changes aimed at a gradual remodeling of the Chinese system as a free market economy, government has carried out an extensive program of land policy reform. With the many positive outcomes associated with these renovations have come problems that are best understood in an historical context. Hence, this chapter provides an overview of land policy prior to 1978 and policy changes since that time. It evaluates the socioeconomic impacts of reform, summarizes issues and challenges faced by policy makers in China's transitional economy, and concludes with a summary of findings and an agenda for future research.

Land Policy: 1949–1978

This section offers a picture of the infrastructure and dynamics of land policy in pre-reform China by reviewing issues of land ownership, land allocation, land supply, land development and spatial land use patterns.

Land Ownership

Before 1949, land was privately owned and could be transferred legally through mutual agreement. A household's wealth corresponded closely to the amount of land it possessed. After taking over the country in 1949, the Communist Party immediately launched a land reform called *tugai*, with the goal of reducing or eliminating social inequality. This was accomplished by confiscating land from the rich (landlords) and redistributing it to the poor. Later, China initiated a series of political movements such as the "big leap" (*dayuejin*) and "people commune" (*ren min gong she*).[1] In rural areas, peasants joined communes ("production coop-erations") by donating their assets, including land and large production materials that had been distributed to them under the previous land reform (*tugai*). This led to the formation of a collectively owned land system that has not been changed since. In urban areas, the state simply confiscated land and declared state ownership. By 1958, land in cities and towns was generally state owned whereas farmland was collectively owned (Yang and Wu 1996; Zhang 1997; Zhao, Bao, and Hou 1998).[2] Private land ownership virtually disappeared and the Chinese Constitution banned land transactions. Thus, land markets vanished and land neither was a commodity nor had value attached to it.

Land Allocation

In urban areas, the state owned the land and allocated it — through the issuance of land use rights — to socioeconomic units, called *danweis*, free of charge for an infi-nite period of time. A danwei was a basic unit of social fabric that functioned dually: as an administrative structure for organizing the society and the economy, and as a political tool for inculcating the socialist collective ethic. A danwei was responsible for both production activities and housing of its members. Because these danweis were either state owned or collectively owned, land use rights and land ownership were legally inseparable. That is, the state owned the land, whereas danweis were granted land use rights for an infinite time period, but were not allowed to transfer land use rights to a third party. Although laws required that danweis should return unused land to the state, this seldom happened because land had no value and there were no economic incentives to return it. Land allocation depended largely on the political powers to whom a danwei was connected, as well as on the political atmosphere in which socioeconomic function and production were planned and organized (Wong and Zhao 1999; Li 1997).

Land Supply

Municipal governments increased their land supply through land acquisition, which meant a conversion of land ownership from collective to state ownership. The Con-stitution stipulated that municipal governments had to compensate farmers' losses. Because there were no land markets, peasants were instead compensated with a pack-age that included job offers (farmers would work for the enterprises established on the acquired land), housing compensation (resettlement fees), compensation for the loss of crops and attached belongings on the ground, and granting of an urban

---

1 The "people commune" movement was divided into three stages, referred to as primary production cooperation, advanced production cooperation and people commune.

2 There were exceptions, such as natural resources (e.g., forests, bodies of water, or minerals) that were owned by the state.

residency license (*hukou*). Although peasants were not paid market prices, they were willing to give their land to the state because, in exchange, they would be granted the hukous that made them eligible for the social welfare services — medical insurance, pension and retirement plans, high-quality schools and subsidized agricultural goods — that were available only to city residents.

Land Development

Under the central planning system, governments were in charge of establishing short-range (one-year) or middle-range (five-year) socioeconomic development plans that would lay out specific economic growth goals (measurable mainly by industrial outputs). After examining existing capacities, governments determined the level of capital investment and improvements required to achieve their socioeconomic goals. Land development was centered in project planning (*xiang mu gui hua*), a process in which land input was the last factor considered. This kind of practice was responsible for substantial amounts of unused land, particularly in industrial sites. These unused lots, obtained free of charge, later entered land markets, causing land market distortion and governments' loss of these state assets. The lack of a land registration system made it difficult to monitor land in administratively allocated parcels and to supervise land development.

Spatial Land Use Patterns and Land Use Structure

Empirical studies have shown an extreme concentration of population in Chinese city centers (Bertaud 1992). This pattern has allowed cities to function with a minimum of investment in urban infrastructure. The concomitant lack of exurban infrastructure helps explain the intensive settlement in central locations, and represents an obstacle in resettling households to the outskirts of cities. Features of this urban compactness include the low per capita consumption of floor space and the prominence of bicycle transportation. In the course of economic reforms, this pattern has not been challenged or changed. The high population density in cities may be seen by planners as a benefit rather than a problem because it not only helps to preserve farmland by preventing rapid urban encroachment into rural areas, but also reduces automobile traffic and commuting time.

During the pre-reform era, industrial use was traditionally one of the dominant land use categories in most Chinese cities, accounting for 20–30 percent of the land, including storage facilities (Ding 2003).[3] Residential use accounted for less than

---

3 Rapid urbanization and massive restructuring, particularly in cities like Beijing, have altered this pattern. The Beijing municipal government is launching a massive plan that will relocate industrial establishments to the outskirts of the city's urbanized area in order to improve the environment for the 2008 Olympic Games. As a result, industrial share is expected to decline dramatically. Few Chinese cities, however, are able to launch such a massive industrial relocation.

TABLE 1

Land Use in Major Chinese Cities by Type, 1991
(as percent of total land use)

	Residences	Industry	Infrastructure[1]	Greenspace	Special Uses
Shanghai*	49.63	30.54	7.28	0	12.55
Beijing*	39.05	20.11	5.54	0	35.30
Tianjin	26.07	35.04	29.56	4.27	4.27
Guangzhou*	35.94	37.00	17.12	0	9.94
Shenzhen	59.86	22.12	14.09	3.02	0.42
Shenyang	29.56	27.95	23.80	6.89	11.79
Chongqing	34.04	33.41	26.99	3.12	5.44
Wuhan	26.84	30.38	24.96	7.00	8.75
Zhenzhou	25.51	28.26	37.76	7.89	0.57
Nanjing	36.79	23.08	9.55	1.85	28.73
Hangzhou	36.17	29.89	15.78	14.94	3.21
Kunming	28.69	23.06	38.47	3.08	6.70
Taiyuan	20.96	26.73	32.83	19.47	0
Xi'an	44.51	29.31	25.91	0.08	0.16
Harbin	38.01	26.34	26.61	6.64	1.84

*Shanghai, Beijing and Guangzhou did not survey greenspace.

NOTE:

1 Infrastructure includes public services, transportation, etc.

SOURCE: Nanjing Institute of Geography and Lake Study (1999)

50 percent of all urbanized land.[4] The share of industrial use in planned economy countries was more than twice that in industrialized countries (Bertaud and Renaud 1992). By comparison, industrial use accounted for only 4–10 percent of built-up areas in most market economy cities (Hong Kong: 5.3 percent, Seoul: 6 percent, and Paris: 5 percent) (Bertaud 1992).

China's land use patterns were consistent with its national policy, which, in the early stage of the Communist Party's regime, was set to achieve rapid industrial growth, even at the expense of other sectors such as agriculture and housing. Industrial goods were overpriced while agricultural goods were underpriced. This pricing difference, called *jia ge jian dao cha*, was administratively created and, at one time, influenced the whole nation with its propaganda of "*sheng chan di yi, sheng huo di er*" ("production first and living second"). Consequently, urbanization did not keep pace with industrialization at the rate that industrialized countries had experienced. This explained the substantial proportion of transient urban population that moved temporarily to wherever jobs were available. The housing and retail sectors were far behind industrial sectors, particularly heavy industry (Dowall 1993). In comparison to developed countries, land was overallocated to industry but underallocated to the housing sector. (For an overview of land use structure midway in the reform era, see Table 1, above.)

---

4 According to Li (1999, 20), residential land accounted for approximately 23 percent in Shanghai, for instance.

Land Policy Reform: 1978–Present

The primary, and compelling, reason for ongoing land policy reform in China is the increasing tension between land supply and the population's need for land, as illustrated through the following facts.

- Population density is high, particularly in eastern China. Henan province, for instance, has only 167,000 square kilometers (1/60 the area of the United States), but hosts a population of more than 100 million (more than 1/3 that of the U.S.).

- China feeds more than 20 percent of the world's population on less than 7 percent of the world's farmland. Its per capita farmland (1,167 square meters) is half of the world average (2,333 square meters).

- Land resources are extremely limited, compared with population. More than 20 percent of land (e.g., deserts and land covered by glaciers and/or snow) is unusable for any purpose; mountainous areas comprise another 30 percent of China's territory. In these areas, agricultural productivity is low, land development costs for urban uses are high and accessibility in general is low. All human activities — economic growth, infrastructure development, environmental and ecological protection, housing and recreation, etc. — demand and compete for land, creating pressure to manage and allocate land in efficient and effective ways.

Land use systems in China have evolved gradually during the last two decades to manage the competing pressures on land through improvement in land management and land use efficiency. Changes include the adoption of a system of land use rights, land use fees and taxation, farmland protection and regulations on urban growth (Liu and Yang 1990; Tang 1989; Zhang 1997).

Land Use Rights

The old land tenure system was first challenged when China adopted its famous "open-door" policy in 1978. The policy not only ended China's decades-long political isolation from the West, but also changed the political and economic environments. Since then, foreign direct investment and the number of joint ventures with foreign companies have increased exponentially. For instance, foreign direct investment totaled only $18.2 million in 1978, but increased to $452.6 million in 1997. The surge of foreign businesses challenged the land use tenure system by demanding access to land use rights (Jiang, Chen, and Isaac 1998). The old land allocation system also conflicted with the ultimate goal of economic reforms that attempted to introduce market mechanisms to improve economic efficiency, correct government failures in land allocation and minimize negative consequences of the land tenure system.

In the early stage of the Chinese transitional period, any effort to reform ownership would provoke vigorous political turmoil. Because public ownership had been the cornerstone of communism and socialism, efforts to change that system faced persistent political resistance from citizens and officials. China addressed this challenge by establishing "special economic development zones" (SEDZs) along its east-coast areas in the early 1980s to attract foreign investment.[5] In these zones, businesses and enterprises enjoyed special policies not available to other geographic areas.

These special policies included access to state-owned land through the separation of land use rights and land ownership (this developed into the land use rights system [LUR], discussed later) and economic development incentives such as tax exemption. The prototype of the LUR, similar to the land leasehold system in Hong Kong, was first developed to accommodate the needs of foreign direct investment. It allowed foreign investors to access land by leasing to them land use rights for a period of time, while the state retained ownership of the land. For this, investors had to pay lump-sum land use rights fees. This early reform in the land tenure system marked a new era of land use policy in modern Chinese history. For the first time, land use rights and land ownership were separable, although this practice was limited to the SEDZs.

Driven by the success of the SEDZs, the Chinese government passed the first Land Administration Law (LAL) in 1986 to institutionalize the LUR nationwide.[6] The 1986 law was at odds with the Chinese Constitution, which banned selling, leasing and transferring of land, so the Constitution was amended in 1988 to clear away any legal barriers to land market development. The 1988 amendment did not change land ownership, but allowed the free transfer of land use rights between land users. As a milestone in the evolution of the Chinese Constitution, the 1988 amendment is significant, because it allowed the state to maintain ownership and at the same time promoted land market development without provoking political turmoil.

To provide concrete legal guidance, in 1991 the State Council announced The Provisional Regulation on the Granting and Transferring of the Land Rights over State Owned Land in Cities and Towns (Provisional Regulation), which established two kinds of land transaction (Hu 1990). One defines the "first" level land market, wherein a municipal government, as a representative of the state, *sells* land use rights to buyers for a fixed period through auction, tender or negotiation. The *transfer* of land use rights defines the "second" level land market. In both markets, the price of

---

5 Initially, there were four special economic development zones: Shenzhen, Shantou, Xianmen and Tianjin. Later, the initiative included eight more, for a total of twelve SEDZs, which were the sites of many policy experiments. Critics of the program charged that it was policy advantages, rather than comparative advantages, that contributed to the rapid growth in these SEDZs. After more than 10 years, policy advantages enjoyed by these SEDZs vanished.

6 The original, 1986 Land Administration Law (LAL) was later amended (in 1988) and implemented in 1991; throughout this volume, this amended version is referred to as the 1988 LAL. Another, revised LAL was adopted in 1998 and implemented 1 January 1999. See Valletta, Chapter 3 in this volume, for more information on the evolution of China's land administration laws.

land use rights depends on land use type, location and density, and on neighborhood externalities. This approximates the way land prices are determined in Western countries, although in China land markets are far from mature (Ding 2003).

The state intends to control land markets through its monopolization of the first-level land markets (that is, through the monopolization of land supply), but is not involved in the transfer of land use rights except for land registration, legal protection and taxation (Liu and Xie 1994; Walker and Li, 1994; Liu and Yang 1990). According to the Provisional Regulation, sale of land use rights means the process by which the state, as landowner, sells land use rights to land users for a specific time period that varies from 40 to 70 years, depending on the types of land use.[7] The sale of land use rights takes the forms of negotiation, tender and auction. Municipal governments act as representatives of the state to sell land use rights and share land revenues with the state. Since land use rights prices vary with the different types of land use, the law requires that the price should be adjusted if the land use changes. To protect the state's land assets, the law mandates that municipal governments have the first rights to buy back land use rights if the price to transfer those rights is significantly below market price. The Provisional Regulation also stipulates that land users who obtain land free of charge through administrative allocation must pay land use taxes. The law prohibits the transfer, lease and mortgage of land use rights obtained free of charge through administrative allocation.[8]

In summary, the objectives and goals of land use rights reforms are to improve land management through land markets instead of administrative channels; improve land use efficiency; make land an important asset that has value attached to it; increase government revenues; manage supply and coordination of land development throughout the country; and preserve farmland and control of illegal conversion from farmland to urban land (Zou 1994).

Land Use Fees and Taxation

In 1989, the state passed the Provisional Act of Land Use Taxation on State Owned Urban Land, meant to improve and rationalize urban land use, adjust land rent differentials, improve land use efficiency and enhance land management.[9] According to the law, all work units (danweis) and individuals were obliged to pay land use taxes or fees if they used land in cities, towns, or industrial and mining districts. The

---

7 Terms for different uses include 70 years for residential use; 50 years for industrial use; 50 years for education, science and technology, cultural, health and sports uses; 40 years for commercial, tourist and recreation uses; and 50 years for other uses.

8 However, there are exceptions. If one of the following conditions is met, land acquired free of charge through administrative allocation can be transferred, leased and mortgaged. A land user must be a company, enterprise, economic entity or individual; have obtained a land use rights license for state-owned land; have legal documents of property ownership of structures and attachments on the property; and/or have paid land use rights prices according to regulations for land use rights selling of state-owned land.

9 A land use tax is also called a land use rights assignment tax.

rates of land use taxes depended on city size and land use types. Total land taxes or fees were calculated by multiplying the size of land parcels by the applicable tax rates. Land taxes and fees were neither differentiated spatially nor dependent on land values. Although land use fees or taxes generated revenue for governments, the proceeds were so minimal that they barely reflected land ownership.

In 1993, the state passed the Provisional Act of Land Value Increment Tax on State Owned Land. It specified that parties or individuals that transferred land use rights were the taxpayers. The act required taxpayers to pay a tax on increases in land value if their net profits from such transfer exceeded more than 20 percent of total costs (including land improvement costs, construction costs, management fees, and transaction fees and taxes). These tax rates were flat but progressive.

Benchmark Land Use Rights Price System

Immediately after the adoption of the LUR, the first real challenge faced by local scholars and officials was determining land prices. Lack of experience and market data made it very difficult. To overcome the problem, a benchmark land use rights price system was developed in the early 1990s to guide the granting and transfer-ring of land use rights (Hu 1990). Its four components are: a land use rights fee paid to the government; infrastructure costs paid to the government for land improve-ment; demolition costs; and land acquisition costs, in most cases paid to tenants either directly or indirectly (Zhang and Li 1997; Yang and Wu 1996; Li and Walker 1996; Ding, Knaap, and Wu 2000).

The formula for calculating the benchmark land price is expressed as:[10]

$$P = \alpha(R) \cdot F + R \cdot I + \beta \cdot D + A \qquad \text{(Equation 1)}$$

Where P = prices of land use rights per square meter;
  F = land use rights fee (see Table 2);
  α = floor-area adjustment coefficient (see Table 3);
  R = floor-area ratio;
  I = infrastructure cost;
  β = demolition adjustment coefficient, which is dependent on land uses;[11]
  D = demolition cost; and
  A = land acquisition cost.

---

10 See Ding, Knaap and Wu (2000) for a detailed discussion of the benchmark land use rights price system and the difference between "*Shu Di*" and "*Sheng Di*" prices. The former reflects developers' payments to governments for urban infrastructure that has been installed, whereas the latter reflects developers' provision of infrastructure, so that infrastructure costs are not a part of land prices but are included in total development costs.

11 β is set to 1, 2 and 4 for residential, enterprise and commercial development, respectively.

TABLE 2
Land Use Rights Fees by Land Grade and Land Use Type, 1996
(in 1,000 RMB)

Land Grade	Land Use Type			
	Commercial	Apartments	Residential	Industrial
1	3,200–5,400	3,000–4,600	2,000–2,700	320–540
2	2,400–3,200	2,200–3,000	1,500–2,000	240–320
3	2,000–2,400	1,800–2,200	1,000–1,500	180–240
4	1,500–2,000	1,400–1,800	800–1,000	140–180
5	1,000–1,500	1,000–1,400	600–800	100–140
6	500–1,000	500–1,000	400–600	70–100
7	400–500	300–500	150–400	30–70
8	70–400	70–300	50–150	25–30
9	50–70	40–70	30–50	20–25
10	45–50	30–40	20–30	15–20

SOURCE: China Land Newspaper (1996)

TABLE 3
Relationship Between Floor-Area
Adjustment Coefficient and Floor-Area Ratio

Adjustment Coefficient of Floor-Area Ratio

Floor-area ratio	<1	2	3	4	5	6	7	8	9	10
Floor-area adjustment coefficient	1	1.91	2.74	3.5	4.2	4.9	5.6	6.3	7	7.7

SOURCE: http://www.law999.net/law/doc/d001/1993/07/06/00035268.html

Clearly, Equation 1 states that land prices depend on land density (floor-area ratio), land grade and land use. Land is classified into 10 levels, or grades, depending on population density, economic and commercial activities, infrastructure and accessibility (Hu 1990). Land use rights fees depend on grades and land uses (see Table 2). The coefficient is determined by the floor-area ratio as illustrated in Table 3. Both parts of infrastructure costs — one for urban infrastructure and the other for community construction — are set as flat rates, as are both demolition and land acquisition costs.[12]

---

12 In Beijing, the rates for urban infrastructure range from 460 to 800 RMB, and for community construction from 150 to 400 RMB.

Farmland Protection

Rapid urban expansion has caused the fast depletion of farmland, particularly in the urban fringes where high-quality and productive land is located. Urbanized areas increased from 9,386 square kilometers in 1985 to 17,940 square kilometers in 1994, a 7.5 percent rate of annual growth.[13] A survey using satellite images, taken between 1986 and 1995, indicated that 31 large cities have expanded their urbanized areas by more than 50 percent (Li 1997). Between 1986 and 1995, farmland had lost more than 1,973,000 hectares to nonagricultural construction (State Statistical Bureau 1996), though some estimates indicate the actual number may have been 2.5 times higher (Li 1997). Although China is the third largest country in the world in terms of the size of its territory, its per capita farmland is well below the world average.

In his 1995 book and 1994 article by the same name — *Who Will Feed China?* — Lester Brown questioned the country's ability to feed its growing population in the twenty-first century. Brown believes that a severe shortage in food supply would not only drive up crop prices in the world market but also destabilize China. His thesis and the reality of rapid farmland loss (due to urban spatial encroachment into rural areas) have alarmed top Chinese officials. Seeing self-reliance in crops as critical to the nation's sovereignty and independence in international affairs, their response has been an elevation of that self-reliance to a top national policy priority, and, in turn, adoption of tough farmland protection measures.

The State Council passed the Basic Farmland Protection Regulation (BFPR) in 1994 to protect farmland so that China could begin to establish self-reliance in crops. The regulation prohibits basic farmland from conversion to nonagricultural activities, and mandates that counties and townships designate the basic farmland protection districts in accordance with provincial farmland preservation plans.[14] The basic farmland protection districts organize land at two levels. The first is high-quality farmland with high productivity; it cannot be converted to nonagricultural uses in the long term. The second level is good-quality farmland with moderate productivity; it cannot be converted to nonagricultural uses during the planned period (usually 5–10 years). The designation of basic farmland protection has to be approved by a higher-level authority and is protected by law.

The new 1998 LAL, implemented on January 1, 1999, may have far-reaching influences on land development and urban form. It intends to protect environmental

---

13 An investigation of 24 large cities indicated that from 1950 to 1980 urbanized area grew at a 3.4 percent annual rate, whereas the annual rate for urban population growth was 2.6 percent. The 1980–1995 rates of growth for urbanized area and population were 4.5 percent and 2.3 percent, respectively.

14 Basic farmland consists of agricultural production bases (such as crops, cotton, edible oils, and other high-quality agricultural products) approved by governments; farmland that has been in production, is highly productive and has good irrigation; vegetable production bases for large and mid-sized cities; and experimental fields for scientific and educational purposes.

and agricultural lands, to promote market development, to encourage citizen involvement in the legislative process and to coordinate the planning and development
of urban land. The law clearly defines the rights and responsibilities of citizens,
enterprises and governmental agencies (Valletta, this volume). Article 33 is the first
of two important regulations that may be most influential; it mandates no net loss
of cultivated land over time:

> People's governments of provinces, autonomous regions and municipalities directly
> under the Central Government should strictly implement the overall plans and
> annual plans for land utilization and take measures to ensure that the total amount
> of cultivated land within their administrative areas remains unreduced. Where
> the total amount of cultivated land is reduced, the State Council shall order the
> government concerned to reclaim land of the same quality and amount as is reduced
> within a time limit. . . . Where individual governments of provinces or municipalities
> directly under the Central Government, for lack of land reserves, can not reclaim
> enough land to make up for the cultivated land they used for additional construc-
> tion projects, they shall apply to the State Council for approval of their reclaiming
> less or not land within their own administrative areas but of their reclaiming land
> in other areas.

The demand for land will continue to rise due to urbanization, increasing
incomes and economic development. Given the fixed territory, the implication of
the article is that land development costs will rise exponentially. This will inevitably
slow the pace of urbanization and urban development unless other policies are introduced to counteract the negative impacts of this regulation.

Article 34 requires that capital farmland shall not be less than 80 percent of total
cultivated land in provinces, autonomous regions and municipalities directly under
the central government.[15] Articles 17–26 include the mechanisms and principles of
planning and implementing overall plans for land utilization. A comprehensive
scheme of urban development has been widely developed across Chinese cities in
order to provide appropriate means to achieve balanced development between society, economy and environment (Tang and Liu 2002). It requires that urban development be coordinated through planning to eliminate redundancy and duplicated
construction, rationalized in layouts so that land use is efficient, and provided with
sufficient infrastructure. It is, thus, expected that urban development patterns will
be different from those of the pre-reform period.

---

15 Protected capital farmland comprises: (1) cultivated land, within bases of grain, cotton and oil crops production,
    that is designated as such with the approval of the relevant departments either under the State Council, or
    of the people's governments at or above the county level; (2) cultivated land with good irrigation and water-
    and soil-conservation facilities, as well as medium- and low-yield fields that are either under improvement
    according to plan, or improvable; (3) vegetable production bases; (4) pilot fields for scientific research
    or teaching of agriculture; and (5) other cultivated land that should be designated as protected capital
    farmland, according to regulations of the State Council.

Land Acquisition

Both the Chinese Constitution and the 1998 LAL specify that the state, in the public interest, may lawfully requisition land owned by collectives. This sets the stage for compulsory land acquisition. Though both documents require that peasants' lives not be adversely affected by land acquisition, implementation of this requirement is difficult, in part because any measures of life changes for peasants are multi-faceted; income is just one of the dimensions.

The 1998 LAL further states that collective communes should be compensated when their land is requisitioned. Rather than being paid full "market" prices, communes are compensated through a package that includes three components: compensation for the land, resettlement subsidies and compensation for attachments to, and young crops on, the requisitioned land. The law stipulates that compensation for the requisition of cultivated land shall be 6–10 times the value of the average annual output of the acquired land for three years preceding such requisition. The size of resettlement subsidies depends on how many people live on the farmland, but each person's resettlement subsidy shall not exceed 6–10 times the value of the annual yield from the occupied farmland. For peasants to maintain their same standard of living, the local governments (provincial and city) may raise the resettlement subsidies, but the total compensation for land and resettlement subsidies cannot exceed 30 times the previous three-year average output value of the acquired land.

Urban Growth Policy

The 1980s saw great debates about how best to achieve urbanization. Despite a lack of empirical evidence, many scholars believed that problems such as congestion and environmental pollution seriously affected the well-being of urban residents and imposed high social costs. During the last two decades, the central government adopted a national policy that strictly controls the population growth of large cities (those with a population >0.5 million); promotes moderate growth of middle-sized cities (those with a population of 0.2–0.5 million); and actively develops small cities and towns (those with less than 0.2 million).[16]

---

16 Urbanization was achieved through three different means in China. The first is migration to urban areas, which stimulates housing demand and helps to form rental markets. The second approach expands existing urbanized areas by converting surrounding agricultural land to urban land uses. The third is the so-called "on site" urbanization, through which farmers become urban residents — without having to leave their land — by converting their villages into towns or cities. This third type of urbanization is obviously not "real" urbanization according to conventional definition since it involves neither career changes nor land development.

Land Policy Reform: Effects and Issues

Effects of Land Policy Reform

Land policy reform in China has resulted in outstanding positive effects on land development, government finance, real estate and housing development, infrastructure provision, urban growth and land use efficiency. The most significant impacts of the LUR may be its contribution to the emergence of land markets in China, and the introduction of price mechanisms to rationalize land use and allocation (Ding, Knaap, and Wu 2000; Xue 1994; Walker and Li 1994). For the first time in modern Chinese history, land has value and can produce economic wealth. Nationally, land sales slowly increased from only 5 lots in 1987 to 545 lots in 1991. Land markets showed a steep rise from 1992 to 1994: the total number of land transactions jumped to 2,800 in 1992, 42,076 in 1993, and 97,405 in 1994, respectively (see Table 4).

The reform period has also witnessed changes in spatial land use structures. Though capital density increased rapidly, population density changed little if any, unlike an increase in floor-area ratio. This is mainly because Chinese cities are overcrowded, particularly in city centers, and socioeconomic development contributes to rising consumption of floor space per capita. Another trend is the reduction of industry and warehousing in central locations and the rising share of commercial and office space. However, by international standards, the industrial segment of Chinese cities still is large, comprising 20–40 percent of built-up areas, as compared with 6–10 percent in industrialized countries.

The impacts on municipal governments of the sale of land use rights are numerous. These transactions account for 25–50 percent of cities' revenues. For example, in Guanghai, in Sichuan Province, sale of land use rights generated 25 percent of

TABLE 4

Land Transactions in China, 1987–1996

Year	Number of Lots	Area (ha)	Value (million RMB)	Price per Sq. M. (RMB)	Average Area per Transaction (sq. m.)	Price per Lot (million RMB)
1987	5	15.7	35.2	223.5	31,460.0	7.0
1988	118	389.1	416.2	107.0	32,972.9	3.5
1989	127	625.2	447.2	71.5	49,229.9	3.5
1990	482	948.2	1,052.0	110.9	19,672.2	2.2
1991	545	1,036.1	1,136.9	109.7	19,011.6	2.1
1992	2,800	2,189.0	52,500.0	2,390.8	7,817.9	18.8
1993	42,076	3,822.5	40,529.3	1,060.3	908.5	1.0
1994	97,405	3,295.5	35,928.5	1,090.2	338.3	0.4
1995	105,473	2,872.8	33,285.7	1,158.7	272.4	0.3
1996	103,921	2,269.9	29,048.4	1,279.7	218.4	0.3

SOURCES: Yang and Wu (1996); and State Statistical Bureau (1990–1996)

the city's total revenues in 1994. Dunhuang, in Gansu Province, earns more than
40 percent of its revenues from the sale of land use rights. Shanghai has collected
more than 10 billion RMB annually since 1992, and Guangzhou Province has realized more than 20.5 billion RMB from the sale of land use rights (Yang and Wu
1996). Local governments' revenues will be multiplied if indirect impacts of land
development, such as employment, and backward and forward linkages, are taken
into account. Extra or off-budget revenues enable local governments to conduct
large-scale infrastructure provision and neighborhood redevelopment. This is
particularly important in city cores where there are many unsafe houses and
insufficient infrastructure (Zhu 1999; Yeh and Wu 1996; Li 1992). Fuzhou, for
instance, collected 2 billion RMB from the sale of land use rights between 1987 and
1993, and used the funds to construct urban infrastructure and housing. It raised
per capita housing consumption from 3.98 square meters in 1980 to 8.2 square
meters in 1993. The proportion of houses with all utilities (gas, electricity, sewer,
water and telephone) increased from 24.43 percent in 1985 to 53.85 percent in
1993 (Yang and Wu 1996).

Issues of Land Policy Reform

Despite the many positive outcomes associated with land policy reform, problems
persist.

Property Rights. Even though the state owns all urban land, the Constitution is
unclear about who represents the state, what constitutes the local government role
in land management, and what rights are assigned to the state entities that actually
occupy land. These uncertainties pose great challenges to land management, land
development monitoring and implementation of land use plans. In addition, the legal
ambiguities of land rights for communes and farmers in rural areas have left farmers unprotected in cases of land development and compulsory land acquisition.

Land Management, Development and Planning. The ambiguities in land rights
lead to confusion and malfunction in land management. First, there are many different government agencies involved — or interfering — with land use and land
development decisions. Sales through the open tender and bidding process account
for only 10–20 percent of all land use rights sales. The majority of the transactions
of land use rights happen through negotiation, which makes it difficult to implement comprehensive land use plans. Second, there is an urgent need to develop
management capacity to cope with issues arising from the development of free markets. For instance, five-year land use plans in many cities cannot provide development guidance — in part because their rigor makes them somewhat inflexible in
dealing with rapid urban development, and in part because administrative systems

have not yet accommodated to the evolution from a planned to a market system, as evidenced by the absence of economic analysis from many comprehensive land use plans.

The revenue-sharing agreement between the local and central governments is blamed for problems such as chaotic and uncoordinated development, an out-of-control, first-level land market and redundant delineation of economic development zones or districts. Local government officials, interested in raising revenue, sell land use rights beyond the levels of municipal need, demand in-kind contributions that actually reduce the central government shares, and exchange land for other commodities such as houses. These overzealous practices yield profound, negative, long-term consequences. First, the revenue-sharing scheme encourages local governments to sell as much land as possible for their own political purposes, leaving less and less land available for future governments' needs. This creates the second problem: how to generate revenue for public services and infrastructure provision if land has been sold out? In some cities, the revenues from the sales of land use rights account for 20 percent of the total budgets that cities can use to finance development. Finally, without land or property taxes, Chinese governments are not able to capture increases in value over time in the framework of a long-term leasehold system. The potential revenue losses will be enormous.

The farmland protection effort has many negative effects on urban development. It explains, in part, new development patterns in southern China, where "every village looks like a city" and "every city is a village." This describes a phenomenon wherein development makes farmers rich, and they in turn build modern houses. Since these modern houses are separated by other farms and are not served by public infrastructure, such new developments look modern at the micro level but chaotic at the macro level. The BFPR tends to create urban villages that are surrounded by urbanized areas when quality farmland is located in fast-growing urban fringes and the law forcefully pushes economic activities further out, leaving farmland in between. Urban sprawl can then result, increasing transportation costs and generating negative externalities.

Hidden Land Markets. Hidden or invisible land markets are very active across Chinese cities, particularly in those with rapidly changing economic development areas. The common forms of these hidden land markets are (Yang and Wu 1996):
- transfer of land use rights through housing sales and rents;
- rental or sale of unused land that was obtained free of charge;
- transfer of land use rights in exchange for housing and other commodities;
- acquisition of stock shares by granting of land use rights; and
- transfer of land use rights through mortgage, merger and restructuring of state-owned enterprises.

Huge profits provide economic incentive for illegal land transactions, while loop-holes in land regulations and laws encourage people to take risks without the worry of getting caught. The coexistence of land allocation systems creates the so-called "double-track" system when the LUR is adopted and at the same time the old land tenure system is still in effect. This results in two ways to obtain land use rights: one is to obtain them without payment, and the other is to buy them from the state or other parties (see Figure 1).

These hidden markets have caused substantial revenue losses to state and local governments, adversely affecting urban development under the guidelines of urban comprehensive plans. They have increased social inequality and corruption, triggered land opportunism and distorted land markets. Both Fushun and Chongqi lost 13 million RMB from land revenues in 1990 (Yang and Wu 1996). Invisible land markets cause distortions so that land prices may not fully reflect market conditions (Ding, Knaap, and Wu 2000; Li and Walker 1996). However, the inability to implement land regulations and control land markets, and the lack of a land registration system, make it difficult to estimate accurately the impacts of hidden land markets on urban land development.

Rising Land Development Costs. Land policy reforms have made land an expensive input for developers. Both the BFPR and the 1998 LAL protect farmland in

---

FIGURE 1
The "Double-Track" Land Allocation System

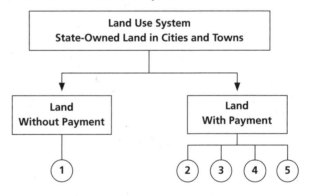

(1) = land use rights granting through administrative allocation (free of charge)

(2) = land use rights granting through administrative allocation (land use
         fees are required)

(3) = land use rights granting through administrative allocation (land users
         are required to pay for land use rights)

(4) = land use rights sale (through tender, negotiation or auction)

(5) = land use rights transfer

order to maintain self-reliance in crops. The laws have achieved their designated goals well, but have also yielded negative impacts on urban land use and urban development. In Beijing, for instance, land costs account for 30–40 percent of total land development costs if the development occurs on farmland. Land costs consist of the prices of land use rights, resettlement of farmers and compensation for agricultural losses, and are approximately equal to construction costs. Land costs, however, can reach 60 percent of total land development costs if development is located in existing urban areas where developers have to resolve resettlement agreement issues with tenants, who can be very demanding and, for instance, refuse to move out unless they are satisfied. Thus, resettlement of tenants can be one of the greatest challenges for developers, and can, along with demolition costs, represent a significant cost component.

Alternatively, developers have aggressively sought cheap land in urban fringes, and cities have rapidly encroached into farmland during the past two decades. The 1998 LAL, however, mandates that developers should be responsible for farmland depletion resulting from their development, and should make up for the farmland losses. Thus, another item, farmland reclamation costs, is added to the cost of land development. Given that political territory is fixed, exploitable land will deplete faster and marginal costs of exploitation will rise exponentially over time. This inevitably makes horizontal land development (urban spatial expansion) more and more difficult and slows down urban development.

Issues in Land Acquisition. Governments are ill equipped to address the issues that have emerged from land acquisition because of lack of preparedness and time lags in legal, institutional and policy responses to rapid change. The first problematic issue in land acquisition is related to the ill-defined concepts of property rights and development rights: who is entitled or empowered to acquire land from peasants for urban development? By law, any entity — including the state, the state's representatives (e.g., provincial, city and county governments, or danweis), or even individuals — that justifies a project as being "in the public interest" may carry out compulsory land acquisition, even though the project may be commercial housing and development, an industrial park (which can attract private investment), or entertainment related (e.g., a golf course), to name only a few examples not genuinely "in the public interest."

This multiparty involvement in compulsory land acquisition has arisen via both societal evolution and an ill-defined legal concept of public interest. For instance, it has been difficult to separate the interests of firms from those of the public because many firms, particularly in cities, were owned by the state. As economic reform and development significantly diminish the roles of the state-owned enterprises, Chinese law will need to reexamine the concepts and definitions of public interest and public projects.

The multitude of players in the land acquisition process has led to widespread patterns of uncoordinated and chaotic urban development and has undercut urban planning efforts. Two urban phenomena stand out. One is the extremely close-set buildings — so close that people can "kiss" each other from the windows of neighboring buildings. Passage between them is so narrow that police, fire, and garbage collection vehicles cannot gain access to the buildings. The other phenomenon is the so-called "*cheng zhong chun*," or village located in the middle of a city. This pattern not only makes a city look unattractive, but also interrupts important urban economic, social and cultural functions. With these patterns, both transportation costs and externalities arising from incompatible land uses will increase substantially.

The second problem is the matter of who is entitled to compensation when land is acquired. The village commune is the basic socioeconomic organization in rural areas. The commune's largest, if not only, asset is the land that is collectively owned by its members. On that basis, both a village commune and its members are entitled to share compensation. The money retained by the village commune is supposed to finance projects and/or causes that benefit all of its members, such as irrigation or village-owned enterprises. Without adequate accounting and auditing systems at the village commune level, however, compensation retained by the village commune committee is widely abused and becomes a source of corruption. To make matters worse, different levels of governments (e.g., township, country and city) each take a cut of the monetary compensation given to farmers who lose their land. Farmers eventually may receive less than one-third of the compensation specified by the 1998 LAL.

For instance, China built a natural gas pipeline from the western to the eastern part of the country. It was a national project, so compensation to peasants was paid by the state, but compensation amounts varied with the different states of economic development of provinces. For example, the state gave 20,000 RMB per *mu* to peasants in Henan province for their land. Given the fiscal structures between governments, these monies were allocated downward to lower levels of government (from the state to province, city, country and township, respectively). At each level, a portion was retained for government use in financing public goods and services. Peasants received only 5,000 RMB in the end.

This practice is rationalized in the principle of value capture, which would hold that because the peasants did nothing to create increased value in the land, they are not particularly entitled to any value increment at its sale. What constitutes a fair division of compensation (into the peasant's share and the government's value-capturing share) is a legitimate question to which there is not yet a satisfactory answer. Certainly, more research will be conducted to address it. The low number of complaints by peasants suggests that their share is sufficient, at least to maintain their living standards, which is one of the legal requirements.

The third issue centers on fairness of compensation — involving both adequacy of compensation and variation in compensation. The 1998 LAL set both a floor and a ceiling for land acquisition compensation. Since there are no market data that can truly reflect the price of farmland, compensation hardly reflects market conditions and varies dramatically from case to case, depending mainly on who plans to develop the land. For instance, profitable projects such as commercial housing and development can afford higher prices for land than can transportation and infrastructure projects such as highways, railroads, airports or canals. If these different kinds of projects (that is, private versus public) occur in one village but at different times, or at the same time but in different neighboring villages, peasants who have been less well compensated feel unequally treated by government. Many complaints involve this inconsistency in compensation over both time and space. Such inequity not only contributes to rising tension and distrust between peasants and the government, but also makes planning implementation and land management difficult.

Finally, it is increasingly difficult and costly to resettle peasants. The 1998 LAL requires that the lives of farmers not be adversely affected by compulsory land acquisition. The law does not specify concrete measures of that goal; consequently, several years after acquisition, many peasants are worse off than before they lost their land. This situation is not difficult to imagine. Farming cannot make peasants rich, but it generates sufficient income to support at least a minimum standard of living. Thus, farmland can provide lifetime security for many peasants, making it challenging to "detach" them from their land. Compensation, on the other end, does not measure up to this kind of lifetime security. Further, without appropriate training and skills in financial management of their lump-sum compensation, and without appropriate investment vehicles (in the event their compensation is even large enough to invest), peasants very commonly end up — several years after land acquisition — with no land to farm, no income stream to support themselves and no job skills with which to compete in tight urban job markets.

Emergence of Urban Sprawl. As noted previously, the BFPR tends to create urban villages surrounded by urbanized areas. The urban growth policy adopted in 1980 to control such urban sprawl failed in several respects. First, it contradicted other national policies, such as the SEDZ initiatives, whereby local governments and enterprises enjoyed the benefits of tax exemptions and were able to access capital resources that were unavailable otherwise. Many zones were established in large cities, including Shanghai, China's largest. Second, large cities have experienced the greatest spatial growth, compared with mid- and small-sized cities (Nanjing Institute of Geography and Lake Study 1999). Third, rapid development and establishment of small towns have depleted agricultural land at an unprecedented rate. In the past 10 years, China's agricultural land decreased by 100 million mu while its population increased by 150 million. Per capita agricultural land decreased to 1.76 mu,

47 percent less than the world average. If farmland protection is the primary goal, the development of small cities and towns should not be encouraged because they consume more land per capita than large cities. Given the anticipated urbanization in the next 20–30 years, large cities and high densities should be encouraged to protect farmland.

Obstacles to Urban Development. Over time, high land development costs and strict farmland preservation regulations, individually or combined, inevitably make horizontal land development (urban spatial expansion) increasingly difficult and slow down urban development.

Deficiencies of the Benchmark Land Use Rights Price System. The benchmark land use rights price system has two major flaws (Ding 2003). The first is the system's use of floor-area ratio as a dominant factor in land price determination, which practice is at odds with urban economic theory. The second is that the system does not provide adequate flexibility for substitution between land and capital inputs, which is key to achieving land use efficiency under market principles. Land costs should be fixed costs in real estate development and should not increase with the scale of development. Unfortunately, land costs do depend on the scale of land development in Chinese cities, which certainly affects market efficiency. Urban planning practices and the benchmark land use rights price system have resulted in high housing prices. In Table 5, the illustrated total project costs of land development are broken into five components: (1) land acquisition, resettlement and demolition; (2) construction; (3) urban infrastructure; (4) taxes and fees; and (5) land use rights. Among these, items 1 and 5 should be subject to a change in floor-area ratio and should be constant, regardless of the scale of land development. Items 2 and 3 should increase with the intensity of land development as measured by capital density. Item 4 may or may not change along with capital density, depending on the way in which it is determined. For simplicity's sake, we assume that item 4 remains constant and both construction and urban infrastructure costs are a linear function of floor-area ratio.

The base case in Table 5 shows a land development project in Wangjing, Beijing, which was launched in a 27,000-square-meter area and was permitted to 110,000 square meters of floor space, for a floor-area ratio of 4.1 (Wang 1997). The housing price per square meter was 5,400 RMB. According to principles of microeconomics, a simple simulation was performed, in which floor-area ratio is allowed to change and cost components are divided into fixed and variable costs. Table 5 illustrates that when floor-area ratio increased from 4.1 to 10, housing price per square meter declined from 5,400 RMB to 3,314 RMB, a striking 40 percent decrease.

TABLE 5
Simulation of Housing Price Change with Free Substitution of Land and Capital Inputs

Development in Old Districts	Price per Sq. M. (RMB)	% of Total Project Costs	Wangjing Base Case	Simulation Scenarios					
				1	2	3	4	5	6
RMB			10,000	10,000	10,000	10,000	10,000	10,000	10,000
Land input (as constant) (in sq.m.)			27,000	27,000	27,000	27,000	27,000	27,000	27,000
Total floor area (sq. m.)			110,000	135,000	162,000	189,000	216,000	243,000	270,000
Floor-area ratio			4.1	5	6	7	8	9	10
Land Development Project Costs									
(1) Land acquisition, resettlement, and demolition	1,890	0.35	20,790	20,790	20,790	20,790	20,790	20,790	20,790
(2) Construction	1,080	0.20	11,880	14,580	17,496	20,412	23,328	26,244	29,160
(3) Urban infrastructure	800	0.15	8,800	10,800	12,960	15,120	17,280	19,440	21,600
(4) Taxes and fees	982	0.18	10,802	10,802	10,802	10,802	10,802	10,802	10,802
(5) Land use rights	648	0.12	7,128	7,128	7,128	7,128	7,128	7,128	7,128
Housing price per sq. m.	5,400		5,400	4,748	4,270	3,929	3,673	3,473	3,314

SOURCE: Ding (2002)

Social Conflict and Injustice. Two types of social conflict have arisen with implementation of land reforms: conflict between urban governments and peasants, and conflict among peasants. The former happens mainly in two cases. Since farmers have been compensated instead of being paid full market prices for their land, and as compensation packages have become less appealing, there is increasing resistance to land acquisition by the government. The second government-peasant conflict case relates to the government compensation packages that cannot match profits farmers can realize if they develop the land themselves. Farmers are reluctant to sell their land use rights to the government, and social conflict arises when the government exercises eminent domain to acquire their land. The social conflict among peasants arises when the law prohibits land development on quality farmland. Farmers find it difficult to resist developing land themselves, when doing so might generate profits 200–300 times higher than net profits from farming. Without income transfers or a spatially differentiated tax-rate system, farmers on quality farmland will be economically disadvantaged compared with farmers whose land is not restricted from development.

Issues in Land Use Taxation. The initial assessment of land taxes in China yielded a mixed result. The Provisional Act of Land Use Taxation on State Owned Urban Land ended the land tenure system that favored free land use, and marked the beginning of the determination of land use through price mechanisms and tax policy. Since then, land use efficiency has improved and there is now an economic incentive for danweis to return unused land that has been allocated free of charge. Fushun, for example, returned 250,000 square meters of unused land to the government in 1985.[17] Land taxes provide a new revenue source for local governments to use in financing long-overdue urban infrastructure. Fushun collected nearly 28.5 million RMB in land use fees from 1984 to 1986, and used these funds to finance infrastructure such as streets, water, gas and heating provision, and greenspace development.

The land tax system does, however, have several drawbacks. First, the many land uses that are tax exempt undermine the role of land taxation in managing and rationalizing land use.[18] Second, there is confusion among officials and scholars because foreign investors are charged land use fees while domestic land users are charged land use taxes. Third, even though tax rates are moderate or low, land use taxes significantly increase costs for large- and medium-sized, state-owned enterprises, many of which are established on large lots of land. Many of these enterprises

---

17 More recent data are unavailable.

18 The following land uses in urban areas are exempted from land taxation: government bureaus, people's organizations and military units; nonprofit enterprises funded by governments; churches, parks and historic preservation districts; transportation networks, public squares, greenspace and other public land uses; agriculture, forestry, pasture and fishing; uses previously established in mountainous, hilly or aquatic areas, and uses on land redeveloped from brownfields; and any other uses — such as energy, transportation, irrigation, etc. — that have been specifically exempted by the department of finance.

have had a hard time balancing their budgets since the 1980s; an estimated 30–40 percent of state-owned enterprises have been in deficit during the last decade. A contributing factor is that land taxes, which are based on size — and not on capital value, site value or rental value — might be significantly higher than those based on value or rent.

Finally, municipal governments may not be interested in tax collection, especially when there are many state-owned enterprises within their administrative boundaries, because most land taxes go to the state rather than to municipal governments. It is challenging for the state to stimulate local governments to collect land taxes actively on one hand, and avoid tax revenue losses on the other. This explains why the revenue-sharing agreements for land use rights sales between the local and central governments have been modified several times in the last 10 years. In addition, the lack of a land registration system and trained staff makes it difficult and expensive to collect land use taxes. Revenues generated from land use taxes have not met expectations: the state expected them to generate revenues of 10 billion RMB annually, but instead collected only 2.5 billion RMB from 1988 to 1990 (Yang and Wu 1996). Overall, it is too early to conclude that the land taxation system in China has achieved the predetermined goals: to rationalize land use allocation, improve land use efficiency and adjust land use structure. Apart from their limited contribution to the financial situations of municipal governments, land taxes may not affect urban land use efficiency as theory has suggested.

Challenges in Land Policy Reform

Supplying land for ongoing, rapid urbanization will continue to be a challenge in years to come. Because public projects cannot offer farmers the same levels of compensation as can developers of profitable projects (like hotels, commercial housing and even entertainment complexes), local governments find it increasingly difficult to acquire land for genuinely public projects, such as highways, railroads, airports or canal systems.

The second challenge is how, in the compulsory land acquisition process, to compensate peasants fairly for their farmland. Low levels of land compensation — whereby governments capture land value increases disproportionately — impose a serious long-term threat to the stability of sustainable development in China. The number of people who live poorly after land acquisition continues to rise. For instance, Zhijiang province alone has more than 2 million *shi di* farmers (farmers who have lost their farmland). In 2002, more than 80 percent of the legal cases filed by peasants against governments in the province were related to land acquisition. This problem is a potential source of instability and could easily escalate in the next decade or two, given the substantial anticipated need for land to accommodate massive urbanization. According to the General National Land Use Comprehensive

Plan, China will need 18.5 million mu of land for nonagricultural uses in the first decade of the twenty-first century. Of that, 90 percent will be acquired from farmers. Based on the number of farmers currently occupying farmland in China, an estimated 12 million farmers will lose their land during this decade of acquisition. Without fair compensation or other efforts to assure their social security over the long term, the plight of these farmers will present enormous socioeconomic problems for years to come.

The third challenge is associated with the rate of urbanization. Given the socioeconomic development objectives laid out in the report of the 16th Communist Party Convention in 2003, the pressure for urban development will be enormous. According to the report, the 2020 growth targets estimate that 55 percent of the population will be in cities and the gross domestic product will quadruple. The total population of China is estimated to be between 1.6 billion and 1.8 billion by that time; the migration from rural areas to cities will be in the range of 10 to 15 million people annually (with the rate of natural urban population growth considered). The need for urban economic development is urgent if the country is to be able to absorb such massive rural-to-urban migration. Providing cheap land to accommodate urban economic growth will be one of the central themes of the national policy agenda.

The fourth challenge is how to achieve a balance between farmland preservation and urban spatial expansion — a question to which there may not yet be any answers. Farmland preservation, by increasing land development costs, slows down urban development. Given the pace of urbanization anticipated in the coming years, pressure to provide jobs will make urban economic growth critical. That economic growth will lead, inevitably, to encroachment into rural areas to take advantage of cheaper land — countering the goals of farmland preservation. How the Chinese government addresses this dilemma remains to be seen.

The fifth challenge relates to the maturing land markets, in which prices will play a more dominant role in land use and land allocation decisions. The dual land markets, hidden land transactions, and ill-defined property rights and responsibilities of state entities all represent challenges to efforts to improve land management capacity. Even though there is no clear division between market determination and government intervention in land use decision making, China will need to reduce its administrative influences in urban policy and management and promote market principles.

The final challenge is how to strengthen the fiscal conditions of local governments, which are pressured to take increasing responsibility for the provision of infrastructure and public services. Local governments need their own revenue sources to be effective in managing, planning and controlling urban growth so as to benefit urban residents socially, economically and environmentally.

Final Remarks

Although policy change in China is typically gradual, land policy reforms have been enacted at a much faster pace and have contributed significantly to the remarkable socioeconomic progress of the past two decades. Land use efficiency has improved, market mechanisms and price principles have been introduced to rationalize land allocation, the government's revenue from land use rights sales has risen, and the quality and quantity of public services have improved. Reforms have also boosted real estate development and created job opportunities.

Yet, numerous problems such as land management, hidden land markets, social conflicts, inequality, corruption and unincorporated urban development have accompanied this progress. Future land policy reform faces the following challenges.

- Balancing the demand for land to satisfy rapid urban growth with the increasing pressure for farmland preservation.
- Reconciling the inconsistencies and conflicts between land regulations and policies. These reflect other conflicts that are deeply rooted in the Chinese political and administrative systems, which sometimes assign dual and conflicting roles to different government authorities. These kinds of problems will not be solved easily in the future without major political reforms.[21]
- Dealing with the increasing social injustice arising from land policy reform. Profit differentials between agricultural and nonagricultural activities make it difficult for government officials to convince farmers not to develop their agricultural land themselves. In addition, the basic farmland protection regulations penalize law-abiding farmers by stripping away their land development opportunities, and indirectly reward farmers who are able to gain windfall wealth from land development of unrestricted sites. Spatially differentiated tax rates may help address this issue.
- Improving land use efficiency. High-density development would seem to be a good solution in the effort to balance the increasing demand for land (due to rapid urbanization) and the rising pressure for farmland protection. This urban development strategy requires changes in land regulations and city policies to ensure the economic profitability of urban redevelopment. However, improving land use efficiency across Chinese cities is currently restricted by predetermined and inflexible floor-area ratios. There is currently no economic incentive for developers to commit to high-density development.

---

21 There are, for instance, conflicts between the LUR and farmland protection. The adoption of the LUR is intended to rationalize land use and land allocation through market principles and price mechanisms. In contrast, the implementation of farmland protection regulations is intended to restrict development of potentially lucrative sites through the designation of farmland protection districts. Society as a whole may be better off if developers are allowed to develop quality farmland at favorable locations, instead of being forced to develop low-quality land at remote locations. Also, conflicts of interest sometimes occur because government ministries are responsible for both drafting and implementing laws and regulations — thus creating dual, and potentially conflicting, roles of legislation and enforcement.

Effective responses to resolve these challenges require not only creative and inno-vative thinking, but also the empirical data and case studies that enable a compre-hensive assessment of the costs and benefits of policy responses and instruments across a wide socioeconomic spectrum. Such an assessment would include, but not be limited to, the following inquiries.

- To what extent is land use efficiency lost under the old land allocation system? This question is largely associated with the degree to which land misallocation occurred under the old policy and administrative regime. The answer to the question also depends on the spatial implication of this misallocated land.

- What are the total costs (direct, indirect and induced) of farmland protection and land administration laws that require "zero net loss" of farmland during urbanization? It may be relatively straightforward to calculate benefits in terms of farmland preservation, but it is more complicated, and usually difficult, to determine the costs. Increases in land development costs will inevitably put some developers out of business, causing housing prices to rise and the demand for construction to decrease. Many industrial sectors also will be hurt in terms of outputs, employment and incomes.

- What are the geographic implications of land policy and how do they affect urban form and the spatial arrangement of urban activities?

- To what extent do urban land policies affect the competitiveness of the urban economy?

- How can governments capture increases in land value that are attributable to public investment? Accumulated public investments have contributed sub-stantively to the differentiation of land values. In turn, property values will continue to affect land and housing values. The need to design a mechanism to capture these land value increments is critical and immediate, and the impacts of associated policy should be fully understood.

These important questions invite future investigation, and it is the authors' hope that this summary and the following chapters in this volume will help shape that investigation and other research and policy discussions to come.

References

Badcock, B. 1986. Land and housing policy in Chinese urban development. *Planning Perspectives* 1(2):147–170.

Bertaud, A. 1992. China: Urban land use issues. Unpublished paper.

Bertaud, A., and B. Renaud. 1992. Cities without land markets. World Bank Discussion Paper #227. Washington, DC: World Bank.

Brown, L. 1994. Who will feed China?: Wake-up call for a small planet. *World Watch* (Sept./Oct.).

———. 1995. *Who will feed China?: Wake-up call for a small planet.* New York and London: W. W. Norton & Co.

Brueckner, J. K. 1986. A modern analysis of the effects of site value taxation. *National Tax Journal* 1:49–58.

———. 1997. Infrastructure financing and urban development: The economics of impact fees. *Journal of Public Economics* 66:383–407.

Chan, N. 1999. Land-use rights in mainland China: Problems and recommendations for improvement. *Journal of Real Estate Literature* 7:53–63.

China Land Newspaper. 1996. April 20.

Ding, C. 2002. Land policy and urban housing development. *Urban Studies* 9(2):61–66.

Ding, C. 2003. Land policy reform in China: Assessment and prospects. *Land Use Policy* 20(2):109–120.

Ding, C., G. Knaap, and Y. Wu. 2000. Land values and the emergence of land markets in Beijing, China. Presented at the Asian Real Estate Society Fifth Annual Conference, July 26–30, Beijing, China.

Dowall, D. E. 1993. Establishing urban land markets in the People's Republic of China. *Journal of the American Planning Association* 59(2):182–192.

Hu, C. Z. 1990. The development, methodology and management of land value appraisal system. Beijing: State Land Administration Internal Report.

Jiang, D., J. Chen, and D. Isaac. 1998. The effect of foreign investment on the real estate industry in China. *Urban Studies* 35(11):2101–2110.

Li, G. Y. 1992. *Real estate development and investment in China.* Tianjin: Tianjin Technical Translation Publisher.

Li, L. H. 1999. *Urban land reform in China.* New York: St. Martin's Press.

Li, L. H., and A. Walker. 1996. Benchmark pricing behavior of land in China's reform. *Journal of Property Research* 13:183–196.

Li, Y. 1997. *Survival and development: Research and thinking on agricultural land preservation in China.* Beijing: China Land Press.

Liu, W., and J. Xie. 1994. *Research on Chinese land rent, tax, and fee systems.* Beijing: China Land Press.

Liu, W., and D. Yang. 1990. China's land use policy under change. *Land Use Policy* 7:198–201.

Mills, E. 1998. The economic consequences of a land tax. In *Land value taxation: Can it and will it work today?* D. Netzer, ed., 31–49. Cambridge, MA: Lincoln Institute of Land Policy.

Nanjing Institute of Geography and Lake Study. 1999. Working Report on Chinese City Development. Nanjing: Chinese Academy of Sciences.

Nechyba, T. 1998. Replacing capital taxes with land taxes: Efficiency and distributional implications with an application to the United States economy. In *Land value taxation: Can it and will it work today?* D. Netzer, ed., 183–205. Cambridge, MA: Lincoln Institute of Land Policy.

Nicholson, W. 1998. *Microeconomic theory: Basic principles and extensions.* New York: The Dryden Press.

State Statistical Bureau. 1990. *China statistical yearbook.* Beijing: China Statistical Publishing House.

———. 1991. *China statistical yearbook.* Beijing: China Statistical Publishing House.

———. 1992. *China statistical yearbook.* Beijing: China Statistical Publishing House.

———. 1993. *China statistical yearbook.* Beijing: China Statistical Publishing House.

———. 1994. *China statistical yearbook.* Beijing: China Statistical Publishing House.

———. 1995. *China statistical yearbook.* Beijing: China Statistical Publishing House.

———. 1996. *China statistical yearbook.* Beijing: China Statistical Publishing House.

Su, J. 1998. *Land property rights guidebook.* Beijing: China Land Press.

Tang, Y. 1989. Urban land use in China: Policy issues and options. *Land Use Policy* 6(1):53–63.

Tang, B., and S. Liu. 2002. Property developers and speculative development in China. Presented at a March 2002 workshop on land and real estate speculation, organized by the Lincoln Institute of Land Policy, Cambridge, MA.

Walker, A., and L. H. Li. 1994. Land use rights reform and real estate market in China. *Journal of Real Estate Literature* 2(2):199–211.

Wang, S. H. 1997. Recommendations for facilitating housing commercialization in Shanghai Pudong. *Beijing City Planning and Construction Review* 4:16–19.

Wong, K. K., and X. B. Zhao. 1999. The influence of bureaucratic behavior on land appointment in China: Informal process. *Environment and Planning C: Government and Policy* 17:113–126.

Wu, F. 1997. Urban restructuring in China's emerging market economy: Towards a framework for analysis. *International Journal of Urban and Regional Research* 21(4):640–663.

Xue, J. 1994. The development trend of the Chinese land market. *Real Estate Market Review* (Oct.):12–15.

Yang, C., and C. Wu. 1996. *Ten-year reform of land use system in China.* Beijing: China Land Press.

Yeh, A. G. O., and F. Wu. 1996. The new land development process and urban development in Chinese cities. *International Journal of Urban and Regional Research* 20(2): 330–353.

Zhang, X. H., and Y. Li. 1997. *China land management handbook.* Beijing: China Land Press.

Zhang, X. Q. 1997. Urban land reform in China. *Land Use Policy* 14(3):187–199.

Zhao, M., G. Bao, and L. Hou. 1998. *Land use system reform and urban and rural development.* Shanghai: Tongji Publisher.

Zhu, J. 1994. Changing land policy and its impact on local growth: The experience of the Shenzhen Special Economic Zone, China, in the 1980s. *Urban Studies* 31(10): 1611–1623.

———. 1999. Local growth coalition: The context and implications of China's gradualist urban land reforms. *International Journal of Urban and Regional Research* 23(3): 534–548.

Zou, Jia Hua. 1994. Intensify reform, strengthen management, and establish a healthy and speedy economic growth. From a speech at the 1994 National Meeting on Land Use Rights Reform.

Chapter 2

The Dual Land Market and Urban Development in China

ANTHONY GAR-ON YEH

Before land reform in 1988, land in China was owned by the government and was normally administratively allocated to users free of any charges. Although experiments with charging land use fees were carried out in Shenzhen, Guangzhou and Fushan (Walker 1991; Yeh 1985; Yeh and Wu 1995), they were limited mainly to land use involving foreign investment. It was not until the First Session of the Seventh People's Congress in 1987 that paid transfer of land use rights (*tudi youchang zhuanrang*) was made official. The clause "The right to use of land may be transferred in accordance with law" was added to Article 10, Section 4 of the Constitution, which stated that "No organization or individual may seize, buy, sell land or make any other unlawful transfer of land." This amendment was approved by the National People's Congress on 12 April 1988, and opened a new era of lawful urban land transactions (Tang 1989). Also in 1988, the State Council announced the Provisional Regulations of the People's Republic of China on Land Use Tax in Cities and Towns, which enabled cities and towns to collect land use taxes. These developments marked the end of free land use and the establishment of urban land markets in China (Dowall 1993).

Although these land markets are operative and land reform measures have introduced land leasing, land that had previously been administratively allocated still exists — and the administrative land allocation system continues. Thus has a dual land market been created in China, comprising both leased and administratively allocated land. This dual system differs from those of Western societies, which tend to have a single, freehold land market. This chapter examines the land development process of this dual land market system and its impact on urban development.

The Land Development Process

The dual land market system has introduced a new land development process in China (Yeh and Wu 1996). There are three main types of land ownership: the first is collective ownership (by farmers) of rural land. The second is titular state ownership of urban land that is occupied by various state work units. The land used by these work units can be described as administratively allocated land. The third type is urban land owned by the state, which can transfer land use rights to users in exchange for payment. This can be referred to as leased land.

Though urban land acquired through the paid transfer of land use rights comprises only a small portion of the existing urban land plus land acquired from rural areas, the transfer of land use rights caused a profound change in the land system in China — the aforementioned dual land market system. As noted previously, most urban land is administratively allocated, while a small portion is leased by the state to users through the paid transfer of use rights.

Under the 1988 Land Administration Law (LAL), transactions of land ownership directly with farmers are illegal. Rural land can be acquired only by state work units or by municipalities; this ensures that the urban land belongs to the state. Transactions between users and farmers are prohibited by a system of land use certificates. Developers must obtain land use certificates from the municipal land administration bureau before proceeding with projects; those that acquire land directly from farmers cannot obtain the necessary certificates.

Urban land is owned by the state and managed by municipalities, and city governments monopolize the supply of leased land. The state work units acquire land through the administrative allocation method and "occupy" the state land, but do not possess the land use rights that could subsequently be transferred to other users. State enterprises can exchange land with each other on a voluntary basis, and the exchange is treated as a special kind of administrative allocation. Land use rights for land acquired by this method are transferable only to other state enterprises. The implication of this policy is that only land acquired through paid transfer of land use rights can be transacted. The dynamics of urban land transactions in China are shown in Figure 1 and described below.

Urban Land Transactions

Type I_1: Acquisition of Rural Land by Work Units for Project-Specific Development

The typical way to acquire rural land for urban development in China is through project-specific development. A work unit that needs land for development can apply for a land acquisition permit from the municipality. With that permit, it can then acquire rural land by paying a standard compensation fee to the farmers of the land parcel. The municipal government would then register the change of land use from agricultural to nonagricultural and issue a land use certificate for the new land use. According to the 1986 LAL, compensation must be 3–6 times the value of the average annual agricultural production of the rural land during the three years prior to land acquisition. The law also requires compensation for buildings and agricultural products attached to the rural land at the time of the acquisition, or for residents if the acquisition involves their relocation. If the acquired land has been in vegetable production, additional payments are made to a fund set up for development of new vegetable cropland.

Before the 1978 economic reforms, economic activities were organized mainly through various ministries of the central government, while municipalities played a relatively minor role. Investment in development projects came primarily from the state budget, without involving local municipal governments; thus, a self-contained development mechanism was adopted. Project investment is normally divided into productive and nonproductive aspects. Compensation for acquiring rural land was counted as productive investment because land leveling had to precede factory construction. It has been noted that urban land is allocated freely to land users. Thus, work units tended to occupy more land than they actually needed (Fung 1981). There is a misconception that municipalities acquire rural land, compensate farmers and allocate the land to work units without charge. In fact, the involvement of the municipality is minimal apart from approving the land acquisition permit. Land acquisition and compensation are directly transacted between the work units and the farmers.

After the establishment of the State Land Administration Bureau (SLAB) in 1986, and of various municipal land administration bureaus in the following year, the power of the municipality increased: land acquisition within the city's jurisdiction now needed to be approved by the city government. The LAL stipulates that the acquisition of more than 1,000 mu of cultivated land, or more than 2,000 mu of

---

FIGURE 1

The Dual Land Market and Land Transaction Types in Chinese Cities

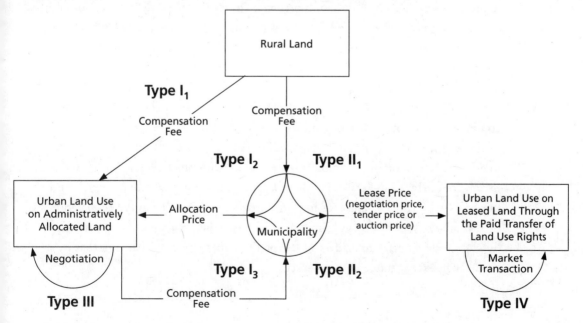

other types of land, needs to be approved by the State Council. Acquisition of cultivated land parcels smaller than 3 mu, or of other types of land parcels smaller than 10 mu, must be approved by local government at the county level (municipalities). However, municipalities can hardly reject the investment from the central ministries. Development is controlled not through local physical plans prepared by municipalities, but through nationwide or provincewide economic plans. The adoption of the paid transfer of land use rights rested on the principle that only state work units (usually large industrial enterprises) could acquire land through administrative allocation, and that such land ought not be leased to foreign investors.

Type I₂: Acquisition of Rural Land by Municipal Governments for Comprehensive Development

Municipalities play an important role in this type of land transaction because they acquire land directly from farmers, develop it comprehensively and then allocate it to users; this kind of transaction has occurred since the 1978 reforms. The purpose of comprehensive development is greater efficiency and timeliness in land acquisition. Because municipalities (instead of users) acquire land directly from farmers for standard compensation fees, negotiations with farmers are streamlined. In addition, associated community facilities, such as parks and playgrounds, can be shared by several work units.

When first introduced in the late 1970s, comprehensive development did not involve much commercial consideration, as most of the land was supplied to state work units through administrative allocation (Yeh and Wu 1999). Later, however, some land also began to be supplied to housing development companies for commercial housing construction. These development companies usually belonged to the municipal housing bureau or construction bureau. In the early stages of housing commercialization, most commercial housing was built on this type of land because it could be obtained less expensively than could land obtained through urban redevelopment (which involves heavy compensation). By securing land from the municipality, developers can set housing prices relatively low, as they have to pay compensation to farmers for agricultural land, rather than the more expensive commercial price of residential land.

However, as for Type I₁ land, users may use the land but cannot transfer it freely to other users, especially foreign buyers. Commercial housing built on Type I₂ land is mainly for use by Chinese buyers, whereas commercial housing built on leased land can be used by either Chinese or foreign buyers. Originating from the cooperation of several work units in building shared housing apartments, comprehensive development has been an artifact of the preliminary market mechanism, that is, a property market without a land market.

Type I_3: Acquisition of Existing Administratively Allocated Urban Land by Municipal Governments for Urban Infrastructure

This type of transaction, usually used for the development of urban infrastructure, involves a municipal government negotiating with the occupiers of the (previously administratively allocated) land that is required for such infrastructure. In theory, because land is owned by the state, and because this kind of transaction involves a change of land users but no change in land ownership, it would seem that no compensation would be necessary. Current users, however, would already have paid compensation (at the time of acquisition) to farmers, and to the municipal government for the costs of leveling and formation of the land. The municipal government, in turn, needs both to compensate the occupiers for their loss and to allocate to them another urban parcel in this kind of transaction.

Type II_1: Acquisition of Rural Land by Municipal Governments for Land Leasing

This is the most recently introduced type of land transaction and is becoming increasingly popular. Rural land is acquired by the municipality and then leased to other users through the market mechanisms of negotiation, tender and auction. Because the municipality monopolizes the supply of this type of land, it can acquire rural land from farmers at a monopolistic price and sell it to developers at market price. A municipality can make a considerable profit because of the great difference between land-acquisition and land-lease prices.

As land acquired through land leasing is more expensive than that obtained through the three types of transactions previously described, most users try to avoid acquiring land through leasing. If foreign users need land for a factory, they can seek various ways to use existing land that is administratively allocated. They might, for example, build a factory as a joint venture with a Chinese partner who can obtain land via administrative allocation methods (Types I_1 and I_2). Currently, it is mainly foreign investors who engage in this type of land transaction, and their development projects are primarily for commercial housing, offices, hotels and industrial buildings. However, municipalities have reported that they face increasing resistance from farmers, who sometimes even resort to violence when their land is acquired by the municipality that will later lease it out on the land market. Farmers are demanding higher compensation because the municipality can secure a higher price in the land market through land leasing.

Type II_2: Acquisition of Existing Administratively Allocated Urban Land by Municipal Governments for Land Leasing

In this kind of transaction, municipalities acquire previously administratively allocated urban land occupied by work units and then lease the land to users who can pay market land prices. Unlike Type I_3, in which municipalities use the land primarily for creation of urban infrastructure (that is, for nonprofit use), this type of transaction (which is similar to Type II_1) is quite profitable. Given the profit-making aspect, compensation to the original users is higher than in Type I_3 because it is difficult for the municipalities to justify paying the same prices as they do for land acquired for nonprofit use (e.g., state construction).

As for land acquired for state construction, the socialist principle is that "local interests should obey national interests and individual interests should obey community interests." Under this principle, users often have been asked to sacrifice for the construction of state projects and community infrastructure; this does not happen in a Type II_2 transaction. Negotiations have to be carried out between the original land users and the municipality until a compromise on profit sharing is reached. It is not surprising that some city governments have to lease out their own compounds (usually located in the city center) and move their offices to other places. Land acquisition through a Type II_2 transaction is much more expensive and difficult for municipal government than acquisition through a Type II_1 process. This explains why leased land comes primarily from the acquisition of rural land and unoccupied urban land, and why Economic and Technological Development Zones (ETDZs), which need large tracts of land, are located at the peripheries of urban areas.

Types II_1 and II_2 transactions are referred to as the *primary land market*. Municipalities acquire land from rural areas (Type II_1) or from existing administratively allocated urban land occupied by various work units (Type II_2), and then transfer the land use rights to users through land leasing by negotiation, tender or auction. Land leasing through negotiation is not much different from the traditional negotiation-and-compromise process. For tender, the conditions of the parcel and the development constraints are announced and tendering is invited. A land auction is an open competition in which the land use rights are awarded to the highest bidder.

Type III: Exchange of Administratively Allocated Land Between Work Units

Work units can exchange their administratively allocated land through negotiation. For example, one side may offer to the other a unit of housing as a medium of exchange. The terms of this kind of exchange, however, do not necessarily respond to market value. Because of the lack of both information and standard practice, such deals are based largely on precedent. Land transactions of this sort can be very time consuming, and the demands of determining compensation and achieving a balance of supply and demand quite challenging.

Type IV: Transaction of Leased Land Between Land Users

Only land that is acquired from the primary market can be transacted through leasing. This is referred to as the *secondary land market*. In newspapers and government documents, transactions of land use rights are sometimes further divided into those among real estate companies and those among ordinary users. The latter is referred to as the *tertiary land market* (Zhou 1992).

Decisions about land supply are still largely centered in the government's administrative system. Market mechanisms operate only in the secondary (leased land) market, and do not affect the majority of land that is administratively allocated. This system differs significantly from that of Western cities, where most land is privately owned under a freehold system. In the West, private initiatives and market mechanisms are the basic processes that decide resource and land allocation. Government intervention, which tries to correct market failures through urban planning, is secondary to these processes (Yeh and Wu 1999).

Impacts of the Dual Land Market on Urban Development

Prior to the introduction of the paid land use system, land users very often would try to acquire more land than was needed because land was allocated free of charges. The new system (the sale of land use rights and collection of land use taxes) is intended to cause land to be used more efficiently. In addition, this change should help strengthen the tax base for construction and maintenance of urban infrastructure.

The new paid land use system has provided city government a new and substantial revenue source unavailable in the past. Land is leased to foreign investors and to local developers for industrial, residential and commercial uses. For example, revenue from the property market (that is, from land leasing, property taxes, etc.), at a peak of the property boom in Hainan province, has been as much as one-fourth of total municipal revenue (Zou 1992). Land-related revenue is used to improve urban infrastructure, which in turn can improve accessibility and open up new land for development. This process increases land value, which then increases government revenue, providing further capital for building more infrastructure. This dynamic is often referred to as "land breeding land development" *(yi di yang di)*.

Guangzhou and many other cities are using the paid transfer of land use rights to finance their underground rail systems. Developers are allowed to develop residential and commercial properties above the underground stations, and the revenue from such development is used to finance part of the construction cost of the underground rail system. The desirability of underground rail transportation generates great demand and high land values. Because land now has monetary value, governments are more willing to invest in infrastructure to improve the environment and accessibility of these station areas, which further increases the land value.

In the past, the so-called "five connections and one leveling" *(wutong yiping)* were the main methods of providing a good investment environment for the special economic development zones (Yeh 1985). These elements of infrastructure — connecting roads, telecommunications, water, electricity, port access and leveling of sites — are actively applied in land development in Chinese cities. With better

FIGURE 2

Amount of Leased and Administratively Allocated Land in China, 1993–1996

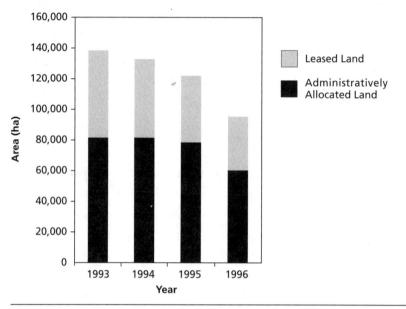

SOURCES: Yearbook of the Land of China (1995, 1996 and 1997)

accessibility and land formation (e.g., leveling of land and infrastructure provision), land can command higher prices in the market.

The provision of roads, water, electricity, telecommunications and site leveling is labor intensive. Because labor costs are relatively cheap, high market land prices mean that the rate of return for the provision of these infrastructure elements is very good. Revenue from land makes possible infrastructure projects (such as roads and telecommunications) that were not possible before the introduction of the land market. Further, the market has enabled the implementation of development plans that would previously have sat dormant for lack of funding.

Despite the introduction of land leasing, a large percentage of land continues to be allocated through the administrative allocation system (see Figure 2). The interactions of the dual land markets are the most influential forces currently shaping Chinese urban development.

The Black Market and Loss of Land Revenue

The dual land market has created a black market, leading to a loss of land revenue for Chinese cities. There are both an urban and a rural form of black market (see Figure 3). The *de facto* owners of administratively allocated urban land — the state work units or individuals who own private housing — can lease their land to other users through negotiation. Urban land has long been leased in the black market through various means, such as the leasing of bars and restaurants in private housing. Because such transactions are illegal, the users cannot obtain land use certificates from the land administration authority. Typically, land users do not own the land and cannot build housing to sell in the market. The land occupier can use land as a form of investment in joint ventures to exchange land for housing or other benefits. By law, land use rights cannot be transacted with other users in the market unless a premium is paid to the municipal government that is the *de jure* owner of the administratively allocated land. However, exchanging land for housing or even cash is very common in the central city. In Beijing, under such black market arrangements, the land occupier can obtain 60 percent of the finished housing units by using the land as a form of joint venture investment.

Black markets also exist in the rural areas at the urban periphery. Farmers rent their land to other users as a form of investment in joint ventures. In the urban fringe, where rural land faces immediate urban expansion, farmers prefer renting their land directly to either foreign or domestic investors because the price is higher than the compensation paid by the municipal government in transaction Types I_1, I_2 and II_1. As a consequence, development in the urban fringe is chaotic.

The difference between the prices of leased land (leased to users at market price through negotiation, tender or auction) and administratively allocated land (allocated to users at an allocation price which is minimal compared with the market price) has led to the development of the black market. The *de jure* system allocates land to state enterprises and institutions at a very low price with the understanding that

FIGURE 3
The Black Land Market in Chinese Cities

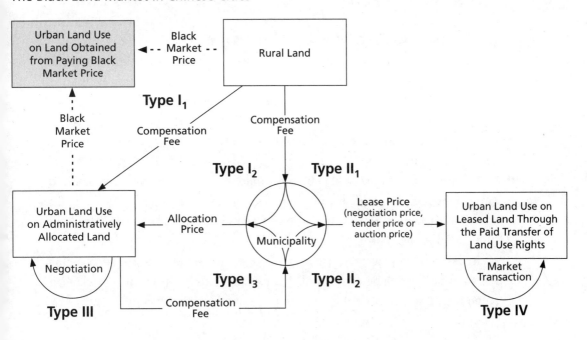

they are the sole users of the allocated land. However, because of the confusion in land ownership, land occupiers (who are the *de facto* owners) of administratively allocated land frequently can sublet their land to other users in the guise of joint ventures. Administratively allocated land transacted in the black market is priced lower than the market price of leased land, but high enough for the land occupiers to make significant profits.

Revenue from such land leasing does not go to the city government but to the land occupiers of the administratively allocated land. Land leasing has the potential to generate large amounts of revenue critically needed by municipal governments for urban infrastructure improvement. In fact, only very little revenue has been generated because most of the revenue from these land transactions has accrued to the work units through the black market.

The existence of the black market has caused enormous losses of land rent; estimates show losses to the state of at least 10 billion RMB (US$1.16 billion) annually (Tian 1994). Unlike land leasing, through which government can obtain substantial planning gains, the black market produces huge benefits that are captured only by the users, while the municipal government bears the cost of infrastructure provision for the increased intensity of land uses. The black market also hinders the development of a competitive land market system, inasmuch as the relatively cheap land secured in the black market enables users to operate businesses in locations that might not prove sustainable in a fair and competitive land market system.

Such a spontaneous conversion of land uses creates the problem of incompatible land uses in Chinese cities. There is an urgent need to regulate land transactions in order to prevent losses of government revenue to the black market and to ensure that planning gains are controlled by the state and used in the public's interest.

Unregulated Land Use Changes and Urban Planning

Unregulated land use changes occur primarily on administratively allocated land. The introduction of economic incentives has been the basic motivation for users to change their land uses to boost profits. Deficiencies in development control make it possible for users to convert the use of land discreetly, without seeking planning permission. The "user discretion" legacy from the project-specific mode of land development is unlikely to change in a short period of time. Administratively allocated land — largely for industry and public organizations — has typically been developed through the project-specific mode of land development (Yeh and Wu 1996). In this model, users acquire land through direct negotiation with farmers, pay for it and have considerable control over it.

In the past, in the absence of markets, there was no reason for the urban planning system to exert development control. The function of urban planning in a planned economy is different from that in a market economy, where private initiatives are the dominant sources of investment and externalities necessitate government intervention. Under China's planned economy, development was managed on a project basis. Thus, the land use of a project was not specified by urban plans; decisions about development intensity, layout and subdivision were left to users. This lack of land management did not lead to chaotic land uses because projects usually fulfilled a government assignment.

The freedom to change land uses becomes problematic, under the dual land system, when land uses are converted spontaneously regardless of compatibility or environmental consequences. Examples include the conversion of the ground floors of some government buildings in Shanghai to retail shops; in Guangzhou, the exhibition of motorcars and lorries within the compound of the Guangdong Science Academy; and the construction of hotels, bars and restaurants on land allocated for military uses.

On the one hand, the *change* of land uses does enhance the *efficiency* of land use, an aspect often neglected under the old system. On the other hand, unregulated land use changes lead to mixed and incompatible uses, chaotic layout, inadequate infrastructure provision, obstacles to future urban development and inconvenience to local people. For example, in Guangzhou, a huge furniture complex has been built by *de facto* users on the site of a proposed city highway junction. Because the project did not apply for a planning permit from the city planning bureau (as required by the 1989 City Planning Act), either the building will have to be demolished or the highway will have to change its path, substantially raising the cost of the project.

Under land leasing, the government can reap substantial planning gains, but from spontaneous and unregulated land use change it cannot capture the benefits that accrue to the users. And, as previously noted, the government has to bear the cost of infrastructure provision for the increased intensity of land uses. This loophole also has negative effects on the establishment of a competitive market system, as the cheap land enables some users to operate businesses that might not survive in a competitive commodity market.

The new land development process also has great impact on urban planning practice. The two-tier structure of urban planning (master planning and detailed layout planning) cannot control development effectively because the master planning process is not an independent component of planning control (Yeh and Wu 1999). It must resort to other measures provided by the planned economy, such as the registration of projects and investment monitoring. But, because of the devolution of power in China from the central government to local governments, these measures have been relaxed and abandoned. The implementation of the master plan has become a serious issue that exacerbates the problem of lack of development control, especially for administratively allocated lands that are undergoing unregulated land use changes in the black market.

In the past, the internal structure of Chinese cities has been strongly influenced by urban planning and state investment. However, these diminish in importance when more and more firms and factories are owned by individual enterprises and foreign investors. The 1989 City Planning Law was ineffective in controlling land development, as its main requirement was the preparation of a master plan by city government. The land use zones of master plans are too broad to control site-specific development (making rejection of a particular project difficult) and leave too much discretion to the building administration and local district governments. Disputes can occur between the applicant and the authority that grants planning permits.

The breadth of the existing land use zones may not control for the location, type and intensity of development along the axes of the master and detailed layout plans. For example, a site zoned for public buildings may be used to build tall office buildings, without regard for the suitability of the site for this use, and depriving the area of cultural and recreational buildings. In the past, most offices, shops and commercial activities were owned and operated by government departments, and all nonresidential land was considered "public building" land.

This differs from the concept of public building land in Western free-market economies. In China's cities, most land considered public building land would, in the West, be considered office and commercial land. There is now more private and foreign investment in Chinese cities because of the post-1978 economic reforms and open economic policies. Consequently, land zoned for public buildings may no longer be under the control of city government, but may be developed into commercial offices by government departments and state enterprises looking to reap greater profits. This can leave inadequate amounts and types of land available for other public buildings that could meet community demand for sports, cultural and recreational facilities.

Again, the broad land use zones make it difficult for city government to ensure that certain kinds of land will be available at the right locations, or will be available at all. For example, land zoned for public buildings can be used for offices and hotels regardless of whether these are suitable uses for the parcels. This explains why office buildings and hotels seem to have been erected randomly in the city, and how, yet again, the availability of appropriate parcels for public buildings for sports, culture and recreation can be at risk.

Unregulated land use changes are occurring very rapidly in China's cities because of the existence of the black market in land and land use. Since the adoption of the paid land use system, land no longer merely provides space for living and production; it has acquired commercial value and become a means to make profit. Land is seen as an input into the production process — a productive factor (capital) that can bring economic return to the landowner. In theory, land is *de jure* owned by the state. In reality, there is no clear understanding about who has the property rights of administratively allocated land. Thus, they are *de facto* owned by the land occupier.

On the black market, the land occupier can "sell" the land to other users, for other uses, in order to capture profits from land prices that are rising due to the introduction of land leasing.

It is difficult for urban planning to control unregulated land use changes because Chinese cities do not operate under zoning legislation. Most land use change is from residential and industrial to commercial uses. This can be observed easily along the main streets of most cities where offices, hotels and restaurants have been erected in place of residential housing. In Shanghai, small companies have redeveloped old two- and three-story flats (previously perceived as high-class, detached private housing) into offices. Since Deng Xiaoping's 1992 tour of southern Chinese cities (during which he famously urged a quickening of the pace of economic reform), pubs and inns have quickly taken over ordinary housing along Zuopu Road in Shanghai. It has become difficult to judge the use of buildings by their appearance. Land use in cities becomes more chaotic and mixed as unregulated land use changes happen at the different structural levels — in buildings, on street blocks and in districts.

To deal with the problem of uncontrolled land use, urban planners are actively proposing the use of detailed development control plans (*kongzhixing xiangxi guihua*), which are very similar to zoning plans but with finer controls, such as plot ratios and site coverage. Attempts are also being made to refine the land use categories in the master plan. The first national land use standard for urban planning in China — the National Standard of Urban Land Use Classification and Planning Standards (National Standard No. GVB137) — was promulgated in 1990 and implemented on 1 March 1991. The standard classifies land uses into 10 main categories, 46 subcategories and 73 subtypes. Some cities, including both Shanghai and Shenzhen, have considered preparing their own zoning ordinances (Yeh and Wu 1999).

Urban Restructuring and the New Urban Form
The dual land market also influences land use restructuring, which under the land leasing system can occur systematically, according to a development plan. And, the land leasing system enables the government to capture the market value of land by leasing it for the use that brings the highest price. Historically, without the land leasing system, city governments have not had the financial resources to restructure land use even when that was desirable. The introduction of the land market has thus made possible elements of urban planning that had previously gone unfunded, and has led to the redevelopment of the city center and the formation of central business districts that Chinese cities have lacked.

The use of land leasing and of BOT (build, operate and transfer[1]) constitutes

---

1 BOT (build, operate and transfer) is a common financing method for infrastructure, in which it is built and operated by the private sector and then returned to government after a term of years, as specified in the original contract.

the current trend in revenue generation for urban infrastructure improvements. Cities such as Beijing and Shanghai are using these mechanisms to attract foreign investment in urban renewal and the construction of the underground rail system. The new paid land use system has provided city governments a new and substantial revenue source unavailable in the past when land was allocated free of charge.

The rapid pace at which land use restructuring is proceeding on administratively allocated land is becoming a major headache for city governments. Because of the underlying problem of development control, owners of administratively allocated land can find ways to convert part or all of their land to uses that generate higher returns, but that differ from the intended use at the time of the original allocation. By subletting their land to other users through joint ventures or other means (which command a good price, given high demand and scarcity of city center land), they can avoid returning the land to the municipal government, and can capture some of the difference between the land's market value and the value of the land that they acquired almost free of charge through administrative allocation.

Land use changes on this type of land, although generally responsive to market demand, tend to be spontaneous and often create urban traffic and environmental problems. Private businesspeople will sometimes identify lots (in residential areas) that they believe have potential as sites for restaurants and nightclubs, and will then buy commercial housing in a suburb to which residents of the urban lots can be relocated. For their trouble, residents can be compensated with sums as great as 10,000–20,000 RMB.

In the past, government has had great difficulty in relocating economic activities and residents from the city center, but now market forces are able to do so. Some streets are evolving toward specialized functions, such as fashion shops on Huaihai Road and clubs and restaurants on Zuopu Road in Shanghai. Visitors to Chinese cities of a decade ago would now find that urban landscapes, particularly those near city centers, have changed dramatically because of land reform (Yeh and Wu 1995; Wu and Yeh 1997; 1999).

The dual land market has led to the development of a new urban form through the urban restructuring process discussed previously. The urban landscape in Chinese cities since land reform in 1988 can be considered a composite of the land use patterns resulting from the more well-planned leased land and from the sporadic development of administratively allocated land (see Figure 4). Leased land is often put on the market for leasing after some form of urban planning, and land development in these areas is normally somewhat orderly. Because of the black market and ambiguity in land use control, administratively allocated land is often converted to land uses that were not intended under the original land allocation. This composite urban form — a patchwork of both well-planned and sporadic development — can be found in every city in China.

FIGURE 4
Dual Land Market and Urban Form in Chinese Cities

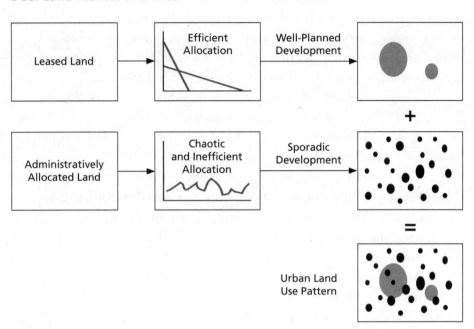

Urban Sprawl

Because it takes time to assemble land in the city center for redevelopment, and because large parcels (for projects such as housing and economic and technological development zones) may not be available, many new developments are decentralized to the urban fringe through acquisition of land from farmers (transaction Types I_1 and II_1). This leads, not surprisingly, to urban sprawl.

Economic and technological development zones (ETDZs) have been used as a mechanism for attracting foreign investment since the 1978 economic reforms. The development of ETDZs was slow before the land reform efforts in 1987, but after the adoption of the paid transfer of land use rights, when land suddenly acquired value, more and more ETDZs were established as municipalities sought to raise revenue through land leasing. In 1990, there were 1,874 ETDZs (Zou 1993); that number reached 2,700 in 1992 (Liang 1993). The total area of ETDZs established in 1992 reached 15,000 square kilometers, exceeding the total area of the built-up portions of China's cities (Song 1995).

Quite a large proportion of ETDZs did not experience substantial development, and that land has been left idle. The rapid increase of ETDZs wasted valuable agricultural land and caused ecological problems by changing the land cover. Only a few ETDZs in the large cities have achieved satisfactory results; Minhang, Hongqiao and Chaohejing in Shanghai are examples. In June 1993 many of the ETDZs that had not attracted any development projects were ordered by the central government to close down.

In addition to the proliferation of ETDZs, the urban fringe has also seen rapid development of large housing projects. Most of the land in the ETDZs is leased out by city government, but for some housing projects land is leased to developers through the black market. In rural areas, farmers prefer leasing directly to developers on the black market — often at lower-than-market prices — because they can secure higher prices than would be possible from the state enterprises (transaction Type II$_1$).

Urban sprawl has led to encroachment on valuable agricultural land (Yeh and Li 1997; 1999; 2000). For example, there has been excessive land conversion and urban sprawl in the Pearl River Delta, north of Hong Kong. As a result of a property boom in the region, rapid land development and agricultural land losses are occurring in Dongguan, located north of Hong Kong at the eastern side of the Pearl River Delta. From 1988 through 1993, 23.7 percent of the total area of Dongguan had undergone changes (Yeh and Li 1997). This is a much higher figure than the 3.2 percent land use change in Hong Kong during the 1987–1995 period (Yeh and Chan 1996).

The spread of urban sprawl (which does not respect urban forms) into valuable agricultural land has produced severe impacts on agricultural production and sustainable urban development, especially the consumption of energy in transportation. It is estimated that if an alternative, compact development were used, it could save as much as 35.7 percent of land development and infrastructure costs, and 34 percent of gasoline consumption in Dongguan (Yeh and Li 2000). Also, as previously noted, the unregulated acquisition of land on the black market for projects at the urban fringe is problematic because very often the potential land use has not been approved by the government. This kind of parcel on the urban periphery may not be provided with water supply and sewer, which leads to environmental problems. Through the black market, land uses in administratively allocated land on the urban fringe have been converted spontaneously, regardless of compatible uses and environmental consequences.

Conclusion: Challenges of the Dual Land Market System

Despite the introduction of land leasing, a large proportion of land in China continues to be allocated through administrative methods, giving rise to a dual land market system. The difference in land prices in the dual land market can be enormous — a reality that often leads to the development of a black market in land. There is constant conflict among the municipalities, developers, existing land users and farmers, all of whom are attempting to capture the differential land value.

The dual land market system may lead to conflict with urban planning. Administratively allocated land is, no doubt, subject to urban plans that can be aligned with the public interest of the time. Leased land, however, is restricted by the lease conditions, as a land lease is a legally protected contract under China's contract law.

The experience of Hong Kong shows that under the leasehold land system there are potential conflicts between land leasing and zoning (Yeh 1994). Lease terms fail as a method of development control because of their rigidity. For lease conditions to be effective as a method of development control, a carefully prepared urban plan has to exist. The current land leasing system in China specifies very clearly the use and development intensity of leased land. If in the future the government wants to change the land use in accordance with a new urban plan, huge compensation liabilities may be incurred.

The dual land market and the resulting black market are vulnerable to corruption: government officials can be bribed to approve development projects or to change the urban plan. Although land auction may capture the best land rent from the market, only a small proportion of land leasing in China is from land auction (see Figure 5). The majority is from negotiation, which may be more susceptible to corruption.

Some changes are urgently needed; the method of land leasing must be changed from negotiation to auction, and land transactions and land use changes must be regulated. This can ensure that the land value gained is under the control of the government and not flowing to the work units or state enterprises, which obtain the administratively allocated land at very low prices. Existing administratively allocated land should be converted to leased status through payment of premiums to city governments.

The administrative allocation system of land distribution is causing losses of land revenue, unregulated land use changes and urban sprawl, and in the long run may have to be abolished. All land, except that designated for community purposes, should be leased land that operates according to land market principles and under the guidance of the urban planning system.

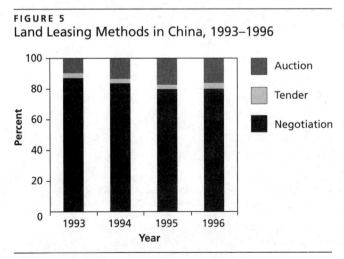

FIGURE 5
Land Leasing Methods in China, 1993–1996

SOURCE: Yearbook of the Land of China (1995, 1996, and 1997)

References

Dowall, David E. 1993. Establishing urban land markets in the People's Republic of China. *Journal of the American Planning Association* 59(2):182–192.

Yearbook of the Land of China. 1995, 1996, 1997. Beijing: China Land Press.

Fung, K. I. 1981. Urban sprawl in China: Some causative factors. In *Urban development in modern China*, Laurence J. C. Ma and Edward W. Hanten, eds., 194–220. Boulder, CO: Westview Press.

Liang, C. 1993. Seven cities chosen as pilot for real estate. *China Daily*. 5 May.

Song, C. H. 1995. Real estate development and urban planning control. *City Planning Review* 2:3–6.

Tang, Yunbin. 1989. Urban land use in China: Policy issues and options. *Land Use Policy* 6(1):53–63.

Tian, Fu. 1994. Review of the problems of real estate business in China. *Urban Problems* 2:51–54.

Walker, Anthony. 1991. *Land, property and construction in the People's Republic of China*. Hong Kong: University of Hong Kong Press.

Wu, F., and A. G. O. Yeh. 1997. Changing spatial distribution and determinants of land development in Chinese cities in the transition from a centrally planned economy to a socialist market economy — a case study of Guangzhou. *Urban Studies* 34(11):1851–1879.

———. 1999. Urban spatial structure in a transitional economy: The case of Guangzhou. *Journal of the American Planning Association* 65(4):377–394.

Yeh, A. G. O. 1985. Physical planning. In *Modernization in China: The case of the Shenzhen special economic zone*, K. Y. Wong and D. K. Y. Chu, eds., 108–130. Hong Kong: Oxford University Press.

———. 1994. Land leasing and urban planning — lessons from Hong Kong. *Regional Development Dialogue* 15(2):3–21.

Yeh, A. G. O., and J. C. W. Chan. 1996. Territorial development strategy and land use changes in Hong Kong. In *Hong Kong and the Pearl River Delta as seen from space*, K. N. Au and M. Lulla, eds., 63–74. Hong Kong: GeoCarto International.

Yeh, A. G. O., and Xia Li. 1997. An integrated remote sensing and GIS approach in the monitoring and evaluation of rapid urban growth for sustainable development in the Pearl River Delta, China. *International Planning Studies* 2(2):195–222.

———. 1999. Economic development and agricultural land loss in the Pearl River Delta, China. *Habitat International* 23(3):373–390.

———. 2000. The need for compact development in fast growing areas of China: The Pearl River Delta. In *Compact cities: Sustainable urban forms for developing countries,* M. Jenks and R. Burgess, eds., 73–90. London: E & F N Spon Press.

Yeh, A. G. O., and F. Wu. 1995. Internal structure of Chinese cities in the midst of economic reform. *Urban Geography* 16(6):521–554.

———. 1996. The new land development process and urban development in Chinese cities. *International Journal of Urban and Regional Research* 20(2):330–353.

————. 1999. The transformation of the urban planning system in China from a centrally planned to transitional economy. *Progress in Planning* 51(3):167–252.

Zhou, Yeping. 1992. *Perspectives on China's real estate business*. Hong Kong: Joint Publishing (HK) Co. Ltd.

Zou, Deci. 1993. An impact by the leasing system of urban land upon urban development. *China City Planning Review* 9(1):27–30.

Chapter 3

The Land Administration Law of 1998 and Its Impact on Urban Development

WILLIAM VALLETTA

In August 1998, China's National People's Congress adopted a revised Land Administration Law (LAL) as part of a series of legislative actions intended to establish the "socialist market with Chinese characteristics."[1] The 14th National Congress of the Chinese Communist Party had first announced this theoretical formula in 1991. It described a mixed system of civil law and market-economic and administrative control mechanisms that the leadership hoped would achieve efficient private initiative along with effective state protection of society and the environment. In this socialist market citizens, enterprises and organizations would have a substantial level of independence, self-reliance and responsibility for the maintenance of economic assets and the outcome of production and trade. They would hold land and real property in forms defined by civil law. This meant that their rights of possession, use and disposition would be defined in written documents, protected by the courts and subject to transfer directly to others without state permission. State agencies would regulate the market in order to prevent abuses. They would retain control of key industries and engage in transactions as parallel legal and economic partners with individuals, enterprises and organizations.

To minimize the risk of social and political disruption, China rejected a "shock therapy" approach and designed these reforms to be adopted and implemented in stages. First, the party and the government worked out the rough ideas and principles. These were then applied in experimental fashion in limited sectors or geographic zones chosen for their high probability of success. When positive results were achieved, the new mechanisms were expanded into more sectors and wider zones (Gao and Chi 1995, 7–16; Liu 1999; Xia 1999).

This pattern of gradual reform was followed in the spheres of land use, land allocation and urban development. The first changes, which introduced elements of contract obligations and leasehold as the basis for land possession, took place in a

---

1 See note 6 in Chapter 1, this volume.

small number of special economic development zones (SEDZs) in the mid-1980s. These mechanisms were applied along with methods of competitive land allocation, streamlined construction permitting and planning, and programs allowing the adjustment of labor, tax and currency laws to stimulate investor interest. The early zones proved successful and municipalities and provinces were permitted to increase the numbers, areas and types of zones (Gao and Chi 1995, 339–358; Gao and Chi 1997, 141–162). Then the new elements of civil law and market transactions were added to laws and administrative regulations applying to selected cities and regions. By the time of the 14th National Congress in 1991, the Communist Party was prepared to extend certain reforms to the country as a whole. Thus, the subsequent legislation, including the 1998 LAL, was adopted in the context of this goal: to accomplish the transition from experimentation to systemic reform.

The process of gradual reform was not linear, however, and it did not involve a one-for-one replacement of old elements with new. Instead, the former administrative mechanisms remained in place for some state enterprises and agencies, while citizens, private enterprises and organizations were made subject to the new mechanisms (Gu and Liu 1999; Gau and Chi 1995, 12–17). This created a double-track system, with each side influencing the other. The new principles and institutions of law, and of economic and planning practice, began to emerge as hybrids.

Today the central problem is determining whether these hybrids are, in fact, achieving the balance intended (for the socialist market with Chinese characteristics), or whether they are leading to an impractical, self-contradictory system, prone to corruption and inefficiency. This chapter is an attempt to begin the analysis. At the outset, it considers the evolution of land law before 1998, in order to clarify the content of the reforms embodied in the LAL of that year.

The Evolution of the Fundamental Concepts Before 1998
The Structure of Landholding

The 1982 Chinese Constitution (amended 1988) fixed a two-part structure of land relations. At the higher level, ownership of land was placed in the state and in collectives, and at a subordinate level, rights of possession and use would be granted to individuals, enterprises and organizations.[2] The 1988 LAL defined the subsidiary forms and specified that certain of these rights would be paid for. It also mandated "overall land use planning" as the method by which decisions to expand developed territory and allocate land parcels for urban uses were to be made. Related to the

---

2 Article 10 of the Constitution of 1982 (amended 1988) provided the framework for the LAL with the following clauses: that land in urban settlements is to be state owned; that rural land is to be owned by collectives, except for portions of such land retained by the state; that the state may "in the public interest" take over land for its use in accordance with law; that no individual or organization may appropriate, buy, sell or otherwise engage in transfer of land by unlawful means; that the right of use of land may be transferred in accordance with law; and that all individuals and organizations using land must make rational use of it.

LAL, the General Principles of Civil Law of 1983 contained basic principles of contractual obligations and transactions among citizens and enterprises.

The systems of land allocation and planning and the methods of payment for
land were detailed in related laws and implementing acts. The 1991 implementation
law for the 1988 LAL defined procedures for creating land parcels for urban development. The Law on the Administration of Urban Real Property of 1994, the Provisional Regulations on the Grant and Assignment to Use State Land in Urban Areas
of 1990, and the Provisional Regulations on Administration of Allocated Land Use
Rights of 1992 further defined the content of urban land use rights. The Law on
Urban Development of 1989 elaborated the system of planning and regulation of
lands within urban areas.

As these laws and regulations took effect, they transformed the occupancy and
use of land from a system of administrative allocation and command to one in which
individuals, enterprises and organizations possessed rights and obligations of a contractual nature. These could not yet be defined as property rights, in the absence of
a comprehensive civil code, but they did establish three key principles: landholders
could make certain decisions about acquiring, using, managing and disposing of
land, independent of the state; they could retain profits from their use of land;
and they were expected to bear the costs and responsibilities of its management.
These rights were subordinate to the overall right of ownership in the state and rural
collectives and had to be exercised within the framework of state planning and
management of land.

After 1988, the structure of landholding involved two forms of socialist public
ownership (state and collective), three forms of subordinate rights of possession and
use, and an experimental form of leasehold.[3] The proper placement of a given land
parcel into these forms was based on its broad use category and the identity or legal
status of its user. The structure could be outlined as follows.

(1) **Agricultural (rural) land** consisted of parcels and territories suitable for agricultural and other surface natural-resource production including cultivation,
livestock grazing, forestry and orchards; and related water bodies, fallow lands
and lands with rural housing and agricultural-industrial facilities. Agricultural
land was to be held under collective ownership.

(2) **Construction land** consisted of all parcels and territories within the administrative boundaries of cities and settlements; lands under roads, transport lines, infrastructure lines and facilities; and industrial complexes
outside the boundaries of settlements. Construction land was retained in state
ownership.

(3) **Unused land** consisted of all lands not otherwise classified, including lands
for nature protection, military and security purposes, mountains, deserts,

---

3 See Chapter 2 of the 1988 LAL, Articles 6–12.

forests, wetlands and other lands with severe natural limitations. Unused lands were retained in state ownership and directly managed by state agencies. Licenses to exploit the resources on these lands could be given to enterprises or individuals (e.g., timber-cutting licenses).

Subordinate to the state or collective ownership, citizens and legal persons (enterprises and organizations) could gain possession and use of land in the following forms.

(1) **Contracts** for occupancy and use of collectively owned land were made available to peasant families for farming and housing purposes, and to rural enterprises and work units for industrial and service purposes. These would be paid for and subject either to a term of years, or to periodic reallocation among the village residents.

(2) **Granted rights of use** of construction land were made available to citizens, domestic nonstate enterprises and other independent institutions for all urban purposes. These would be paid for and carry a limited term of years.

(3) **Allocated rights of use** of construction land were made available to state enterprises and public agencies and institutions for limited industrial, energy, transportation and public-service purposes. These would be transferred without payment and without a term of years.

(4) **Leases** of construction land within SEDZs were made available to foreign-owned, joint-venture and certain domestic enterprises meeting the functional criteria for the given zone. The lease transferred the right of possession and occupancy of a parcel along with the right to develop a project in accordance with an approved design and an approved plan for industrial production or service. The lease carried a fixed term of years, usually with a right to renew. In some zones, the lease could be sold or transferred to another enterprise, which agreed to be bound by its terms and conditions. The lease might also be mortgaged.[4]

Planning, Allocation and Land Use Regulation

In conjunction with the reforms of landholding, the 1988 LAL introduced the overall land use plan, which was to serve as the framework in which decisions would be made about creating land parcels, determining their use and placing them into legal forms, as outlined above. The plan was to be part of a broad planning system and was to draw its underlying data and policies from the economic, social, environmental, land use and urban development plans defined in other laws.

In essence, this planning system rested on the Marxist-Leninist theory of affiliation, which holds that various resources (including land and real property)

---

4 The three forms of granted rights, allocated rights and contracts were provided for in the 1988 LAL, to be applied throughout the territory of China. The leasehold was found only in the regulations governing certain special economic zones. In practice, the lease has been strongly influenced by the experience of Hong Kong land leasing.

ought to be affiliated with the various needs of society by means of scientific measurement and classification (rather than market demand and supply). Any decision about occupancy and use of a land parcel would match the characteristics of the land (natural content, location, and level of improvement) to the needs of the user. The laws on planning described a four-stage process.

First, to define the needs of society, the economic and social development plans were to be created for the nation as a whole, including its subordinate provinces, districts and municipal subdivisions. These five-year plans would identify all of the activities in agriculture, industry, trade, infrastructure and housing that would need land. Second, at the level of cities and urban settlements, the general plans would detail the type and intensity of activities foreseen and would consider their most efficient placement within each territory. Third, a parallel hierarchy of overall (spatial) land plans was to be prepared, based on the data assembled about the quality and quantity of the land, water and other resources in each region. With greater detail at the lower levels, these plans were to indicate the best location for each new activity from the standpoint of land capacity. Fourth, each overall land use plan was to be transformed from qualitative analysis to a quantitative calculation. There would be determined, for each major category of social needs, the amounts of land that could be newly allocated during the next five-year period. These amounts would be set as annual quotas of land to be made available for those needs. In particular, for growing cities the key quota was the amount of rural land that could be transformed each year into construction land.[5]

To ensure that the quota of rural land was strictly maintained, the law made use of both political and administrative methods. First, the plan and its quota could not be adopted by the administration of the territorial level to which it was to apply. Instead, the higher-level government had to consider and adopt the plan. For example, the overall land use plan for a major city had to be prepared by the provincial administration and adopted by the provincial council. Second, the law required a four-stage administrative requisition procedure to transform rural land to urban land. This involved (1) the transfer of ownership from the collective to the state; (2) the reclassification of the land from agricultural use to appropriate urban use; (3) the inclusion of the land within the administrative control of the city; and (4) its reallocation to the new industrial, commercial or housing users. Local governments at the municipal level could approve the requisition of rural land in very

---

5 Chapter 3 of the 1988 LAL described the overall land use plan and required governments at all levels to prepare such plans (Article 15). Further, the law required that "urban planning shall fit in with the overall land use plan" and that, in turn, "the use of land within an area covered by an urban plan shall be consistent with such urban plan" (Article 16). Governments at all levels were required to "adopt measures to protect cultivated land" and to improve soil and prevent erosion. The law included the following standard in Article 20:

> Economy must be practiced in using land for state construction and township and village construction; cultivated land shall not be used when wasteland can serve the purpose; good land shall not be used when poor land is available.

small amounts (not more than 3 mu [0.2 hectare] of cultivated land and not more than 10 mu [0.7 hectare] of other rural land).[6] Larger projects needed the vote of the provincial council and the largest (more than 1,000 mu [70 hectares] of cultivated land and 2,000 mu [140 hectares] of other land) required national State Council approval.[7]

For urban land, the law prescribed a less cumbersome process involving only three steps: (1) the land would be reclassified to accommodate a proposed use by amending the city general plan or adopting a new neighborhood detailed plan; (2) on this basis, the local administration and council would withdraw the land from its present user; and (3) they would reallocate it to the new user.

Taken together, these procedures were expected to change the balance of political interests involved in land use decisions by steering new development projects away from rural land and toward land already within urban classifications. By requiring higher-level decisions, it was expected that the parochial interests of municipal officers in expanding urban development would be offset by regional concerns. These political and administrative impediments to the use of rural land were to be reinforced by economic methods in the process of payment for land.

Payment for Land

The 1988 LAL introduced the requirements of payment for urban construction land, and of compensation when agricultural land was requisitioned for urban needs.[8] Initially, it was not intended that these payments would be based on market prices, since the primary transactions would involve state administrative activity, rather than competitive activity among independent individuals or enterprises. The law described the land transfer fees in terms of compensation of the value of the resource being taken from the existing landholder and the particular sector of the economy. A land value reflecting the purposes of the new user was not relevant and could not be considered because to do so would encourage speculation.

The 1988 LAL described land acquisition fees in two circumstances. When farmland was to be requisitioned, the following three payments would be required:

(1) compensation for the land, calculated by taking the average annual output value of its crop or livestock production for the three preceding years and multiplying by a factor of 3–6;[9]

---

6 A mu is the basic unit of land measurement in the Chinese survey system; it equals approximately 1/15 hectare. See the Glossary for more information on land measurement and equivalences.

7 See the 1988 LAL, Article 25.

8 See the 1988 LAL, Articles 27–32.

9 Average annual output value is measured by averaging the monetary value of grain or other crops produced on the land during three harvests.

(2) resettlement fees, calculated by determining the average land area per person (displaced from the land taken), multiplied by the average output value (as in item 1), and then multiplied by a factor of 2–3; and

(3) specific compensation for the replacement value of any improvements on the land and the discounted agricultural output price of any growing crops or perennial plants on the land.

Taken together, the total of these payments was capped at 10 times the output value of the land. Local district- and municipal-level governments were to have some power to adjust these amounts to fit local conditions. When urban land was to be acquired, the following three payments would be required:

(1) a land compensation fee, set as an average per-meter value by the local administration, based on factors measuring the relative location and carrying capacity of the land, and its planning designation;

(2) payment for any losses caused by the withdrawal of the land from the present user; and

(3) payment of all costs related to moving the existing user to another site.

Local administrations could use available market data to set the basic land compensation fee by making reference to the secondary market in leasehold rights or by offering the rights to particular land parcels at auction or by tender. The 1988 law made no reference to the calculation of payment for land in any secondary transaction that might occur. It was unclear whether this omission reflected an expectation that such transactions were not authorized and would not occur, or whether there was intention to allow unregulated negotiation between the parties.

Problems in Applying the 1988 Land Administration Law

Despite the theory behind the 1988 LAL — that its combination of political, administrative, economic and civil law mechanisms would induce disciplined use of land — it was soon obvious that it was failing. Large areas of agricultural land were being transformed to urban land.[10] An increase in eroded and degraded land, and the occurrence of devastating floods attested to the continued mismanagement of rural and forest land. In many cities there was speculation in land and overinvestment in

---

10 As a national policy, China has calculated that it must maintain a minimum of 275 million acres (127 million hectares) of cultivated land to guarantee sufficient production of grain. By 1992 cultivated land had declined to 130 million hectares and in 1994 it fell below the "danger level" of 125 million hectares (Gao and Chi 1997, 102). Sichuan provincial authorities reported that 175,900 hectares of agricultural land were taken out of production each year between 1987 and 1996. Total agricultural land in this mountainous province stood at 6.59 million hectares in 1996 and comprised 13.49 percent of the land mass of 48.88 million hectares. With a population of more than 85 million, cultivated land in Sichuan was only 0.08 hectare per capita, the second lowest ratio in China (Committee Staff and Consultants' Report on Local Environmental Protection and Natural Resources Conservation Legislation of Sichuan Province. Submitted to the Environmental Protection and Natural Resources Conservation Committee of the National People's Congress, Beijing, October 1999).

office buildings, retail premises and luxury housing. Incidents of official corruption involving land and real estate deals proliferated.[11] These problems were, in part, the result of shortcomings in the 1988 LAL.

Under the law, contractual land rights were not property rights, and their holders had no incentive to take a long-term view in managing and improving the land, or to defend actively against its irrational use. In particular, the peasant landholders had no ability or incentive to resist losing the land to urban development.[12] A peasant family's land contract was usually for a very short term of one, three or five years. The family typically made no capital investments and passively relied on the collective-farm management to direct all activities and fund any improvements. If the land were marked for requisition, the peasant would be directed onto another field and would have no share in the proceeds from the compensation fees. The collective or the state or municipal agencies would retain the fees and would apportion them without any accountability.

The urban land contracts, similarly, offered few incentives for their holders to take a long-term and protective view. These granted use rights usually carried long terms and the allocated land use rights were perpetual. Thus, they seemed to meet the need for secure possession during the life of industrial, commercial or housing investments. However, other aspects of their incomplete definition tended to undermine this security. For one thing, the law failed to anticipate that circumstances could change over time and a landholder might be required to dispose of the land and its improvements. In the regulations of some of the SEDZs, the leaseholds were expressly recognized as alienable, or subject to sale, sublease and mortgage.[13] But under the 1988 LAL applicable outside the zones, no reference was made to a right of alienation or disposition. This made it necessary for the municipal and regional officials to have a role in every secondary transaction, withdrawing the right from the first holder and reallocating it to the second. Of course, the public officials would claim a role in the financial "deal." Because the law guaranteed for the existing landholder only compensation for relocation costs and direct losses, it would be claimed that the state (the municipality) was entitled to any other gain in land and real property value. This discouraged enterprises that used land inefficiently from taking

---

11 Jiang criticizes the way in which local governments have competed with each other in "blindly" launching development zones, and estimates that such zones have resulted in the transfer of 24 million mu (1.6 million hectares) of cultivated land out of agricultural use (Jiang 1999).

12 The relationship between the terms and conditions of the land contract and the peasants' willingness to manage and improve the land is discussed in detail in Gao and Chi (1997, 103–108). See also, Du Ying, Experience gained and problems unresolved in experiments on building the land system. In FBIS *China: Unresolved problems noted in land reform*, trans. from Beijing Renmin Lutan, http://www.wnc.fedworld.gov/cgi-bin.

13 In the Shenzhen Special Economic Zone the holder of a "residential property right" — which included both building ownership and the land use right — was given the authority to transfer the right to another person by sale, gift, exchange or inheritance, and to mortgage the right. See Regulations of the Shenzhen Special Economic Zone on the Management of Commodity House Property, Article 6, adopted by the 4th Session of the Standing Committee of the Sixth People's Congress of Guangdong Province (ChinaLaw Computer Assisted Research Center, Document No. 175, 13 November 1983).

active steps to relinquish their excess holdings, and it hindered the redevelopment of built-up areas.

The problem was remedied in part in 1991 with the adoption of the Interim Regulations on Granting and Transferring the Right to Use State Owned Land in Cities and Towns (Interim Regulations of 1991). Through this regulation, the holder of a land grant, who had constructed buildings or improvements (as per plan), could subsequently transfer to a new party, by sale, exchange or gift, the land right along with the buildings rights for the duration of the term. This law reserved for the municipal officers the ability to intervene only if it were determined that the sale price was significantly below the market price, or unreasonably higher. In the case of a low price, the municipality could exercise a preemptive right to purchase at that price. In the case of a higher price, the regulations stated only that the municipal government could "take necessary measures."[14] This law unleashed secondary land and real property sales, along with various mechanisms designed to conceal from public officials the true prices paid.

In other ways, it became clear that the combination of administrative, political, economic and civil law elements in the 1998 LAL were working at cross-purposes, rather than reinforcing one another. There was a significant mismatch between the land planning system and the processes of urban land acquisition and development. The processes of scientific planning were slow, cumbersome and inaccurate, while real investors — those with ready money available to purchase land — quickly determined the locations that were best for their needs, and deals were made without consideration of the plans. These transactions were adjusted after the fact, if at all, by retroactive amendments.

Similarly, the structure of two different methods of valuation — one for rural land being requisitioned, and the other for urbanized land being acquired for development — exposed the great disparity in respective values in some regions. In many requisition deals a large windfall of new value resulted from the reclassification of the land. The requisition procedure was designed to capture all of this value for the state or municipality. That is, the state agency initiating the requisition would pay to the collective the land- and relocation-compensation fees based on agricultural value. After reclassification, the agency would offer the land (by auction, tender or negotiated sale) to industrial, commercial or housing developers as *urban* land, and for a high price. Problems arose because, in reality, the state was not a single, unified organization, but a group of separate, competing agencies. With large amounts of money on the table, the requisition deals attracted intense interest from all the state and municipal units that possessed any claim to jurisdiction over the land.

---

14 Several provinces adopted more detailed regulations. See, for example, the Rules of Guangdong Province on the Assignment (Alienation) of Real Estate in Cities and Towns, adopted 18 January 1994 by the Sixth Session of the Standing Committee of the Eighth Guangdong People's Congress.

Thus, rather than providing a strong disincentive to the transformation of agricultural land, the process spurred bureaucratic units to go out looking for land requisition deals.

Another problem arose because of the inability to keep separate the paid-for, granted land use rights, and the free, allocated land use rights. The law, in theory, prohibited any state enterprise from engaging in a secondary transaction with its allocated land. The planning process was supposed to ensure that these enterprises did not receive excess land beyond their needs as defined in the economic plans. In reality, of course, the growing value of urban land was a strong incentive for state enterprises to claim and hoard as much land as possible and, in various ways, to profit from unauthorized transactions with the surplus.

The failure of the overall land use planning process to discipline state and municipal agencies and state enterprises was a direct result of the weak mechanisms of civil law and the persistence of unrestrained administrative discretion. Public officials in all levels of government retained broad discretionary powers to decide land use questions with no open public review, no audits or financial accountability, and no legal appeals for citizens or enterprises whose rights might be affected. In theory, it was the plans — economic, social, spatial, city development and overall land use — that were supposed to compel the public officials and bureaucratic units to make rational, scientifically directed decisions about land use. But without the necessary methods of coordination, the agencies each prepared plans most favorable for their own mandates and interests. The councils of people's deputies were supposed to ensure that, in the adoption of any plan, other agencies with parallel and overlapping interests would be consulted and disputes resolved. In reality, however, the underlying assumption that each plan was scientifically determined made it very difficult to change any draft at its final stage. The agency sponsoring a plan would employ skillful political maneuvering to get it adopted without challenge, and the legislative bodies and the Communist Party always sought to avoid substantive debate and controversy. Thus, for many territories, particularly on the peripheries of cities, there emerged overlapping plans with different mandates for the same land.

The purpose of the overall land use plan and its quotas was, presumably, to cut across all other plans and solidify clear policy choices for each area. To accomplish this, strong mechanisms were needed to force interagency confrontation and resolve the ensuing disputes. Unfortunately, the 1988 LAL contained only the simplest statements about the requirements of governments to create the plans. It did not mandate participation of parallel agencies in the planning process, and set forth no procedural details for the creation and implementation of the overall land use plan. It did not provide for any mechanism of public participation through which constituencies of citizens could be rallied in support of the plan. Thus, the overall land use plans were ineffective in curtailing the requisition of rural land or the hoarding of urban land.

Adjustments Made by the Land Administration Law of 1998

The drafters of the 1998 LAL sought to remedy the shortcomings of the previous (1986, amended 1988) law by including more mechanisms of economic self-discipline, along with mechanisms to strengthen the effectiveness of planning and the protection of agricultural and unused land. However, they did not intend to alter the fundamental system of landholding. Even though some legal scholars and economists were studying whether to adopt civil law property rights in full as the basis of economic relations, a comprehensive proposal to revise civil law would not be ready for several more years. Thus, the 1998 law retained the four forms of land tenure: agricultural contract, urban granted rights of use, urban allocated rights of use, and lease. However, it refined certain details of these forms in an effort to strengthen peasant and urban landholder participation, and to recalibrate the balance of costs in the development of rural, rather than urban, land. Similarly, the overall land use plan was retained as the primary mechanism for controlling urban expansion, but elements of its procedures and legal mandate were adjusted in an effort to strengthen its effectiveness. These changes appeared in eight content areas in the 1988 LAL.

(1) The definition of the agricultural land contract

New provisions added to the definition of the rural land use contract were intended to strengthen the long-term interests of the peasants and give them an active role in protecting their land against requisition. Previously, municipal-level officials and collective-farm managers had full discretion to set the terms and conditions of the land contract. In most villages they set terms of very few years, and frequently reallocated the fields among the village residents. On one hand, this system had the beneficial purpose of ensuring that every village resident kept an approximately equal share of land as people died or moved away, and others married and reached the age of majority. On the other hand, the system discouraged long-term investment and left the peasant family with a passive role.

Under Article 14 of the 1998 law, the land contract was redefined to carry a 30-year term. Any process initiated by the village or collective-farm administration to change the contract terms within that period would require a two-thirds vote of the village council and would have to be approved by the higher-level township council. The resulting security of a longer term and increased stability in status would, it was expected, encourage peasant families to manage and improve the land more successfully, and to take a stronger interest in its preservation in agricultural use.

(2) The method of calculating the payment for requisition of agricultural land

The status of the peasant family as protector of the land was further reinforced by provisions for the calculation and allocation of fees for land requisition. Formerly, the three-part fee of land compensation, relocation costs, and compensation for improvements and current crops was paid in full to the collective-farm management and village administration. These officials, after transmitting the required amount to higher levels of government, could control the disposition of the funds without any accounting to the farm members or the displaced peasant families.

Article 47 of the new law changed the fee structure and accounting process in three ways. First, the basis for the fees was substantially increased. The land compensation element was now set at 6–10 times the average annual output value for the three preceding years. (Under the 1988 law, a factor of 2–3 was used.) The other fees were similarly increased, and the provincial administration could make further adjustments, based on local conditions, allowing the combined fees to rise to 30 times the output value.

The law also adjusted the administrative process by which the municipal officials and farm managers would make decisions allowing the requisition of land. The affected peasant families were given the rights to receive notice and to review the requisition plan or any other plan to reorganize the holdings of families. The law also required local officials to publish the resettlement plans and fee calculations, and to issue a subsequent accounting of all monies received and disbursed. Although the peasant family had no right to receive a specific portion of the income or to appeal an inadequate settlement, the publication and review requirements were expected to give them stronger leverage to influence the outcome of a requisition plan.

(3) The procedure for approving the requisition of agricultural land

Another change in the procedure for requisitioning farmland involved the level of government empowered to approve such a requisition. Article 45 of the 1998 law removed from the level of municipal administration any power to approve the requisition of rural land, no matter how small a parcel. Henceforth, any transfer of agricultural land in the classification of the richest soil would require approval by the State Council, the highest national level. Similarly, a State Council vote would be necessary to approve any transfer of 35 hectares (530 mu) or more of cultivated land of moderate fertility, and 70 hectares (1,060 mu) or more of any other rural land. The transfer of smaller tracts of land in these categories had to be approved by the provincial council.

It was thought that this would end the practice of local agencies segmenting development projects into small pieces, and would discourage enterprises and bureaucratic units from seeking to requisition rural land because of the more difficult and costly process at the provincial level.

(4) The definition of the (paid-for) grant of urban land use

The previous version of the LAL (1986, amended 1988) had been silent on the ability of the holder of a granted land use right to transfer it to another party or to mortgage it. However, the Interim Regulations of 1991 had set out provisions under which this could take place. Article 63 of the 1998 law stated that an enterprise holding a granted land use right could sell, lease or mortgage it if circumstances made this necessary or convenient. This appeared to mean that the long-term user of the land could engage in a direct, civil law transaction to dispose of its land right. Some ambiguity still remained with respect to the ability of municipal government units to intervene in these transactions.

(5) The definition of (unpaid) allocated rights of use of urban land

In an effort to curb the abuses of unpaid allocation of land to state enterprises, Article 54 of the 1998 LAL limited such allocations to four categories of state users:

(1) governmental units of the state and the military;

(2) public utilities and public welfare organizations;

(3) energy, transportation and water-conservancy projects; and

(4) other uses expressly stated in laws and regulations.

State industrial, commercial and service enterprises would now be excluded from receiving free land, except to the extent that groups of them could muster the political support to secure a new law or regulation.

As a matter of balance to this limitation, it was recognized that a state enterprise with land (previously acquired by allocated right of use without payment) should have the ability to change the holding of that land to a granted right of use by paying the state some portion of the value of the land. Terms of such transactions could be determined by negotiation. The enterprise could then sell, sublease or mortgage the land right to some other party in a direct transaction. It was expected that many state enterprises would be willing to give up for redevelopment parcels of urban land being used inefficiently.

(6) The power to withdraw granted or allocated rights of use of construction land

In conjunction with the provisions allowing granted rights of use to be alienated in direct, civil law transactions, the 1998 law refined the power of state and municipal governments to withdraw these rights. The new provisions, in Article 58, defined a process of expropriation for public needs, rather than a routine administrative process of withdrawal and reallocation.

There were five permissible reasons for which land, already granted or allocated, could be subsequently withdrawn before the end of its term of use:

(1) public welfare needs;

(2) implementation of a city redevelopment plan;

(3) expiration of the contract of the grant and failure of the landholder to renew;

(4) dissolution of a state enterprise holding a (free) allocated right, its removal from the site or its failure to actively use the land; and

(5) large-scale transportation projects, sanitary landfills and mining operations.

This provision was expected to put to rest the question of whether state or municipal agencies could interfere as third parties in the secondary market for land rights. In conjunction with the language of Article 63, it appeared that private parties could now engage in direct, civil law transactions to sell, mortgage or sublease granted land use rights.

(7) Registration and legal protection of granted land rights

As a further method of providing legal protection to urban landholders, the 1998 LAL, Article 11, mandated the creation of a land registration system by agencies of the local and provincial governments, and the issuance of certificates that would "affirm the right of use of such land."

The landholder could secure, from the registry office, legally sufficient proof of its rights to engage in transactions and seek protection in the courts and administrative tribunals. The full details of how registration was to work were not spelled out in the law, but would await further legislation and regulation. There were a number of shortcomings in the description of the registry system. In particular, several different bureaucratic units were given the responsibility for registering lands of various types. The registry was not viewed as a unitary system, and this would complicate its administration and legal status in the future. Nevertheless, inclusion of the principles of registration and certificates of proof was an important step in the movement toward a civil law basis for landholding.

(8) The status of the overall land use plan

In order to remedy the ineffectiveness of the overall land use plan in resolving competing claims to control of land, Articles 17–30 of the 1998 law included five new mechanisms and principles.

First, the law offered more detail about the calculation of the hierarchy of quotas for construction land. The plans at lower levels (i.e., localized administrative entities) were each to contain a portion of the quota set at the higher level, and in the aggregate these lower plan quotas could not exceed the total amount. A new standard of no net loss of agricultural land was set, mandating that, at the level of provinces and of municipalities (rural districts), the total amount of agricultural land had to remain constant or increase. Thus, when a quota of new construction land was permitted in one area, it had to be offset by the creation or improvement of agricultural land in another area.

Under a new Chapter 4 of the law, all agricultural land was to be classified by fertility. The areas with the best soils for grain and seed-oil production, other high-quality soils and irrigated fields were to be marked as "basic agricultural production land." In each province, at least 80 percent of the existing cultivated land had to be so classified. Reclassification of this land for construction or nonagricultural use, except in the most compelling circumstances, would be prohibited. For those areas with fewer parcels of high-quality land, requisition would be allowed in conjunction with a program of fertility improvement (to bring the land into the basic agricultural land classification), or a program to transform wasteland into productive agricultural land by melioration, irrigation or drainage.

Second, Article 20 of the law introduced zoning as a regulatory element of the overall land use plan. Each township-level plan was to fix the zones for various purposes and, in this way, "determine the land use purpose for every piece of land with public announcements."[15] This appeared to mean that the use classification of all parcels of urban land would be determined prior to specific proposals for development in the given territory. This would support more rational decisions about location and dampen somewhat the windfall-value effect on lands being reclassified from low-value to high-value uses.

Third, the 1998 law contained further elaboration of the hierarchical process of adopting the overall land use plans. It retained the fundamental idea of "kicking upward" the authority to approve a plan, but now required dual approval by the two higher levels. For example, the plan of a major city would be prepared by the land agency at the provincial level and then submitted both to the provincial council and to the State Council for approval. The higher levels, it was presumed, would ensure that the plan did not improperly favor local development interests at the expense of agriculture and natural resources protection.

Fourth, Articles 22–25 of the new law made reference to other plans, including city general plans, environmental plans for rivers and other water bodies, economic and social plans, and plans for industrial growth and development. These provisions were intended to coordinate the ministries and to establish, as a legal matter, the supremacy of the overall land use plan in determining the allocation of land for all activities. In Article 26, the law stated that, if deviation from the overall land use plan were necessary to accomplish a major project for energy, transportation or hydropower, then amendment of the plan, involving its full redocumentation, would be required.

Finally, in Articles 27–30, the law provided more detail about the responsibilities of monitoring, gathering statistics on, analyzing and reporting on, and complying

---

15 The translation of the text of the law to include "land with public announcements" refers to rural areas where the method of public notice may be a handwritten sign posted on the door of the communal farm-equipment shed.

with the overall land use plans. The state land management agency would have these responsibilities, which were designed to provide the basis for strict enforcement of the plan in the issuance of construction permits, land allocations, and grants and leases.

Assessing the Impacts of the New Law on Urban Development and Land Use
Implementation of the 1998 Law

The revised LAL took effect on 1 January 1999. In accordance with the Chinese legislative system, it was necessary to adopt subsidiary regulations and, in each province, an act to implement the law at the levels of regional and local administration. The Ministry of Land and Natural Resources promulgated the implementing regulations in April 1999, and Sichuan Province was the first to adopt a provincial law in December 1999. Both of these acts repeated the principles and procedures of the national law, adding detail with respect to the allocation of administrative tasks and responsibilities at the national, regional and local levels. These statutes clarified certain issues. For example, the implementing regulations of the national ministry stated that governments at all levels had the power to allocate urban lands by lease as well as by administrative grant in areas outside the SEDZs. The choice between these two forms would be made by the government body issuing the grant or lease and would reflect economic strategy and the bargaining power of the enterprise acquiring the land. If the lease form were chosen, the terms would be negotiated and the up-front payment to acquire the lease would be relatively low. The grant terms would be administratively determined, and the initial purchase price would likely be higher than that for a lease, with a lower annual fee.[16]

In one important aspect — creating strong public interest in the law and in land preservation — the 1998 LAL realized significant success. This was the result of the process by which the law was considered, adopted and put into effect. For the first time in modern China's legislative process, the Standing Committee of the National People's Congress published the draft LAL prior to its consideration. In the spring of 1998, the full draft text appeared in newspapers and journals with an invitation to citizens to offer written comments and to attend hearings on the law. These took place in provincial cities and drew groups of experts, local officials and citizens, who debated the merits of the new law and made numerous recommendations for changes. The record of public comments was compiled along with responses prepared by the Environmental Protection and Natural Resources Committee. The compilation and analysis, together with a redrafted law, were delivered to the Standing Committee of the National People's Congress during the early summer of

---

16 For a discussion of the implementing regulations see Chan (1999).

1998.[17] After the law was adopted, the process of its implementation at the provincial level included outreach by the National People's Congress committee staff. In Sichuan Province, where the "model" provincial law was drafted, a similar procedure of hearings and public comments took place.[18]

Public interest in the new LAL was considerable, both because of this process of public involvement and because of the timing of its adoption. In August 1998 China had just suffered a series of devastating floods in its central river valleys, and it was well understood that poor land and forest management had been important contributing factors. The government publicized the new law as part of its decisive response to the disaster. Thus, the law was launched with a high degree of expectation and with commitment to implement its provisions.

An Approach to Measuring the Impact of the 1998 Law

Because so few years have passed since implementation of the law, conclusions about its impact on development trends in urban areas would be premature. It is appropriate, however, to begin to structure methods for this analysis. Initial reference can be made to the annual statistics on urban and rural land use, compiled by the Ministry of Environment and the provincial land management agencies (see Appendices 1 and 2, pp. 80–85). Over time, these statistics should indicate a decreasing trend in the loss of farmland to urban development and an increasing trend in density of development within cities. The start of this trend may be reflected in the most recent statistical reports on urban land, issued on a province-by-province basis. The reports show a somewhat smaller amount of land requisitioned for construction in 1999 for the eastern provinces, when compared with the large amounts of land requisitioned for specific cities in the 1988–1996 period and for the list of provinces in 1996. This may reflect a strengthening of farmland protection, and improved planning and enforcement.

As would be expected, the statistics after 1996 reflect a shift in accord with the announced policy of encouraging development in the western provinces. These western urban regions will offer a more revealing test of the success of the law, because in those predominantly mountainous and desert areas, the main urban centers are situated in the same well-watered valleys in which the very limited productive agricultural land is found. In comparison with eastern cities, the existing density of development in the western cities is quite low, suggesting that these cities can gain population and intensified industry and services without significant expansion of their land areas.

---

17 Legislative Department of the Environmental Protection and Natural Resources Conservation Committee of the National People's Congress, Legislative Report on the Land Law, Asian Development Bank Technical Assistance Project of Legislation, Beijing, September 1998.

18 Implementation Measures of Sichuan Province on the Land Administration Law of the People's Republic of China, adopted at the 12th meeting of the Standing Committee of the 9th People's Congress of Sichuan Province on 10 December 1999.

Real property market prices are another set of measurements that should show the impact of the law. In many eastern cities (in Beijing, Shanghai and Guangzhou, in particular) the secondary markets in land and real property are lively and well monitored.[19] During the past 10 years, they have developed the patterns typical of urban markets. There is differentiation among properties, based on industrial, commercial, housing and other uses, and among subcategories of these, such as luxury domestic housing, housing for foreign residents, and housing for industrial and service workers. There is also differentiation among properties based on the factors of location, like central and peripheral locations, quality of environment, level of urban services, etc. As would be expected in the major cities, real property prices have fluctuated based on levels of construction, vacancy rates and rates of demand for space.[20] After 1997, when the downturn in Asian economies took place, there was a direct impact on prices and rents, exposing the very high level of overbuilding in many sectors — in luxury housing and in office and commercial premises, in particular.

If the law is successful in encouraging growth in secondary-market activity, there should be two beneficial effects. First, more enterprises and other organizations that use land inefficiently will make it available on the market for redevelopment. In conjunction with more effective limitation of farmland requisition, this should increase redevelopment and urban density, and rationalize landholding patterns within existing built-up areas. Second, by creating a more accurate record of prices and values (differentiated among categories of use and location) the secondary market should influence investors to make more precise choices about the types and timing of projects to pursue. Cycles of boom and bust should flatten toward more typical levels seen in urban areas around the world.

Persistence of the Double-Track Economy in Land

The major problems that the 1998 LAL did not solve are those that result from the maintenance of the double-track system. Despite some adjustment — the limitation on free land allocation to state enterprises, in particular — there remain a significant number of spheres in which the former administrative system still functions. This fact reflects the theory of a balanced socialist market economy with Chinese char-

---

19 See the work of Raymond Y. C. Tse and his colleagues, comparing the fluctuations of rents and prices for office space in Shanghai, Guangzhou and Shenzhen. Their analysis shows how these markets developed quickly after the cities were opened to investment from foreign and Hong Kong firms. Starting from a nonexistent base in 1987, by 1997 these cities were major office markets, with prices and rents showing normal market functioning. In the initial rush to supply pent-up demand, there were strong levels of investment and construction activity combined with rising rents and prices; this situation lasted until 1995 when supply caught up with demand. Continuing addition of new space, paired with leveling and declining demand in the economic downturn of 1997–1998, caused both rents and prices to fall, a trend that continued through 1999. Tse and his colleagues attributed the overbuilding to the tendency of the new development enterprises to rush ahead with projects that were inadequately based on future financial analysis. They were inexperienced in calculating the timing of real estate cycles, and were eager to get projects finished for fear that the government might rescind development rights or expropriate returns (Tse, Chiang, and Raftery 1999; Tse and Webb 2000; and Choi 1998).

20 See, for example, Jones, Lang, and LaSalle, Inc. Year 2000 ULI market profiles for Pacific rim cities, in which the Shanghai property market is analyzed for 1998–1999.

acteristics, but achieves little in the way of practical solutions. The overdevelopment of luxury commercial and housing projects in cities, the unrestrained requisitioning of farmland and the over-reliance on development of the periphery (rather than redevelopment of central districts) all can be recognized as symptoms of the double-track economy in land. Certain enterprise managers, along with municipal, regional and provincial officials, have had access to land, without payment or at low cost, through the systems of allocated land use rights, requisition and negotiation. Thus, they have initiated many urban development projects with the prime motivation of securing state assets and resources. These projects have taken place without consideration of demand, and without a clear calculation of future costs and returns. They have gone forward with the intent of establishing their sponsors as players holding assets. In this way, the problem of speculation, which the socialist market is supposed to prevent, has arisen not as the result of an unrestrained market side, but as a result of unrestrained bureaucratic power and political influence.

The LAL of 1998 did not make an essential change in this situation. It has added some clarity to the mechanisms of land contracts, grants and leases; it has limited free allocation; it has kicked upward to higher levels of political and administrative power the authority to approve requisitions of farmland; and it appears to have removed the process of withdrawal-and-reallocation from routine dispositions of granted land use rights. However, it has allowed each of these processes to remain as an element of the primary land system, and it has preserved broad discretion in their use by bureaucratic units and administrative and legislative bodies, which are guided by political decision making.

In response to past abuses, the law drafters curtailed the powers of municipal- and district-level officials, and required key decisions on planning and requisition to be made at provincial and national levels. This reflects the assumption that, at these latter levels, decisions will be guided by more thorough scientific assessment, and that the political forces representing agriculture and natural resources protection will have a stronger balancing influence on decisions. This assumption does not appear to have a strong basis in past experience. It is just as likely that, with the decision-making powers having been kicked upward, the corrupt practices will move upward as well. Because it will now be more expensive and require greater political influence to benefit from land deals, these deals will likely involve a smaller number of large-scale interests linked to major government department and Communist Party cadres.

What remains missing in the new LAL are adequate mechanisms for public scrutiny of land deals, and for clear accounting of costs, values, expenditures and receipts involved in land transactions. On 1 June 2001, the Xinhua News Agency reported on a policy statement of the Ministry of Land and Natural Resources, indicating that it would mandate the use of public bidding and auctions for commercial projects in order to improve transparency in the transfer of state-owned land. Hu

Cunzhe, Director of Land Use Management in the ministry, was quoted as saying that currently, only 5 percent of state-owned land is dealt with by auction or tender. "Irregularities in land supply, resulting from behind-the-scenes dealing, have caused 10-billion-yuan losses in land revenues," Mr. Hu stated. In response, the ministry ordered all cities and townships to adopt regulations providing for auctions and tenders for land for commercial purposes, and to raise their base land transfer prices before the end of that year.

The permissive authority to use auctions and tenders has existed since 1988 and has been the routine method of leasing in some of the SEDZs. However, as is clear from the Xinhua News Agency report, municipal, regional and provincial officers have avoided these open methods in favor of negotiation and behind-the-scenes dealing. In conjunction with a low base price, the negotiation process gives maximum flexibility to apportion the money on the table in any development deal. Ministry regulations may help to achieve more open and accountable procedures, but without a clear mandate in the law, and given the double-track system, their success is improbable.

Conclusion

The pressure on China's limited land resources will continue, whatever the outcome of the implementation measures for the 1998 Land Administration Law. The Tenth Five-Year Plan for National Economic and Social Development (2001–2005) anticipates continued strong growth of industry, commerce and services — at or above 7 percent of gross domestic product (GDP) per year. Further, the plan anticipates that large numbers of rural residents will leave the land, allowing consolidation of farm holdings and modernization of farm techniques.[21] Taken together, the growth of urban production and services, and the migration of new populations to cities will sustain the strong pressure to bring more land into urban use.

If this strong demand becomes more accurately reflected in urban land prices, as appears to be happening, the disparity between the values of urban and rural land will continue to grow, creating a greater challenge for the land management and planning agencies. In this situation, the role of a strong land use planning system becomes even more critical. But, it is in this aspect of planning that the law is weakest. Despite its new language exhorting agencies and enterprises to subject their economic planning to the overall land use plans, and its kicking upward of the authority to approve these plans, the fundamental structure of the planning process has not been improved.

To be successful, the planning process should be one in which every new national-, provincial- and regional-level action with the potential to affect the need for land is reviewed openly and critically for its impact. Trade-offs among the

---

21 The main elements of the Tenth Five-Year Plan have been reported in Frankenstein (2000).

interests should be made clear. For example, every new highway proposal should be carefully studied to determine how much land it is going to require, and whether its width might be narrowed, its length reduced and its location shifted away from agricultural and prime urban land. However, there is nothing in the planning process, as defined by the 1998 LAL, requiring that this kind of critical analysis take place, and no mechanisms appear in the law to force conflicting policies, plans and projects to be openly revealed and debated.

Achieving 7 percent annual growth in GDP will require very large investments in infrastructure and the encouragement of strong industrial and service expansion. China has demonstrated its commitment to carry forward such projects. Finding the balance of economic growth with environmental protection and preservation of farmland will need a similar commitment. So far, the planning mechanisms and structures of civil law and regulatory enforcement do not appear to be sufficiently developed to provide the necessary balance.

Appendix I

TABLE 1.A
Enterprise Growth and Land Development, 1997–1999

Indicator	1997	1998	1999
Number of new enterprises registered			
Total	21,286	24,378	25,762
State-owned		7,958	7,370
Collective		4,538	4,127
Hong Kong-/Taiwan-owned	1,989	3,214	3,167
Foreign-owned	2,095	1,204	1,173
Domestic private			
Employment in new enterprises			
Total	683,200	825,900	880,300
State-owned		332,800	312,200
Collective		134,900	127,400
Hong Kong-/Taiwan-owned	50,000	83,800	80,200
Foreign-owned	54,300	33,400	32,900
Domestic private			
Land used for development (in hectares)			
Land area developed	7,371.3	7,730.1	9,319.6
Land area acquired	6,641.7	10,109.3	11,958.9

SOURCE: State Statistical Bureau (2000, Table 6-35)

Appendix I

TABLE 1.B
Urban Growth Indicators, 1988–1999

Four Autonomous Cities	Developed Area (sq. km.)	Requisitioned for Construction (sq. km.)	Population Density/ sq. km.	Floor Space in All Buildings (1,000 sq. m.)	Floor Space in Resid. Buildings (1,000 sq. m.)
Beijing					
1988	391.00	3.90	2,250		
1989	395.40	4.40			
1992	429.40	5.20		199,200	99,530
1993	454.10	11.60			
1994	467.00	12.90		248,280	122,890
1996	476.80	9.80		230,630	117,410
1999	488.28	0.15	2,562	274,300	142,110
Tianjin					
1988	315.50	7.60	1,315		
1989	321.80	7.70			
1992	337.50	5.70			
1993	338.00	0.00		120,560	60,210
1994	339.30	11.60		125,090	63,490
1996	374.30	3.16		136,080	68,040
1999	377.90	0.00	1,381	150,420	98,310
Shanghai					
1988	247.20	39.00	20,727		
1989	248.30	42.20			
1992	253.70	120.60			
1993	300.00	0.00		202,370	105,609
1994	390.20	632.80		208,880	110,430
1996	412.27	32.90		235,930	131,350
1999	549.58	44.00	2,872	318,020	193,100
Chongqing					
1988	84.10	3.60	1,909		
1989	84.10	0.40			
1992	101.50	2.20		61,270	29,680
1993	106.30	4.70			
1994	116.10	10.30		63,500	30,010
1999	302.61	3.94	588		

SOURCE: Constructed from data in State Statistical Bureau (2000, Table 11–8; 1996, Table 10-8; and 1994)

(continued)

Appendix I

TABLE 1.B
Urban Growth Indicators, 1988–1999 *(continued)*

Eastern Provincial Centers	Developed Area (sq. km.)	Requisitioned for Construction (sq. km.)	Population Density/ sq. km.	Floor Space in All Buildings (1,000 sq. m.)	Floor Space in Residential Buildings (1,000 sq. m.)
Guangzhou					
1988	240.70	22.10	2,418		
1989	182.30	4.80			
1992	206.00	4.00		87,230	46,520
1994	216.20	4.80	2,614	91,570	50,230
Shenzhen					
1992	72.00	33.00	1,444		
1993	80.90				
1994	84.00		4,069		
Guangdong Province					
1996	1,551.90	177.28	806		
1999	1,628.56	12.18	1,433		
Fuzhou					
1988	48.30	0.10	1,199		
1989	48.80	0.20			
1992	54.80	3.90			
1993	60.70				
1994	64.00		1,298		
Fujian Province					
1996	345.48	14.03	1,103		
1999·	420.30	11.89	1,223		
Hangzhou					
1988	67.10	2.00	3,053		
1989	67.90	1.10			
1992	85.20	2.40			
1993	90.20	4.20			
1994	96.40	6.20	3,286		
Ningbo					
1988	56.40	0.80	1,011		
1989	57.80	1.10			
1992	63.30	5.40			
1993	77.70	10.10			
1994	61.40	2.90	1,073		
Jiangsu Province					
1996	1,186.30	47.06	2,112		
1999	1,297.00	22.39	2,243		
Wuhan					
1988	187.40	1.60	1,613		
1989	110.90	2.80			
1992	193.90	3.30			
1993	210.90	16.90			
1994	226.80	15.90	2,412		

Appendix I

TABLE 1.B
Urban Growth Indicators, 1988–1999 *(continued)*

Western Provincial Centers	Developed Area (sq. km.)	Requisitioned for Construction (sq. km.)	Population Density/ sq. km.	Floor Space in All Buildings (1,000 sq. m.)	Floor Space in Residential Buildings (1,000 sq. m.)
Chengdu					
1988	81.90	2.50	1,949		
1989	83.20	4.80			
1992	88.90	28.20			
1993	92.20	9.30			
1994	97.10	2.80	2,181		
Sichuan Province					
1996	1,089.74	119.89	540		
1999	956.00*	13.12	540		
Lanzhou					
1988	162.50	2.20	888		
1989	162.50	0.10			
1992	162.50	1.40			
1993	162.50	1.90			
1994	162.50	1.00	987		
Gansu Province					
1996	403.30	1.92	280		
1999	413.30	4.67	294		
Xian					
1988	135.00	2.70	3,007		
1989	135.80	0.50			
1992	148.00	9.40			
1993	148.00	18.40			
1994	148.00	20.20	2,739		
Shaanxi Province					
1996	379.20	7.64	1,342		
1999	470.20	4.86	1,456		
Kunming					
1988	93.70	4.10	712		
1989	94.30	4.10			
1992	95.20	5.30			
1993	98.00	6.50			
1994	116.00	17.50	784		
Yunnan Province					
1996	260.65	17.12	244		
1999	318.80	15.53	271		

*This figure does not include Chongqing.

Appendix 2

Urban Growth Indicators by Province, 1966 and 1999

Province	Developed Area (sq. km.)	Requisitioned for Construction (sq. km.)	Population Density/ sq. km.
Hebei			
1996	893.30	9.04	1,771
1999	941.89	8.97	1,769
Shanxi			
1996	556.00	6.63	592
1999	600.36	4.01	747
Liaonang			
1996	1,456.00	20.19	1,218
1999	1,536.00	10.71	1,184
Jilin			
1996	815.00	6.43	751
1999	767.30	17.87	737
Heilongjiang			
1996	1,282.00	2.19	226
1999	1,248.20	3.36	231
Jiangsu			
1996	1,186.30	47.06	2,112
1999	1,297.00	22.39	2,243
Zhejiang			
1996	833.73	36.08	988
1999	868.50	32.48	1,207
Anhui			
1996	767.40	48.51	1,480
1999	835.90	8.29	1,548
Fujian			
1996	345.48	14.03	1,103
1999	420.30	11.89	1,223
Jianxi			
1996	481.83	16.81	436
1999	513.90	3.95	446
Shandong			
1996	1,342.99	26.26	571
1999	1,475.50	26.28	617
Henan			
1996	917.50	22.43	1,780
1999	1,017.20	18.93	1,326

SOURCE: Constructed from data in State Statistical Bureau (2000, Table 11-5; and 1997, Table 10-8)

Appendix 2

Urban Growth Indicators by Province, 1966 and 1999 *(continued)*

Province	Developed Area (sq. km.)	Requisitioned for Construction (sq. km.)	Population Density/ sq. km.
Hubei			
1996	1,539.70	341.75	410
1999	1,271.30	20.80	424
Hunan			
1996	645.42	22.43	1,780
1999	743.40	22.35	921
Guangdong			
1996	1,551.90	177.28	806
1999	1,628.50	12.18	1,433
Guangxi			
1996	509.12	11.56	391
1999	566.80	4.43	464
Hainan			
1996	180.33	8.71	2,051
1999	254.60	4.65	2,295
Sichuan			
1996	1,089.74	119.89	540
1999	956.00	13.12	540
Chongqing			
1999	302.61	3.94	588
Guighan			
1996	229.33	4.57	286
1999	254.90	8.26	324
Yunnan			
1996	260.65	17.12	244
1999	318.80	15.53	271
Gansu			
1996	403.30	1.92	280
1999	413.30	4.67	294
Shaanxi			
1996	379.20	7.64	1,342
1999	470.20	4.86	1,456
Ningxia			
1996	109.17	0.68	267
1999	121.63	4.24	618
Total China			
1996	20,214.18	1,018.05	367
1999	21,524.54	340.47	462

References

Alsen, Jonas. 1996. An introduction to Chinese property law. *Maryland Journal of International Law and Trade* 20(Spring):1.

Baker, Mark B. 1995. Forgotten legal China. *Houston Journal of International Law* 17 (Spring):363.

Cai, Yunlong. 1998. The protection of farmland in urban development in China. *China Environment News*, 6 June, p. 6. Land Science Center, Beijing University.

Chan, Rico. 1999. Green acres. *China Business Review* 26(July-Aug.):14.

Choi, Sonsu. 1998. A housing market in the making. *China Business Review* 25(6/Nov.-Dec.):14.

The Economist. 2000. Survey of China. 8 April.

Frankenstein, John. 2000. China's tenth five-year plan: Statement of intent and targets. *China Business Review* 27(3/May-June).

Gao, Shangquan, and Fulin Chi. 1995. *Theory and reality of transition to a market economy.* Beijing: Foreign Language Press.

———. 1997. *Several issues arising during the retracking of the Chinese economy.* Beijing: Foreign Language Press.

Gao, Shangquan, Guoguang Liu, and Junru Ma. 1999. *The market economy and China.* Beijing: Foreign Language Press.

Gu, Shutang, and Xin Liu. 1999. Focal points and the difficulties of changing China's double-track economic system into a market economy. In *The market economy and China*, S. Gao, G. Liu, and J. Ma, eds., 267–291. Beijing: Foreign Language Press.

Institute of Public Administration (New York) and Institute of Finance and Trade Economics (at the Chinese Academy of Social Sciences). 1995. China's urban housing reform. Report of Joint Research.

Jiang, Chunze. 1999. The marketization process of the Chinese economy and the current macroeconomic situation. In *The market economy and China*, S. Gao, G. Liu, and J. Ma, eds., 47–54. Beijing: Foreign Language Press.

Jones Lang La Salle, Inc. 2000. Year 2000 Urban Land Institute market profiles for Pacific rim cities.

Kwok, R. Y., William Parrish, Anthony Gar-on Yeh, and Xueqiang Xu, eds. 1987. *Chinese urban reform — what model now?* Studies on Contemporary China. New York: M. E. Sharpe.

Liu, Guoguang. 1999. Establishing a socialist market economic framework. In *The market economy and China*, S. Gao, G. Liu, and J. Ma, eds., 30–46. Beijing: Foreign Language Press.

Miles, Micheal, and Jianping Mei. 1994. Real estate investment opportunities in China: How risky? *Real Estate Finance* 11(2/Summer):66.

Ping, Jiang. 1997. The improvement of the Chinese land law system — an outline. Report presented to the Environmental Protection and Resource Conservation Committee of the National People's Congress, September 18, 1997. Reproduced in *Inception report of the capacity building for natural resources legislation project*, Asian Development Bank, TA No. 2375-PRC, November 1997.

Roberts, Dexter. 2000. China's wealth gap. *Business Week* 15 May:170.

State Statistical Bureau. 1994. *China statistical yearbook.* Beijing: China Statistical Publishing House.

———. 1996. *China statistical yearbook.* Beijing: China Statistical Publishing House.

———. 1997. *China statistical yearbook.* Beijing: China Statistical Publishing House.

———. 2000. *China statistical yearbook.* Beijing: China Statistical Publishing House.

Stewart, Richard, and William Valletta. 1999. Reform of environmental and land law legislation: Two case studies from China. New York University Center on Environmental and Land Use Law, Asian Development Bank, TA No. 2375-PRC, July 1999.

Tse, Raymond Y. C., Y. H. Chiang, and John Raftery. 1999. Office property returns in Shanghai, Guangzhu and Shenzhen. *Journal of Real Estate Literature* 7(2):197.

Tse, Raymond Y. C., and James Webb. 2000. Regional comparison of office prices and rentals in China. *Journal of Real Estate Portfolio Management* 6(2/April):141.

Xia, Zhenkun. 1999. Clearing up some doubts about China's change to a market economy. In *The market economy and China*, S. Gao, G. Liu, and J. Ma, eds., 134–143. Beijing: Foreign Language Press.

Xinhua News Agency. 2001. Report available from CND Global News. 1 June. www.cnd.org.

Yao, Liang Huang, and Zhao Hua Xie. 1995. China on the horizon: An overview of China's real estate law. *John Marshall Law Review* 28(Spring):593.

Zhu, Jieming. 1994. Changing land policy and its impact on local growth: The experience in the Shenzhen Special Economic Zones, China, in the 1980s. *Urban Studies* 31(10/Dec.): 1611–1623.

Chapter 4

China's Land Resources and Land Use Change

GEORGE C. S. LIN AND SAMUEL P. S. HO

C hina has seen significant changes in land use and land management in the past two decades as it has embarked on market reforms and active engagement with the forces of globalization. Until recently, scholarly attempts to understand the magnitude, extent, and cause-and-effect relationships of land use changes had been hampered by a lack of accurate and reliable data. For years, China's policy makers and Western researchers have been confused by the existence of multiple and contradictory statistics on land resources and land use. Estimates of the total area of China's cultivated land, for instance, have ranged from 94.97 to 160 million hectares.[1] There was virtually no systematic information on China's nonagricultural land except for various statistical reports on the elusive *chengshi jianchengqu* (urban built-up area) encircled by the ever-changing administrative boundaries.[2] Despite several important attempts to address the lack of accurate and reliable data, ambiguity and confusion remain about the size of China's territory, how the land has been used and how land use has changed over time and across space.[3]

Yet, issues of land resources and land use change are of great significance. With more than 20 percent of the world's population living on less than 7 percent of Earth's cultivated land, China's land resources are extremely scarce in comparison to

---

1 Gerhard Heilig (1997, 144) identified three sets of estimates for China's cultivated land, including 94.97 million hectares from China's State Statistical Bureau, 125.23 million hectares from China's State Land Administrative Bureau and 136.4 million hectares from Chinese geographers. Vaclav Smil (1999, 423) argues that a tally of China's farmland should include aquacultural ponds and orchards because of their growing contributions to the Chinese diet. Such an accounting would lead to an estimate of China's 1997 farmland in the range of 146–160 million hectares. China's official State Statistical Bureau reported in 1995 that China had cultivated land of 94.97 million hectares; it then stopped releasing any information until the year 2000. See State Statistical Bureau 2000, 373.

2 The Chinese statistical authorities defined *chengshi jianchengqu* (urban built-up area) as "a largely continuous area covered by urban constructions and urban facilities. Water surfaces such as rivers and lakes are also included." (State Statistical Bureau, Team for Urban Social and Economic Surveys 2000, 488.)

3 For detailed discussions, see Orleans 1991, 403–417; Crook 1993, 33–39; Heilig 1997, 139–168; Ash and Edmonds 1998, 836–879; Smil 1999, 414–429; and Yang and Li 2000.

the world average.[4] Dramatic economic expansion since the 1978 reforms has brought about massive land developments throughout the country, leading to an alarmingly rapid loss of cultivated land. Chinese statistical authorities have reported that between 1978 and 1995, total cultivated land shrank substantially from 99.39 to 94.97 million hectares, whereas the total population of the nation continued its rise, climbing from 962.59 million to 1.21 billion people (State Statistical Bureau 2000, 69 and 355). Given the sheer scale of both land area and population, the widening gap between a growing population and a rapidly shrinking land resource base has raised concerns about the capability of the Chinese to feed themselves and the possible implications of that for global food security.

The urgent need for accurate and reliable data on China's land use has caught the attention of agricultural and land administration authorities. A large-scale national land survey, the first of its kind since the founding of the People's Republic of China (PRC) in 1949, was conducted from 1984 to 1996.[5] The purpose of the nationwide survey was to gather systematic county-level data on the types, area and location of land use, as well as the distribution of land under different ownerships.

The survey adopted a standardized land classification scheme consisting of 8 one-digit categories and 46 two-digit categories, and was based primarily on the reading, verification, classification and measurement of different land uses from the most recent aerial photos, Landsat images and maps available at the time. The survey covered 2,843 counties, 43,000 towns, 740,000 villages, 25,000 farms and 400,000 administrative units. It involved more than two million people and cost more than one billion yuan, of which the central government contributed 0.315 billion yuan, while the balance was covered by provincial and local governments. Most of the survey was conducted between 1990 and 1995, but it was subsequently decided that all surveys would be adjusted to a standard date of 31 October 1996 (a methodology similar to that used in the national population census). The results of the survey included a set of raw land use data gathered on various dates between 1981 and 1995, and a set of land use data adjusted to 31 October 1996.

This chapter analyzes data obtained from the 1996 national land survey, which provides the first systematic measurement of China's land. Given the country's great geographic and technological variation, the data may not be entirely free of error, discrepancy or inconsistency despite the official effort for verification and

---

4 China's per capita cultivated land in 1996 was a mere 0.106 hectare — more than 50 percent smaller than the world average of 0.236 hectare. See Li 2000, 6.

5 Prior to 1949, important attempts had already been made to investigate land utilization in China. See, for instance, Buck (1937). Since 1949 a number of land surveys have been conducted by the Ministry of Agriculture and the Chinese Academy of Sciences, but none was on a scale comparable to that of the 1996 national land survey (see Appendix, p.119).

correction.[6] Compared with many other estimates derived from various Chinese and Western sources, however, the results of the 1996 land survey stand out as the most comprehensive and coherent quantification of China's land currently available. As China conducts the land survey periodically, as it does with the national population census, the 1996 survey will provide the foundation for future comparative studies of the dynamics of land use change over time.

The chapter begins with an assessment of China's land resources and the structure of land use in 1996, and proceeds with an analysis of changes in land use since 1949 — especially during the 1990s, when dramatic changes in land use took place as a result of accelerated economic growth. Special attention is given to an evaluation of changes in cultivated land, as this issue has concerned both academics and policy makers.[7] The authors conclude with a summary of major findings and discussion of their implications for better management of China's precious land resources.

China's Land Resources

When Mao Zedong proclaimed the founding of the People's Republic of China in October 1949, he was told by the surveying soldiers of the People's Liberation Army (PLA) that the territory over which he ruled had a land mass of 9.6 million square kilometers. This estimate was derived from measurement of topographical maps for military purposes (Ma 2000, 6). The figure became the official estimate quoted in students' textbooks, statistical yearbooks and government documents. It was only after October 1996 that China was finally able to modify the official estimate of its land area on the basis of scientific surveys. The 1996 national land survey revealed that the size of the Chinese mainland was actually 9,506,763 square kilometers, a smaller figure than the one reported to Mao 47 years earlier. Even when the three non-Communist enclaves of Taiwan (36,000 square kilometers), Hong Kong (1,098 square kilometers) and Macao (23.8 square kilometers) were taken into account, the nation had a territory of only 9.54 million square kilometers.

The results of the 1996 national land survey challenged the long-standing and widely held Chinese belief that their country had "a vast territory with abundant resources" (*dida wubo*). Although the country's territory ranks as the world's third largest, next only to Russia (17.7 million square kilometers) and Canada (9.97 million square kilometers), and slightly larger than the U.S. (9.36 million square kilometers), about two-thirds of the territory is mountainous (46.4 percent) or hilly (20 percent). Arable land accounted for only 14.5 percent of China's total land

---

6 A quality assessment exercise conducted by China's State Land Administrative Bureau (on the basis of 12,000 sampled land slots) reported a discrepancy of 19,812 mu out of 2.023 billion mu (a ratio of 1:102,126) between the reported and verified areas of cultivated land (1 mu = .0667 hectares; see Glossary for table of equivalences). See Ma 2000, 249.

7 In this study, the term "cultivated land" is used interchangeably with "farmland."

area.[8] China's poor land resource conditions were exacerbated by the unbalanced geographical distribution of its population: more than 40 percent of the Chinese people lived in East China on less than 14 percent of the country's total land area. On the other hand, West China, with more than 56 percent of the land, housed only 23 percent of the population.[9]

The structure of land use, according to the 1996 survey, is outlined in Table 1. Upon scrutiny, three important points become obvious. First, China's land use was predominantly agricultural, with approximately 67 percent of the land devoted to various agricultural activities, including crop cultivation, orchard, forestry and pasture. This figure corresponded closely to the 75.6 percent of the population that was defined as agricultural — an interesting correspondence, given the growing importance of the nonagricultural sector of the economy and the rising level of urbanization.[10] Human settlements and stand-alone industrial and mining sites occupied slightly more than 2.5 percent of China's territory, suggesting a remarkably high density and intensity of urban and industrial development in such a populous country.

Second, the main users of China's construction land (that is, land developed for human settlements, and for industrial and transportation construction) were primarily in the countryside. Rural settlements accounted for more than two-thirds (68.35 percent) of the construction land, while the 69 percent used for transportation comprised predominantly rural roads. This pattern appeared to be the result of a distinctive process of rural industrialization and urbanization, in which extensive land developments, scattered around the country rather than concentrated in a few large cities, have occurred spontaneously.

Third, there was considerable geographic variation in land use. Among the three macro regions, East China used a significant portion of its land for crop cultivation (28 percent), compared with Central China (19.93 percent) and West China (6.88 percent). Likewise, settlements and industrial and transportation developments absorbed a greater proportion of the total land in East China than in Central or West China (see Table 1).

---

8 Chinese geographers reported in 2000 that plains accounted for 33.6 percent of China's land mass. However, 59 percent of the plains areas (or 20 percent of the total land mass) was located in regions of harsh environmental conditions, including Inner Mongolia, Xinjiang, Qinghai and Tibet — leaving the country with less than 14 percent of its land cultivable. Cultivable land included 130 million hectares of cultivated land (accounting for 13.68 percent of the total land area) and another 8 million hectares (0.84 percent of the national land area) of land that was believed to be suitable for cultivation after reclamation (Li 2000, 10–11).

9 The Chinese statistical definition of East China includes Liaoning, Beijing, Tianjin, Hebei, Shandong, Jiangsu, Shanghai, Zhejiang, Fujian, Guangdong, Hainan and Guangxi. Central China includes Heilongjiang, Jilin, Nei Mongol, Shanxi, Henan, Anhui, Jiangxi, Hubei and Hunan. West China includes Sichuan (including Chongqing), Guizhou, Yunnan, Qinghai, Xizang, Shaanxi, Ningxia, Gansu and Xinjiang (Li 2000, 7).

10 The Chinese statistical authorities reported that the Chinese population in 1996 was 75.6 percent agricultural (State Statistical Bureau 1997, 373). It is a well-known fact, however, that people who are officially classified as part of an "agricultural population" may not necessarily be engaged in agricultural activities or live in the countryside.

TABLE 1
China's Land Use Pattern by Region, 1996
(area in square kilometers or 100 hectares)

	China			East China[1]			Central China[2]			West China[3]		
	Area	% of Total	% of Subtotal	Area	% of Total	% of Subtotal	Area	% of Total	% of Subtotal	Area	% of Total	% of Subtotal
Total area	9,506,762	100.00		1,318,901	100.00		2,815,902	100.00		5,371,960	100.00	
Agricultural land	6,337,365	66.66	100.00	934,192	70.83	100.00	2,224,323	78.99	100.00	3,178,850	59.17	100.00
Cultivated land	1,300,392	13.68	20.52	369,559	28.02	39.56	561,189	19.93	25.23	369,645	6.88	11.63
Other agricultural land	5,036,973	52.98	79.48	564,633	42.81	60.44	1,663,134	59.06	74.77	2,809,206	52.29	88.37
Yuan di[4]	100,238	1.05	1.58	55,145	4.18	5.90	22,215	0.79	1.00	22,878	0.43	0.72
Forest	2,276,087	23.94	35.92	488,685	37.05	52.31	915,574	32.51	41.16	871,828	16.23	27.43
Pasture	2,660,648	27.99	41.98	20,803	1.58	2.23	725,346	25.76	32.61	1,914,499	35.64	60.23
Settlements & ind.-mining sites	240,753	2.53	100.00	91,648	6.95	100.00	94,482	3.36	100.00	54,624	1.02	100.00
Cities & towns	26,503	0.28	11.01	12,521	0.95	13.66	9,736	0.35	10.31	4,245	0.08	7.77
Rural settlements	164,558	1.73	68.35	58,001	4.40	63.29	69,182	2.46	73.22	37,375	0.70	68.42
Stand-alone ind.-mining sites	27,688	0.29	11.50	13,789	1.05	15.05	9,557	0.34	10.12	4,342	0.08	7.95
Other	22,005	0.23	9.14	7,337	0.56	8.01	6,007	0.21	6.36	8,661	0.16	15.86
Land used for transportation	54,677	0.58	100.00	18,371	1.39	100.00	23,059	0.82	100.00	13,248	0.25	100.00
Railroads	3,230	0.03	5.91	931	0.07	5.07	1,721	0.06	7.46	579	0.01	4.37
Highways	13,263	0.14	24.26	4,860	0.37	26.45	4,696	0.17	20.36	3,708	0.07	27.99
Rural roads	37,730	0.40	69.01	12,339	0.94	67.17	16,548	0.59	71.77	8,843	0.16	66.75
Other	454	0.01	0.83	241	0.02	1.31	94	0.00	0.41	119	0.00	0.89
Water area	423,088	4.45		117,755	8.93		139,083	4.94		166,251	3.09	
Unused land	2,450,879	25.78		156,935	11.90		334,955	11.90		1,958,989	36.47	

NOTES:

[1] Liaoning, Beijing, Tianjin, Hebei, Shandong, Jiangsu, Shanghai, Zhejiang, Fujian, Guangdong, Hainan and Guangxi

[2] Heilongjiang, Jilin, Nei Mongol, Shanxi, Henan, Anhui, Jiangxi, Hubei and Hunan

[3] Sichuan (including Chongqing), Guizhou, Yunnan, Qinghai. Xizang, Shaanxi, Ningxia, Gansu and Xinjiang

[4] Orchards, vineyards and plantations

SOURCES: Li (2000, Table 2-2-1); and Liu (2000)

The percentage of unused land declined from West China to the east, as would be expected because land use depends on the natural environment, population density and level of economic development. East China is endowed with a favorable natural environment suitable for intensive crop cultivation. In 1996 the region also had a population density two-and-one-half times that of Central China, and nearly eight times that of West China. Per capita gross domestic product (GDP) in East China was approximately 80 percent higher than that in Central China, and nearly 130 percent higher than that in West China.

Other things being equal, higher population density and a better-developed regional economy will create greater demand for land for settlements, and for industrial as well as transportation developments. China's unused land consisted primarily of bare stone (42 percent), sand (20 percent), and waste grassland (20 percent), although the latter covered more than one-quarter (25.78 percent) of China's total land mass. The bulk of unused land (79.9 percent) was found in West China, where the natural environment is harsh.

Among the different kinds of land use, cultivated land has received the greatest attention from scholars and policy makers. This is not surprising because cultivated land remains the most important "rice bowl" for the huge Chinese population. It has been estimated that the limited (and shrinking) cultivated land in the country provided 88 percent of the food for the Chinese people (Li 2000, 7). Therefore, it was believed that changes in cultivated land would have significant impacts on food security. Scholars are divided, however, on the seriousness of China's problem of farmland loss, and the extent to which it could undermine the capacity of the Chinese to feed themselves. The disagreement has revolved around differing estimates of how much cultivated land China actually has, where such land is located (that is, whether the loss of cultivated land in one place can be replaced by newly reclaimed land elsewhere), and how intensively arable land may be used (i.e., single cropping versus multiple cropping).[11]

The results of the 1996 national land survey provided new insights. Table 2 lists data on China's cultivated land at the provincial level in 1996. China's cultivated land totaled 130 million hectares in 1996, according to the national land survey. Those provinces whose cultivated land accounted for five percent or more of the national total were clearly clustered in three regions: the Sichuan Basin, the North China Plain (Hebei, Henan and Shandong), and the frontier of Inner Mongolia-Heilongjiang. The first two regions correspond with population concentrations and

---

11 Lester Brown's widely discussed projection that China would not be able to feed itself by 2030 if the current trend of farmland loss continued is representative of a rather pessimistic view intended to be a "wake-up call" for China. On the optimistic side, Vaclav Smil and Gerhard Heilig are among those who believe that China actually has 40–50 percent more cultivated land than has been claimed by the statistical authorities. This, coupled with other factors like the dietary change from cereals to animal foods, increased intensity of land use through multiple cropping, and technological advances (e.g., fertilizer, irrigation, better agronomic practices, etc.) should give China "a fairly hopeful outlook." See Smil 1999, 429; Heilig 1997, 144; and Brown 1995.

TABLE 2
China's Cultivated Land, 1996
(area in hectares)

Province	Land Survey Cultivated Land (ha)	% of National Territory	Per Capita (ha)	State Statistical Bureau Data (ha)	Discrepancy (%)
Beijing	343,921.35	0.26	0.03	399,533.33	-13.92
Tianjin	485,598.01	0.37	0.05	426,133.33	13.95
Hebei	6,883,347.65	5.29	0.11	6,517,333.33	5.62
Shanxi	4,588,612.27	3.53	0.15	3,645,133.33	25.88
Nei Mongol	8,200,950.34	6.31	0.36	5,491,400.00	49.34
Liaoning	4,174,785.53	3.21	0.10	3,389,733.33	23.16
Jilin	5,578,386.23	4.29	0.21	3,953,200.00	41.11
Heilongjiang	11,772,951.13	9.05	0.32	8,995,333.33	30.88
Shanghai	315,076.68	0.24	0.02	290,000.00	8.65
Jiangsu	5,061,672.29	3.89	0.07	4,448,333.33	13.79
Zhejiang	2,125,342.72	1.63	0.05	1,617,800.00	31.37
Anhui	5,971,720.63	4.59	0.01	4,291,133.33	39.16
Fujian	1,434,692.11	1.10	0.04	1,204,000.00	19.16
Jiangxi	2,993,434.94	2.30	0.07	2,308,400.00	29.68
Shandong	7,689,286.67	5.91	0.09	6,696,000.00	14.83
Henan	8,110,338.71	6.24	0.09	6,805,800.00	19.17
Hubei	4,949,534.51	3.81	0.09	3,358,000.00	47.40
Hunan	3,952,960.77	3.04	0.06	3,231,733.33	22.32
Guangdong	3,272,159.34	2.52	0.05	2,317,333.33	41.20
Guangxi	4,407,937.20	3.39	0.01	2,614,200.00	68.62
Hainan	762,068.05	0.59	0.10	429,200.00	77.56
Sichuan	9,169,098.94	7.05	0.08	6,189,600.00	48.14
Guizhou	4,903,499.41	3.77	0.14	1,840,000.00	166.49
Yunnan	6,421,570.71	4.94	0.16	2,870,600.00	123.70
Tibet	362,593.47	0.28	0.15	222,133.33	63.23
Shaanxi	5,140,480.40	3.95	0.15	3,393,400.00	51.48
Gansu	5,024,741.81	3.86	0.20	3,482,533.33	44.28
Qinghai	688,012.78	0.53	0.14	589,933.33	16.63
Ningxia	1,268,798.61	0.98	0.24	807,200.00	57.19
Xinjiang	3,985,656.17	3.07	0.24	3,128,333.33	27.41
Total	**130,039,229.45**	**100.00**	**0.11**	**94,953,466.67**	**36.95**

SOURCES: Li (2000, 93); and Liu (2000)

FIGURE 1
Cultivated Land in China per Capita, 1996

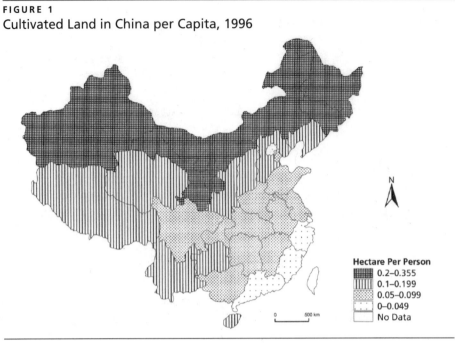

Hectare Per Person
0.2–0.355
0.1–0.199
0.05–0.099
0–0.049
No Data

N

0   500 km

SOURCE: Liu (2000, 76)

established agricultural traditions. The location of cultivated land in the northern and northeastern frontier is clearly a result of recent reclamation, as discussed later in this chapter.

When the impact of population concentration is taken into account, cultivated land per capita displayed a neat pattern (Figure 1). Availability of cultivated land decreased from north to south and from the interior to the southeastern coast. The seemingly abundant supply of land resources in the northern and northeastern frontiers should be discounted, however, because the natural environment there is less favorable for cultivation than that of the southeastern coast. Differences in productivity or land use intensity between the North and South, or interior and coast, can be illustrated by the geographic variation in the multiple cropping index (MCI) — the ratio between the total area sown in a year and the area of cultivated land. As shown in Figure 2, provinces in the northern and northeast regions are all characterized by an MCI of less than 100, suggesting that these regions are suitable for no more than a single cropping per year. In contrast, regions in the southern and southeastern coast, where multiple cropping has been the norm, all feature an MCI greater than 200. This situation suggests that the limited land resources in the southern and southeastern regions of the country are more precious than those on the northern frontier. Therefore, any loss of farmland in the South may not be sufficiently compensated by land reclamation in the North.

It has been well documented that China's local officials have tended to underreport the areas of cultivated land in order to evade state production quotas and

FIGURE 2
Distribution of Multiple Cropping Index (MCI) in China, 1995

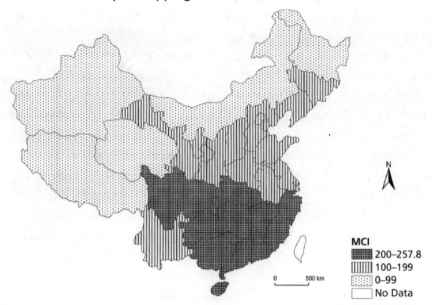

SOURCE: Li (2000, 157)

taxes (Orleans 1991, 404; Crook 1993, 33–39; Heilig 1997, 143; Ash and Edmonds 1998, 844; Smil 1999, 417). The extent of under-reporting and the reasons for it have not been entirely clear, however.[12] Table 2 compares the figures from the 1996 land survey with those of the State Statistical Bureau. For the country as a whole, the total area of cultivated land reported by the statistical authorities (94.95 million hectares) was smaller than the surveyed figure (130 million hectares) by about 37 percent. With the exception of Beijing, all provinces and special municipalities showed under-reporting of their cultivated land. The two provinces that had an abnormally high discrepancy (of more than 100 percent) are Guizhou and Yunnan, both mountainous provinces in the southwestern interior. Other provinces in which under-reporting exceeded 50 percent included those at high elevations (Tibet), in isolated locations (Hainan), and in hilly regions (Ningxia, Shaanxi and Guangxi).

The reasons for under-reporting land area are many, including attempts to incur reduced production quotas and taxes, or to inflate average yields for promotion. These motives do not, however, explain why under-reporting has been more serious in the hilly and mountainous regions than elsewhere. Several technical reasons should not be overlooked. First, the statistical data set was built by adding net real changes annually to the original measurements done in the early 1950s, when land was first

---

12 After comparing the official 1985 figures with the land census data from Frederick W. Crook (1993, 34), Robert Ash and Richard Edmonds (1998, 844–845) observed that the statistical figures under-reported China's cultivated land by 44.2 percent, and that the degree of under-reporting has tended to be greater for hilly and mountainous regions. Vaclav Smil (1999, 429) suggested that the Chinese official figures may have under-reported farmland by 40–60 percent.

assigned to peasants using varying local units of measurement. The discrepancies may be a smaller problem in plains areas where land is relatively uniform and easy to measure, and a larger problem in mountainous and hilly regions, where the likelihood of errors is greater.

Second, the Chinese government has, since the 1950s, encouraged land reclamation in the less developed regions. Newly reclaimed land was entitled to tax exemption only for the first three years and was tax liable afterward. To avoid that liability, a considerable amount of reclaimed land in the newly developed regions was never reported to the government. Third, when land was contracted to peasants, the less productive slope land in hilly and mountainous areas was allocated with extra acreage beyond the amounts registered, in recognition of poor quality.[13]

Finally, when cultivated land was expropriated by the state for the construction of large projects, the expropriated land area was removed from the statistical yearbook once the projects were approved. There have been cases in which approved projects never were completed and the expropriated land was eventually returned to farmers for cultivation, but the returned land area never was entered back into the statistical record (Li 2000, 94). The chance of project failure has typically been higher in the less-developed hilly or mountainous regions than in the economically advanced and more accessible regions where the demand for land development is higher.

Land Use Change

Assessment of land use changes in China over time has long been hindered by the lack of accurate and comparable data. Data that have been made available as a result of the land surveys conducted in the mid-1980s, 1990 and 1996 were conflated to identify the long-term trend in land use change since 1949 (see Table 3), and to examine more closely the pattern of change in recent decades[14] (see Tables 4 and 5).

China's land use, as it existed in 1949, was characterized by its low level of development. The two types of land that represented the lion's share of China's land mass

---

13 Vaclav Smil (1999, 417) reported that 1.25–1.5 mu of less-productive land would be assigned to peasants but registered as only 1 mu.

14 The data used for analysis here include those for 1949, the mid-1980s, 1990 and 1996. The 1949 data were first published in Wu and Guo 1994, 77. It was derived by the geographers of the Chinese Academy of Sciences from both census materials provided by relevant agricultural departments and estimates based on sampled surveys and readings of topographic maps. For instance, the area of cultivated land and *yuan di* (orchards and fruit tree plantations — see note 15) was derived from the Ministry of Agriculture, whereas the area of forested land was obtained from the Ministry of Forestry. The figures for pastureland came from the national annual agricultural statistics; areas of other land use types were calculated from either sampled surveys or reading of maps. While the 1949 data set may not be as accurate as one would expect, it remains an important benchmark — the only available one with a classification scheme comparable to those for subsequent national land surveys. The land surveys conducted in the mid-1980s, 1990 and 1996 were all based on analyses of aerial photos and Landsat images in combination with field surveys. Only a small number of provinces carried out the land surveys at the county level in the mid-1980s (1980–1984), and the results were published in four volumes for internal use in Chinese Academy of Sciences, Commission for Comprehensive Surveys of Natural Resources 1989. Data for both 1990 and 1996 were the results of the recent nationwide land survey. The 1990 raw data were gathered in the first round; the 1996 data were updated to a standard point in time (31 October 1996). See: note 6; Chinese Academy of Sciences (1989); Li 2000, 126; Liu 2000; and Appendix, p.119.

TABLE 3

Changes in Land Use in China, 1949–1996
(area in 1,000 hectares)

	Area		Change		Land Use		Change
	1949	1996	Area	%	1949 (as % of total)	1996 (as % of total)	(in percentage points)
Total area	950,676.20	950,676.20			100.00	100.00	
Cultivated land	97,881.30	130,039.20	32,157.90	32.85	10.30	13.68	3.38
Orchards/plantations	1,066.70	10,023.80	8,957.10	839.70	0.11	1.05	0.94
Forest	125,000.00	227,608.70	102,608.70	82.09	13.15	23.94	10.79
Pasture	391,918.70	266,064.80	-125,853.90	-32.11	41.23	27.99	-13.24
Settlements & ind.-mining	4,733.30	24,075.30	19,342.00	408.64	0.50	2.53	2.03
Transportation	2,000.00	5,467.70	3,467.70	173.39	0.21	0.58	0.36
Water area	22,533.30	42,308.80	19,775.50	87.76	2.37	4.45	2.08
Unused land	305,542.90	245,087.90	-60,455.00	-19.79	32.14	25.78	-6.36

SOURCE: Li (2000, 126)

were pasture-grassland (41 percent) and unused land (32 percent). During the subsequent 47 years, both pasture-grassland and unused land were converted in large measure to other uses: cultivation, orchards and plantations, and construction.[15] Pastureland shrank by 125.85 million hectares (32 percent) and its proportion of total land area dropped from 41.2 to 28 percent.[16] Conversion from pasture to cultivation and construction took place primarily in three provinces: Inner Mongolia, Heilongjiang and Xinjiang. Unused land had gone through a similar process of conversion, losing more than 91 million hectares to forestry and cropland, but gaining 30.66 million hectares from forestry and cultivation due to desertification or other natural hazards. The net loss was 60.45 million hectares of unused land, nearly 20 percent of what it had been in 1949.

While pasture and unused land shrank in both absolute amount and proportion, the land used for cultivation and construction demonstrated significant expansion as a result of population growth and economic development. The largest

---

15 Land used for orchards and plantations has been identified in China as "yuan di," which has often been translated as "horticulture." However, this is misleading; the Chinese definition of yuan di actually excludes gardens (acreage in vegetables is included in the definition of "cultivated land"). Yuan di includes orchards and plantations — land planted with perennial plants and trees — that yield products such as fruit, mulberries, tea, rubber, cocoa, coffee, tong oil, spices, and medicinal plant products. For the Chinese definition of yuan di and other categorization of land, see Ma 2000, 13–14.

16 The amount of pastureland converted to cultivation and construction between 1949 and 1996 was estimated at 130.329 million hectares. In the same period, an estimated 4.475 million hectares of cultivated land were returned to pasture. The net reduction in pastureland was 125.853 million hectares or 32.11 percent of the 1949 area (Li 2000, 129).

proportional gain occurred in *yuan di* (orchards and plantations), which showed a dramatic increase of 840 percent since 1949. This expansion is in part due to its very small base in 1949, but is also a result of the profound structural changes in Chinese agriculture since the 1978 economic reforms (discussed in detail later). Most of the growth of yuan di took place in East and South China, where the market demand for cash crops is high and the natural environment is favorable.

Following orchards and plantations in proportional gain was land used for human settlements and industrial-mining sites (more than 400 percent), and transportation infrastructure (173 percent). The forces of industrialization and urbanization clearly have driven such expansion.[17] Between 1949 and 1996, the number of designated cities increased from 132 to 666, and designated towns from 5,402 (in 1953) to 16,126 (in 1996). The urban population grew from 57.65 to 359.5 million and the level of urbanization rose from 10.6 percent to 29.37 percent. Urban built-up area in 1996 reached 1.388 million hectares, which was 2.6 times the amount in 1949 (State Statistical Bureau 1998, 105; Ma and Cui 1987, 388; Chan 1994b, 245; Li 2000, 131; Lin 2002, 307–308).

Most of the new construction land was taken from cultivated land, forest, pasture and unused land. It was estimated that about 80 percent of new land for human settlements and industrial-mining sites was acquired through conversion from cultivated land. Geographically, most of the land development for settlements, industrial facilities and transportation infrastructure had taken place along the eastern coast, particularly in major metropolitan regions (Yeung and Hu 1992; Lin 2001; Logan 2002).

The two other types of land use that merit discussion are cultivated land and forest land, both of which demonstrated considerable gain in absolute amount and proportion. Between 1949 and 1996, an estimated 38.647 million hectares of cultivated land were lost to construction, orchards and plantations, forestry and various natural hazards. At the same time, additional cultivated land, estimated at 70.8 million hectares, was reclaimed from unused, pasture and forest lands. The lost cultivated land was fertile land located primarily in coastal provinces, especially Shandong, Liaoning, Jiangsu, Beijing, Tianjin, Shanghai and Fujian. On the other hand, land reclamation took place mostly in the border and frontier regions such as Heilongjiang, Inner Mongolia, Yunnan, Guizhou, Guangxi and Xinjiang. This pattern suggests that the availability of cultivated land has not improved as much as the 70.8 million–hectare figure suggests, because the newly reclaimed land in the border regions is of poorer quality than the lost fertile land.[18] A similar pattern was observed for forested land, although the reforestation of cultivated land on slopes

---

17 For a detailed discussion, see Ho and Lin 2001b.
18 This pattern is consistent with the observations of several earlier studies. See Ash and Edmonds 1998, 843; and Yang and Li 2000, 78–79.

in recent years — implemented for environmental reasons — had contributed a considerable amount of newly added forest land.

Beginning with the 1978 reforms, and most dramatically since the early 1980s, China has undergone rapid economic growth and dramatic social and structural changes, including a pattern of land use change slightly different from that of the 1949–1996 period, as previously outlined. The population has been on the move as a consequence of a relaxation of China's past policy restricting rural–urban migration, and the rate of urban growth has accelerated. Rising per capita income and increased exposure to the outside world have also changed the lifestyles and consumption habits of a significant portion of the population. These developments — rising per capita income, industrialization, migration, urbanization and changing life-styles — have altered the country's land use significantly.

In the early 1980s, the Chinese Academy of Sciences initiated a project to survey land resources at the county level. Most provinces surveyed only a few of their coun-ties, but several surveyed all. Subsequently, these provinces were surveyed as part of the 1996 national land survey. Thus, for a small number of provinces, these two observations of land use pattern are available. Table 4 compares these two sets of land use data for three provinces, one from each of the three main regions — Shandong in eastern China, Hunan in central China, and Shaanxi in western China. In a comparison of the results, it is important to remember that the 1996 results show how land was used on 31 October 1996, while the pre-1985 land use data are simple aggregates of county survey results obtained at different times between 1980 and 1984.[19]

The provincial land use patterns presented in Table 4 show that between the early 1980s and 1996 two important changes occurred: land use within agriculture altered in significant ways; and more land was converted to nonagricultural use. Cultivated area declined in all three provinces, but most severely in the more devel-oped and faster-growing coastal province of Shandong. Cultivated land as a percent of Shandong's total area declined from 54.45 percent in the early 1980s to 48.96 percent in 1996, a drop of more than five percentage points in just a decade. Culti-vated land as a percent of total area also declined during this period in Hunan and Shaanxi, but only by one to two percentage points. The decline in cultivated land was caused largely by a restructuring of the agricultural sector, that is, a shift of cultivated land to other agricultural uses. For example, in Shandong between the early 1980s and 1996, cultivated land declined by 844,000 hectares while yuan di increased by 740,000 hectares. In Shaanxi, the shift was apparently from cultivated land and pasture to forest, and in Hunan, both cultivated land and pasture declined, the latter by more than one million hectares. The data also show that unused land

---

19 For example, Shaanxi surveyed 12 counties or city districts (*shi qu*) in 1980, 17 in 1981, 31 in 1982, 32 in 1983, and 13 in 1984. See Chinese Academy of Sciences 1989, 198–203.

TABLE 4

Land Use Change in Three Chinese Provinces, 1983 and 1996
(area in hectares)

Province	Year	Total Area	Agricultural Land				
			Subtotal	Cultivated Land	*Yuan di*	Forest	Pasture
Shandong	1983	15,671,690	10,307,378	8,533,000	293,096	1,339,486	141,796
	%	100.00	65.77	54.45	1.87	8.55	0.90
	1996	15,705,241	10,079,682	7,689,287	1,033,388	1,315,276	41,731
	%	100.00	64.18	48.96	6.58	8.37	0.27
difference, 1996–1983		33,551	-227,696	-843,713	740,292	-24,210	-100,065
Hunan	1983	21,191,387	17,457,833	4,195,540	298,207	11,827,620	1,136,467
	%	100.00	82.38	19.80	1.41	55.81	5.36
	1996	21,185,469	16,314,530	3,952,961	501,417	11,753,885	106,267
	%	100.00	77.01	18.66	2.37	55.48	0.50
difference, 1996–1983		-5,918	-1,143,304	-242,579	203,210	-73,735	-1,030,200
Shaanxi	1983	20,523,631	17,885,045	5,483,429	196,889	7,780,829	4,423,898
	%	100.00	87.14	26.72	0.96	37.91	21.56
	1996	20,579,460	18,198,235	5,140,480	479,202	9,398,908	3,179,645
	%	100.00	88.43	24.98	2.33	45.67	15.45
difference, 1996–1983		55,829	313,190	-342,948	282,313	1,618,079	-1,244,253

SOURCES: Chinese Academy of Sciences (1989, vol. 3: 142–151, 152–159 and 198–203); and Liu (2000)

increased significantly, suggesting that pastures were converted to unused land. Table 4 shows that land allocated to nonagricultural use increased, and that some of the increase was the result of conversion of agricultural land to nonagricultural use. The rise in nonagricultural use was particularly dramatic in Shandong, where land allocated to nonagricultural uses as a percent of total area increased from 11.61 percent in the early 1980s to 14.55 percent in 1996, a rise of nearly three percentage points. Most of the increase was caused by the expansion of settlements and of industrial-mining sites.

TABLE 4
Land Use Change in Three Chinese Provinces, 1983 and 1996 *(continued)*
(area in hectares)

Province	Nonagricultural Land					Transportation Land	Water Area	Unused Land
		Settlements and industrial and mining sites						
	Subtotal	Subtotal	Settlements	Stand-alone ind.-mines	Other			
Shandong	1,818,714	1,365,759				452,955	1,715,035	1,830,563
	11.61	8.71				2.89	10.94	11.68
	2,285,569	1,826,710	1,450,818	245,453	130,439	458,859	1,685,266	1,654,725
	14.55	11.63	9.24	1.56	0.83	2.92	10.73	10.54
	466,855	460,952				5,904	-29,770	-175,839
Hunan	910,527	737,213				173,313	1,440,947	1,382,080
	4.30	3.48				0.82	6.80	6.52
	1,164,751	1,010,981	891,915	87,100	31,966	153,769	1,670,428	2,035,760
	5.50	4.77	4.21	0.41	0.15	0.73	7.88	9.61
	254,224	273,768				-19,544	229,482	653,680
Shaanxi	673,592	461,024	405,767	28,047	27,209	212,568	409,393	1,555,602
	3.28	2.25	1.98	0.14	0.13	1.04	1.99	7.58
	811,657	675,950	587,075	51,186	37,689	135,708	399,113	1,170,456
	3.94	3.28	2.85	0.25	0.18	0.66	1.94	5.69
	138,065	214,926	181,308	23,139	10,480	-76,861	-10,280	-385,146

The spectacular land development brought about by the late Deng Xiaoping's visit to Shenzhen in the spring of 1992 also influenced China's land use structure. Table 5 analyzes changes in land use between 1990 and 1996. For the country as a whole, yuan di continued to experience the greatest expansion in that period, followed by transportation infrastructure, and settlement and industrial-mining sites. This pattern underscores the importance of agricultural restructuring, industrialization and urbanization in land use change, and is consistent with the long-term trend identified for 1949–1996. At the regional level, the locus of agricultural restructuring

TABLE 5
Land Use Changes in China Between 1990 and 1996 (area in hectares)

	Year	Total Area	Agricultural Land				
			Subtotal	Cultivated Land	Yuan di	Forest	Pasture
China	1990	950,650,010.41	633,906,886.64	134,890,238.52	8,041,791.76	225,358,378.63	265,616,477.73
	1996	950,676,195.05	633,736,518.46	130,039,229.45	10,023,795.59	227,608,718.63	266,064,774.79
difference, 1996–1990		26,184.64	-170,368.18	-4,851,009.07	1,982,003.83	2,250,340.00	448,297.06
%		0.00	-0.03	-3.60	24.65	1.00	0.17
East China[1]	1990	131,863,934.23	93,810,315.62	38,821,233.74	4,648,602.27	48,237,376.42	2,103,103.19
	1996	131,890,052.74	93,419,224.07	36,955,887.60	5,514,544.99	48,868,494.79	2,080,296.69
difference, 1996–1990		26,118.51	-391,091.55	-1,865,346.14	865,942.72	631,118.37	-22,806.50
%		0.02	-0.42	-4.81	18.63	1.31	-1.08
Central China[2]	1990	281,589,991.16	223,591,138.45	57,998,342.49	1,780,367.47	90,132,929.59	73,679,498.90
	1996	281,590,106.74	222,432,293.25	56,118,889.55	2,221,452.68	91,557,403.15	72,534,547.87
difference, 1996–1990		115.58	-1,158,845.20	-1,879,452.94	441,085.21	1,424,473.56	-1,144,951.03
%		0.00	-0.52	-3.24	24.78	1.58	-1.55
West China[3]	1990	537,196,015.00	316,505,432.55	38,070,662.29	1,612,822.01	86,988,072.61	189,833,875.64
	1996	537,196,035.58	317,885,001.14	36,964,452.31	2,287,797.92	87,182,820.68	191,449,930.23
difference, 1996–1990		20.58	1,379,568.59	-1,106,209.98	674,975.91	194,748.07	1,616,054.59
%		0.00	0.44	-2.91	41.85	0.22	0.85

NOTES:

[1] Liaoning, Beijing, Tianjin, Hebei, Shandong, Jiangsu, Shanghai, Zhejiang, Fujian, Guangdong, Hainan and Guangxi

[2] Heilongjiang, Jilin, Nei Mongol, Shanxi, Henan, Anhui, Jiangxi, Hubei and Hunan

[3] Sichuan (including Chongqing), Guizhou, Yunnan, Qinghai: Xizang, Shaanxi, Ningxia, Gansu and Xinjiang

TABLE 5
Land Use Changes in China Between 1990 and 1996 (continued)
(area in hectares)

	Year	Total Area	Nonagricultural Land			Water Area	Unused Land
			Subtotal	Settlements and Ind.-Mines	Transportation		
China	1990	950,650,010.41	27,218,853.61	22,198,289.07	5,020,564.54	41,442,397.97	248,081,872.19
	1996	950,676,195.05	29,542,981.61	24,075,286.14	5,467,695.47	42,308,826.81	245,087,868.17
difference, 1996–1990		26,184.64	2,324,128.00	1,876,997.07	447,130.93	866,428.84	-2,994,004.02
%		0.00	8.54	8.46	8.91	2.09	-1.21
East China[1]	1990	131,863,934.23	10,005,982.76	8,344,075.32	1,661,907.44	11,573,152.07	16,474,483.78
	1996	131,890,052.74	11,001,852.03	9,164,773.23	1,837,078.80	11,775,492.07	15,693,484.57
difference, 1996–1990		26,118.51	995,869.27	820,697.91	175,171.36	202,340.00	-780,999.21
%		0.02	9.95	9.84	10.54	1.75	-4.74
Central China[2]	1990	281,589,991.16	10,968,185.58	8,848,913.77	2,119,271.81	13,424,106.08	33,606,561.05
	1996	281,590,106.74	11,754,036.94	9,448,165.35	2,305,871.59	13,908,259.54	33,495,517.01
difference, 1996–1990		115.58	785,851.36	599,251.58	186,599.78	484,153.46	-111,044.04
%		0.00	7.16	6.77	8.81	3.61	-0.33
West China[3]	1990	537,196,015.00	6,244,615.27	5,005,229.98	1,239,385.29	16,445,139.83	198,000,827.35
	1996	537,196,035.58	6,787,092.65	5,462,347.56	1,324,745.09	16,625,075.20	195,898,866.59
difference, 1996–1990		20.58	542,477.38	457,117.58	85,359.80	179,935.37	-2,101,960.76
%		0.00	8.69	9.13	6.89	1.09	-1.06

SOURCE: Liu (2000)

and economic development has been on the eastern coast. The increase in land area used for orchards and plantations was greatest in East China, while the rate of growth of yuan di ascended from the eastern coast to the western interior because of the different bases involved.

Human settlements and industrial-mining site use also experienced the largest gains (in both area and growth rate) in East China, where rural industrialization and urbanization have been most intense. During the 1960s and 1970s, transportation development strategy focused on frontier expansion in West China; since the 1980s it has concentrated on branch sophistication and internal upgrading in East China. Concordantly, the growth rate of land used for transportation infrastructure descended from the eastern coast to the western interior, although the net gain in land area was slightly greater in Central than in East China. Finally, unused land continued to shrink because of the growing demands of population growth and economic development. The bulk (2.1 of the 2.99 million hectares, or more than 70 percent) of the land reclaimed from unused land was located in West China.

Two major features distinguish the pattern of land use change between 1990 and 1996 from the long-term trend for the period of 1949–1996. First, unlike the substantial reduction of pastureland in the earlier period, there was a slight increase in pasture from 1990 to 1996. Pastureland continued to shrink in East and Central China because of the higher demand for cultivation and construction. This loss was offset, at least in terms of area, by the gains in West China, primarily through the reclamation of unused land and the return of cropland on slopes to pasture to stop soil erosion. Chinese leaders seemed finally to have learned the lesson: the marginal gain in food production through overcultivation on slope land in West China (where major rivers originate) simply could not compensate for the tremendous losses from devastating floods in Central and East China caused by severe soil erosion upstream.

The most striking feature separating recent land use change from the long-term trend since 1949 has been the net loss of large quantities of cultivated land. Whereas cultivated land recorded a net gain of 32.15 million hectares between 1949 and 1996 (primarily because of continued land reclamation in the border regions), it shrank by 4.85 million hectares (3.6 percent) in the first six years of the 1990s. Such large-scale farmland loss has been most noticeable in East and Central China where the conversion of fertile land from cultivation to other purposes accounted for 77 percent of the country's total farmland loss. The reduction of precious cultivated land has been so alarming that the State Council and the Central Committee of the Chinese Communist Party imposed, in May 1997, a one-year moratorium (subsequently extended to 1999) on arable land conversions (Ho and Lin 2003). The importance of cultivated land merits a detailed assessment of the magnitude, location and sources of farmland loss in recent decades, with special attention to a period before the moratorium was imposed — from the mid-1980s to the early 1990s.

Data from China's State Statistical Bureau are used to analyze historical trends, and those from the 1996 land survey are used to examine the location and sources of farmland loss.[20]

Changes in Cultivated Land

Historically, China has a long tradition of land cultivation. Better land for cultivation, and therefore, a more stable food supply, was one of the major forces driving the frontier territorial expansion of the Chinese empire from the cradle of the Yellow River Basin to the Yangtze and Pearl river deltas in the East and the South. Two eras saw remarkable expansion of China's cultivated land: the Song Dynasty (A.D. 960–1279), when the nation experienced a large-scale southward migration, and the late Qing Dynasty (1644–1911), when the agricultural economy enjoyed prosperity. However, these two periods of farmland expansion corresponded with significant growth of the population (Heilig 1997, 147). The net outcome, therefore, was a continued drop of cultivated land per capita from 0.3 hectare in the Qin (221 B.C.) to 0.18 hectare in 1949 (see Table 6).

The founding of the PRC set off a new era of land reclamation and development. From 1949 to 1957 the country underwent massive land reclamation carried out by soldiers of the PLA, who settled first in Xinjiang and then in Heilongjiang, frontier provinces in the northwest and northeast regions, respectively. Reclamation increased the stock of cultivated land from 97.88 million hectares in 1949 to a peak of 111.83 million hectares in 1957, a net growth of nearly 14 million hectares, or 14.25 percent, in nine years.

However, this initial period of land reclamation was immediately followed by one of land development on a comparable scale. Mao's disastrous industrialization campaign of the Great Leap Forward (1958–1960) brought with it not only enormous abuse of human and financial resources, but also unprecedented devastation of China's precious and fragile land. During those three years, the country lost an estimated 14.53 million hectares of cultivated land primarily to the irrational and unrealistic industrialization campaign to "overtake the U.K. and catch up to the U.S. in 15 years." When the continuing reclamation of marginal land is taken into account, the net loss of farmland was still 6.97 million hectares (see Table 6).

The economic readjustment engineered by the liberal leadership from 1963 to 1965 did curtail the misuse and mismanagement of China's human and land resources, resulting in a small surplus of cultivated land by 1965. The recovery of the national economy and its land resources did not last long, however, because China underwent another disastrous decade of domestic turmoil and revolutionary

---

20 The data from China's State Statistical Bureau suffer from the problem of under-reporting, but this problem is believed to have been consistent throughout the years. The situation has been recognized in several previous studies (Yang and Li 2000, 74; and Smil 1999, 417).

TABLE 6
China's Changing Cultivated Land (area in hectares)

Year	Cultivated Land	Change Area	Change %	Population (in millions)	Ha per Capita
221 B.C.	6.0000			20.00	0.300
A.D. 2	15.8700			59.50	0.267
775	14.0700			52.90	0.266
110	27.6700			104.00	0.266
1578	31.0000			130.00	0.238
1766	52.0500			208.10	0.250
1851	80.0000			410.00	0.195
1934	82.0000			462.00	0.177
1949	97.8813			541.67	0.181
1950	100.3560	2.4747	2.53	551.96	0.182
1951	103.6713	3.3153	3.30	563.00	0.184
1952	107.9187	4.2474	4.01	574.82	0.188
1953	108.5287	0.6100	0.57	587.96	0.185
1954	109.3547	0.8260	0.76	602.66	0.181
1955	110.1567	0.8020	0.73	614.65	0.179
1956	111.8247	1.6680	1.51	628.28	0.178
1957	111.8300	0.0053	0.01	646.53	0.173
1958	106.9007	-4.9293	-4.41	659.94	0.162
1959	104.5793	-2.3214	-2.17	672.07	0.156
1960	104.8613	0.2820	0.27	662.07	0.158
1961	103.3107	-1.5506	-1.48	658.59	0.157
1962	102.9033	-0.4074	-0.39	672.95	0.153
1963	102.7267	-0.1766	-0.17	691.72	0.149
1964	103.3120	0.5853	0.57	704.99	0.147
1965	103.5940	0.2820	0.27	725.38	0.143
1966	102.9580	-0.6360	-0.61	745.42	0.138
1967	102.5640	-0.3940	-0.38	763.68	0.134
1968	101.5533	-1.0107	-0.99	785.34	0.129
1969	101.4600	-0.0933	-0.09	806.71	0.126
1970	101.1347	-0.3253	-0.32	829.92	0.122
1971	100.6993	-0.4354	-0.43	852.29	0.118
1972	100.6147	-0.0846	-0.08	871.77	0.115
1973	100.2127	-0.4020	-0.40	892.11	0.112
1974	99.9120	-0.3007	-0.30	908.59	0.110
1975	99.7080	-0.2040	-0.20	924.20	0.108
1976	99.3880	-0.3200	-0.32	937.17	0.106
1977	99.2473	-0.1407	-0.14	949.74	0.105
1978	99.3893	0.1420	0.14	962.59	0.103
1979	99.4980	0.1087	0.11	975.42	0.102
1980	99.3053	-0.1927	-0.19	987.05	0.101
1981	99.0373	-0.2680	-0.27	1,000.72	0.099
1982	98.6060	-0.4313	-0.44	1,016.54	0.097
1983	98.3593	-0.2467	-0.25	1,030.08	0.095
1984	97.8540	-0.5053	-0.51	1,043.57	0.094
1985	96.8460	-1.0080	-1.03	1,058.51	0.092
1986	96.2300	-0.6160	-0.64	1,075.07	0.090
1987	95.8887	-0.3413	-0.35	1,093.00	0.088
1988	95.7220	-0.1667	-0.17	1,110.26	0.086
1989	95.6560	-0.0660	-0.07	1,127.04	0.085
1990	95.6727	0.0167	0.02	1,143.33	0.084
1991	95.6533	-0.0194	-0.02	1,158.23	0.083
1992	95.4253	-0.2280	-0.24	1,171.71	0.081
1993	95.1013	-0.3240	-0.34	1,185.17	0.080
1994	94.9067	-0.1946	-0.20	1,198.50	0.079
1995	94.9707	0.0640	0.07	1,211.21	0.078
1996					

SOURCE: Li (2000, 84 and 91)

upheaval during the notorious Cultural Revolution (1966–1975). The overwhelming political agenda interrupted the reclamation of land but did not stop the continuing encroachment on farmland. The result was a decline of total cultivated land from 102.95 to 99.7 million hectares — a net loss of 3.88 million hectares during the decade of the Cultural Revolution.

Economic reforms instituted in 1978 by the post-Mao leadership significantly redefined the relationship between land reclamation and development. Reclamation of marginal land in the border regions during the prior three decades had already exhausted available land resources. Excessive land reclamation in ecologically fragile regions had damaged the natural environment, causing problems like soil erosion, desertification and deforestation (Ash and Edmonds 1998; Yang and Li 2000). Decentralization of decision making, and marketization and globalization had driven peasants to reallocate farmland and engage in nonfarm activities that could generate greater profits than could the cultivation of food staples (Ash 1988; Lin 1997b). The subsequent processes of agricultural restructuring, spontaneous rural industrialization and urbanization removed a large amount of land from cultivation to be put to more profitable uses.

Between 1978 and 1996, cultivated land shrank from 99.39 to 94.97 million hectares, a net loss of 4.42 million hectares or 4.4 percent. The loss of farmland was most severe in the mid-1980s, when the country experienced accelerated economic growth. For 1984–1986, the Chinese statistical authorities reported a net loss of 2.1 million hectares of farmland, primarily to urban and rural development and through agricultural restructuring. In the meantime, population continued to grow from 962.59 million to 1.21 billion, leading to a drop in cultivated land per capita from 0.104 hectares in 1978 to 0.079 hectares in 1995 (see Table 6).

Figure 3 maps out the spatial distribution of changes in cultivated land from 1949 to 1996. The magnitude of those changes appears to cluster in three regions: provinces and special municipalities along the eastern coast that suffered from a reduction of farmland because of their high population density and advanced level of economic development; provinces in the western interior and northern frontier that show significant expansion of cultivated land because of continued land reclamation; and (not identified on the map) provinces whose farmland showed a marginal increase during the period.

When Figure 3 is compared with Figure 2, an interesting spatial pattern emerges. It is obvious that provinces that lost cultivated land are all associated with an MCI higher than 100, suggesting that the lost land was highly fertile and suitable for annual multiple cropping. In contrast, most of the provinces that had gained farmland (Xinjiang, Qinhai, Tibet, Heilongjiang and Inner Mongolia) carry an MCI lower than 100. This inverse association between change in land area and MCI

FIGURE 3
Changes in Cultivated Land in China, 1949–1996

Percent Changed
- ▓ 100–207.06
- ▥ 50–99.99
- ░ 0–49.99
- ⠐ -11.9–0
- ☐ No Data

0   500 km

SOURCE: Li (2000, 93)

further substantiates the contention that newly reclaimed marginal land in the western interior or northern frontier simply cannot compensate for the loss of fertile land in the southeastern coast.[21]

The decrease in cultivated land has been accompanied not only by a decline in quality but also by the ever-growing and unevenly distributed population. The changing availability of cultivated land per capita between 1949 and 1996 is mapped out in Figure 4. With the exception of Tibet, Guizhou and Yunnan in the southwestern region, China's provinces invariably showed a reduction of cultivated land per capita. This has been particularly evident in three clusters of provinces, including those in the Shandong Peninsula: the North China Plain, the southeastern coast, and the Qinghai Loess Plateau. The substantial decline in farmland in the first two regions clearly has been driven by the forces of population growth and economic development, whereas the worsening situation in the Qinghai Loess Plateau may be

---

21 It has been estimated that the loss of 1 mu of cultivated land in South China is the equivalent of the loss of 1.56–1.59 mu in the North. See Special Team of Investigation on the Issue of Farmland Protection 1997, 3. Another issue to be noted is that the figures for land reclamation may have been over-reported. The 1998 Land Administration Law (LAL) aims to maintain a dynamic balance of the farmland stock. Under it, any construction project taking away primary farmland must either reclaim an equivalent amount of land or pay a land reclamation fee. Thus, it is not surprising that, analogous to the previous practice of under-reporting the amount of cultivated land in order to avoid paying state grain quotas and taxes, local cadres began to over-report land reclamation so as to avoid paying the land reclama-tion fees (G. P. Brown 1995, 927).

FIGURE 4
Decline of Cultivated Land in China per Capita, 1949–1996

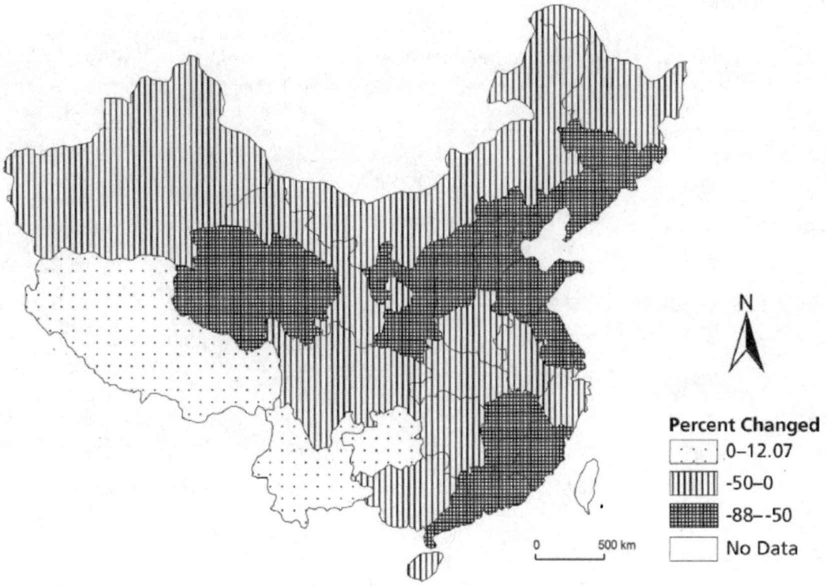

N

Percent Changed
- ┌┈┈┐ 0–12.07
- ▓▓▓ -50–0
- ███ -88--50
- ☐ No Data

0   500 km

SOURCE: Li (2000, 157)

a result of natural hazards and environmental degradation.[22] An exploration of the causes or sources of farmland loss yields better understanding of the dynamics of change in cultivated land.

The drastic loss of farmland in the mid-1980s was sufficiently alarming to catch the attention of the Chinese government. Among the responses of the state were the enactment of a Land Administration Law (LAL) and the establishment, in 1986, of a new hierarchical system of land administrative bureaus to regulate land use conversion. Since then, all construction projects that involve the conversion of cultivated land to other purposes must apply to the State Land Administrative Bureau (SLAB) at the appropriate level, as determined by the amount of farmland needed.[23] This requirement has allowed the development of important databases that are compiled

---

22 It was reported that soil erosion in the Qinghai Loess Plateau covered an extensive area of 45 million hectares, or 79 percent of the total land area of the plateau (Li 2000, 132). Robert Ash and Richard Edmonds (1998, 860) reported that environmental degradation affected approximately 83.2 million hectares, or 60 percent of China's revised total arable area. Soil erosion — resulting from deforestation, cultivation on slopes, overgrazing, etc. — was identified as the most important factor in this environmental degradation, accounting for 48 percent of arable land damage in China in 1996.

23 The original Land Management Law enacted in 1986 required state construction projects using up to 3 mu of farmland (or up to 10 mu of nonagricultural land) to report to the State Land Administrative Bureau at the county level for approval. Those projects using between 3 mu and 10 mu of farmland (or between 10 mu and 20 mu of nonagricultural land) were required to get approval at the prefecture level; others using between 10 mu and 1,000 mu of farmland (or between 20 mu and 2,000 mu of nonagricultural land) were to get approval at the provincial level. This requirement was revised in the 1998 version of the Land Administration Law (LAL), which requires all construction projects that would use cultivated land to submit land use applications to governments at the provincial level or higher for approval. For a detailed discussion, see Ho and Lin 2003.

TABLE 7
China's Farmland Loss by Cause, 1986–1995
(area in 1,000 hectares)

Year	Farmland Loss	Agricultural Readjustment		Construction		Natural Hazards	
		Area	%	Area	%	Area	%
1986	1,108.3	684.6	61.8	252.6	22.8	171.1	15.4
1987	877.2	556.5	63.4	194.0	22.1	126.7	14.4
1988	676.3	394.7	58.4	122.2	18.1	159.4	23.6
1989	417.3	231.1	55.4	89.2	21.4	97.0	23.2
1990	346.4	207.7	60.0	82.7	23.9	56.0	16.2
1991	448.3	234.8	52.4	102.5	22.9	111.0	24.8
1992	707.3	452.9	64.0	155.5	22.0	98.9	14.0
1993	625.3	423.4	67.7	134.5	21.5	67.4	10.8
1994	785.1	511.1	65.1	133.1	17.0	140.9	17.9
1995	798.1	511.8	64.1	160.5	20.1	125.8	15.8
Total	6,789.6	4,208.6	62.0	1,426.8	21.0	1,154.2	17.0
Average	679.0	420.9	62.0	142.7	21.0	115.4	17.0

SOURCE: Li (2000, 159)

from the land use applications submitted to the SLAB, and thus, made possible closer scrutiny of the sources of farmland loss.

Table 7 lists the causes of farmland loss for the period from 1986 to 1995, according to data released by the former SLAB. During those 10 years, an estimated 6.79 million hectares of cultivated land were converted to other uses. Of the total farmland removed, 62 percent was taken for agricultural production rather than the cultivation of food staples, 21 percent went into construction projects carried out by the state and collectives, and the remaining 17 percent was altered by natural hazards and environmental degradation.

The single most important source of farmland loss has been structural change within the agricultural sector. A breakdown of the category of agricultural restructuring reveals that 39 percent of lost cultivated land was converted to use for yuan di (orchards and plantations), 33 percent to forest and woodland, 20 percent to pasture, and 8 percent to fish ponds.[24]

---

24 See Li 2000, 158. This pattern is consistent with the findings of several earlier studies. Ash and Edmonds (1998, 847–848) observed that structural change within the agricultural sector accounted for more than half of the shrinkage of China's cultivated acreage between 1987 and 1991. Vaclav Smil (1999, 425–426) identified three factors responsible for China's farmland loss between 1987 and 1995, including conversion to forest and pasture (accountable for 33 percent of the loss), conversion to orchards (22 percent) and natural hazards (17 percent). Yang and Li (2000, 84) pointed out, however, that much of the land reported as converted from cultivated land to forest and pasture was actually fallow or abandoned land in the arid and semi-arid western interior. Local cadres made such reports of land conversion for political considerations.

A more detailed analysis of the data released by the SLAB in 1994 (see Table 8) shows that agricultural restructuring accounted for more than 65 percent of total farmland loss.[25] The balance was due to natural hazards (18 percent) and construction (17 percent), including state and collective construction as well as rural housing. Conversion to yuan di accounted for 40 percent of farmland conversion due to agricultural restructuring. Immediately following yuan di are forest (30 percent) and pasture (21 percent). Agricultural restructuring played a more significant role in Central and West China than in the East. This is hardly surprising given the fact that much of the conversion to forest and pasture had taken place in Central and West China. The fact that conversion to yuan di accounted for more than 57 percent of agricultural restructuring in West China suggests that the forces of marketization had penetrated well beyond the eastern coast into the interior.

The construction category refers primarily to industrialization, urbanization, transportation infrastructure development and rural housing. Although construction land took less than one-fifth of the total lost farmland, much of the converted land was valuable, fertile land in economically advanced regions. Within the category of state construction, land used for city, town, and stand-alone industrial-mining sites accounted for nearly 60 percent of the land conversion due to construction — a testimony to the importance of urbanization in land use change. At the regional level, the shares of state and collective construction as well as rural housing were all significantly higher in East China than in its Central and West China counterparts.

The category of natural hazards includes flooding, drought, soil erosion, desertification, salinization and alkalinization. The reason for the greater significance of natural hazards in farmland loss in East China than in the central and western regions is unclear. One possible explanation is the flooding that affected China during the summers of 1993 and 1994. The effects of the flooding were more severe in East China than elsewhere because it is home to the lower reaches of some of the country's major rivers.

The results of our analysis of the national data are not dissimilar to those of a survey of 294 sampled counties conducted by China's Ministry of Agriculture in 1994 (see Table 9).[26] According to the ministry's survey, on average counties lost 419.27 hectares of cultivated land. The degree of farmland shrinkage declined from East (433 hectares per county) to Central (421 hectares) and West China (403 hectares), reflecting the geographical variation in population density and level of economic development. Agricultural restructuring accounted for the lion's share

---

25 The figure for total area of farmland loss reported in Table 8 (785,236 hectares) is slightly different from the one that appears in Table 7 (6,789,600 hectares) because of different data sources. This difference should not affect the pattern of structural change analyzed, however.

26 Of the 294 sampled counties, 93 were chosen from East China, 104 from Central China, and the remaining 97 from West China (Li 2000, 158).

TABLE 8
Decline in China's Cultivated Land by Cause, 1994
(area in hectares)

Land loss	China			East China[1]			Central China[2]			West China[3]		
	Area	% of Total	% of Category	Area	% of Total	% of Category	Area	% of Total	% of Category	Area	% of Total	% of Category
Total	785,236	100.00	100.00	243,652	100.00	100.00	348,128	100.00	100.00	193,455	100.00	100.00
To state construction	89,794	11.44	100.00	52,425	21.52	100.00	22,895	6.58	100.00	14,474	7.48	100.00
Cities	16,072	2.05	17.90	11,444	4.70	21.83	2,610	0.75	11.40	2,019	1.04	13.95
Towns	20,421	2.60	22.74	13,885	5.70	26.49	3,087	0.89	13.48	3,450	1.78	23.83
Stand-alone ind.-mining sites	16,858	2.15	18.77	10,238	4.20	19.53	4,741	1.36	20.71	1,879	0.97	12.98
Railroads	5,059	0.64	5.63	1,358	0.56	2.59	2,802	0.80	12.24	900	0.47	6.21
Highways	17,310	2.20	19.28	9,945	4.08	18.97	5,237	1.50	22.88	2,127	1.10	14.70
Water conservancy	7,981	1.02	8.89	1,412	0.58	2.69	3,429	0.99	14.98	3,140	1.62	21.70
Other	6,094	0.78	6.79	4,145	1.70	7.91	989	0.28	4.32	960	0.50	6.63
To collective construction	31,620	4.03	100.00	13,821	5.67	100.00	14,012	4.02	100.00	3,787	1.96	100.00
Rural roads	7,451	0.95	23.56	2,351	0.96	17.00	4,277	1.23	30.52	823	0.43	21.73
Irrigation	11,199	1.43	35.42	2,741	1.12	19.83	6,960	2.00	49.67	1,499	0.77	39.57
Township-village enterprises	9,712	1.24	30.71	6,808	2.79	49.26	2,085	0.60	14.88	819	0.42	21.63
Other	3,259	0.42	10.31	1,922	0.79	13.91	690	0.20	4.93	646	0.33	17.07
To rural housing	11,726	1.49		4,075	1.67		3,718	1.07		3,933	2.03	
To other agricultural uses	511,125	65.09	100.00	99,304	40.76	100.00	265,904	76.38	100.00	145,917	75.43	100.00
Yuan di[4]	205,648	26.19	40.23	54,408	22.33	54.79	67,365	19.35	25.33	83,876	43.36	57.48
Forest	154,380	19.66	30.20	17,375	7.13	17.50	91,792	26.37	34.52	45,213	23.37	30.99
Pasture	109,596	13.96	21.44	1,242	0.51	1.25	93,393	26.83	35.12	14,961	7.73	10.25
Fish ponds	41,501	5.29	8.12	26,279	10.79	26.46	13,355	3.84	5.02	1,867	0.96	1.28
To natural disasters	140,971	17.95		74,028	30.38		41,599	11.95		25,344	13.10	

NOTES:

[1] Liaoning, Beijing, Tianjin, Hebei, Shandong, Jiangsu, Shanghai, Zhejiang, Fujian, Guangdong, Hainan and Guangxi

[2] Heilongjiang, Jilin, Nei Mongol, Shanxi, Henan, Anhui, Jiangxi, Hubei and Hunan

[3] Sichuan (including Chongqing), Guizhou, Yunnan, Qinghai. Xizang, Shaanxi, Ningxia, Gansu and Xinjiang

[4] Orchards, vineyards and plantations

SOURCE: Constructed from data in China State Land Administrative Bureau (1996, 148–149)

TABLE 9

Average Loss of Cultivated Land by Land Use Change in 294 Sampled
Counties, 1994
(area in hectares)

	China		East China[1]		Central China[2]		West China[3]	
	Area	%	Area	%	Area	%	Area	%
Total per county	419.27	100.00	433.28	100.00	421.35	100.00	403.74	100.00
State construction	67.60	16.12	95.00	21.93	59.87	14.21	49.73	12.32
Collective construction	32.20	7.68	38.67	8.93	25.47	6.04	33.27	8.24
Peasant housing	16.00	3.82	11.87	2.74	17.47	4.15	18.47	4.57
Natural hazards	41.14	9.81	40.47	9.34	59.67	14.16	21.80	5.40
Agricultural restructuring	262.33	62.57	247.27	57.07	258.87	61.44	280.47	69.47
Forest	58.87	22.44	9.14	3.70	83.74	32.35	79.87	28.48
Pasture	29.40	11.21	1.00	0.40	24.20	9.35	62.27	22.20
Yuan di	137.53	52.43	181.13	73.25	106.80	41.26	128.73	45.90
Fish ponds	36.53	13.93	56.00	22.65	44.13	17.05	9.60	3.42
Subtotal	262.33	100.00	247.27	100.00	258.87	100.00	280.47	100.00

NOTES:

[1] Liaoning, Beijing, Tianjin, Hebei, Shandong, Jiangsu, Shanghai, Zhejiang, Fujian, Guangdong, Hainan and Guangxi

[2] Heilongjiang, Jilin, Nei Mongol, Shanxi, Henan, Anhui, Jiangxi, Hubei and Hunan

[3] Sichuan (including Chongqing), Guizhou, Yunnan, Qinghai. Xizang, Shaanxi, Ningxia, Gansu and Xinjiang

SOURCE: Li (2000, 158)

(62.6 percent) of farmland conversion, and showed a steady increase from the eastern coast to the western interior — primarily because forest and pasture took up a larger proportion of the converted land in the West than in the East (see Table 9).

Yuan di, the most significant source of agricultural restructuring, accounted for more than 70 percent of the converted land within the agricultural sector in East China, a greater proportion than was the case in Central and West China. This pattern is consistent with that identified from the national data, the only difference being the significance of construction and natural hazards. The 1994 survey revealed that urban and rural construction were responsible for a substantially greater proportion of lost farmland than was reported to the SLAB. State and collective construction as well as peasant housing were responsible for 27.6 percent of farmland loss, according to the counties survey, a significantly larger proportion than the one we have identified from the 1994 data reported to the SLAB (16.96 percent).[27]

27 Several earlier studies also disagreed on the importance of urban and rural construction as a source of China's farmland loss. Vaclav Smil (1999, 425) reported that urban and rural construction had been responsible for less than one-fifth of China's farmland loss between 1987 and 1995. Ash and Edmonds (1998, 847) showed that the share of farmland taken by state and collective construction rose from 18 percent during the 1986–1990 period to 29 percent for 1991–1996. Yang and Li (2000, 79) found that urban and rural construction accounted for 20–40 percent of farmland loss between 1978 and 1996.

However, the proportion of loss due to natural hazards was lower than that in the SLAB statistical record. It is not surprising that local cadres under-reported the extent of land conversion from crop cultivation to construction and over-reported the effect of natural hazards, because these would minimize their accountability. Despite minor discrepancies between the data of the two surveys, it appears certain that China's farmland loss in recent years has been the result of three concurrent processes: agricultural restructuring, industrialization and urbanization in city and countryside, and environmental degradation.

Discussion and Conclusions

China's enormous population size and its growing interaction with the world economy have underscored the global significance of land resources and land use. Until recently, studies of China's land utilization had been hampered by the lack of accurate and reliable information. Researchers had to piece together data obtained from different sources and struggle with the inevitable discrepancies that can lead to further confusion and unnecessary disputes. For the first time since the founding of the PRC in 1949, the 1996 nationwide land survey has provided detailed and systematic information on the status of land resources and land use.

Mao and his comrades would have been disappointed to learn that the nation's territory has turned out to be smaller than the Chinese had claimed during the past five decades. The long-standing Chinese belief that the country occupied a "vast territory with abundant resources" has become questionable if not untenable. Slightly less than 14 percent of China's land is cultivable and more than 56 percent of its territory lies in the western interior region, where population is sparsely distributed and environmental conditions are undesirable for economic development. The most encouraging result from the land survey is the fact that China has 35 million hectares, or 37 percent, more cultivated land than had been reported to the statistical bureau. Even this seemingly encouraging surprise has to be tempered by the fact that most of the "discovered" or unreported farmland was located in hilly or mountainous regions where the productivity of land is low. In summary, the 1996 land survey did not provide strong evidence for optimistic speculation about the condition of China's land resources. Yet, there is pressing need for China's efficient and effective use of its limited land resources — for the sake of its own growing population and the globalizing world.[28]

---

28 This is by no means an attempt to sketch a catastrophic scenario for China. The issue of food security, for instance, depends less on how much farmland China has, and more on how the land is used. As several studies have correctly suggested, China may still be able to cope with its food needs in the foreseeable future because of such new developments as: the change in diet from cereal to animal foods; improved carrying capacity of the land due to technological advances; and increased imports of food grain coupled with exports of high-value-added farm commodities. These new developments cannot, however, change the fundamental situation that available per capita land resources in China are below the world average.

How land is used depends on population density, level of economic development, urbanization, changes in diet and the land management system (Heilig 1997; Ho and Lin 2003; Kung and Liu 1997; Liu, Carter, and Yao 1998; Verburg, Chen, and Veldkamp 2000; Kung and Cai 2000). China evidences this theory by the considerable land area and intensity devoted to cultivation and construction in East China, compared with the dominance of pasture and unused land in the west of the country. What distinguishes China from the universal norm are the way in which institutional changes have so profoundly influenced land use decisions and the resulting peculiar patterns of land use.

During the past five decades, Chinese leaders have been preoccupied by two overarching political mandates: to feed the ever-growing population of the nation so as to maintain social stability, and to develop an industrialized economy strong enough to defend itself against any possible foreign attacks. These mandates have driven changes in land use since 1949. The imperative to maintain social stability by providing enough food for its people has motivated the Communist regime to launch campaigns of land reclamation since the 1950s. At the same time, the ambition to build an industrialized economy has compelled land development to accommodate industrial and transportation infrastructure as well as human settlements. The aggregate result has been an expansion of both cultivated and construction land at the cost of unused land and pastureland. Under Mao's philosophy of "man is bound to conquer nature" (*ren ding sheng tian*), the two political mandates have been fulfilled largely at the expense of the natural environment. Despite continued land reclamation, the per capita availability of farmland has not improved because of the burgeoning population.

The transition of the political economy since 1978 from principles of authoritarianism to local corporatism, and from plan to market, has ushered in a new institutional setting for changes in land use. Relaxed state control over the rural economy has allowed farmers to reallocate land from food grain production to horticulture that promises better profits. The ideological shift from egalitarianism to comparative advantage has given rise to the spectacular expansion of cities and towns as well as development zones on the eastern coast. At the same time, excessive reclamation of land during the prior three decades in environmentally fragile frontier regions brought nature's revenge in various forms of natural hazards. The outcome of agricultural restructuring, increased industrialization and urbanization, and human-made environmental hazards has been a drastic loss of cultivated land. The trend of farmland disappearance has been further fostered by the recent introduction of a land system that permits farmland to be expropriated cheaply from farmers and then sold to commercial users at much higher prices.[29]

---

29 For detailed discussions of China's land system, see Ho 2001; Guo 2001; Ho and Lin 2003; Yeh and Wu 1996; Keng 1996; Chen and Wills 1999; Yang and Wu 1996; and Li 1997.

Judged from an ecological perspective, the expansion of farmland at the expense of pasture and unused land in Mao's era was more regrettable than desirable. By comparison, the shrinkage of China's farmland in recent years may have reflected an irreversible trend of growing marketization, urbanization and globalization that should be accepted rather than deterred. Since the mid-1980s, the Chinese government, concerned over the issue of food security, has attempted to control the conversion of land from agriculture to construction. These attempts have not been successful, however, because of strong local resistance and circumvention.

The current approach has been to maintain a "dynamic equilibrium of farmland" by asking potential developers of cultivated land (for construction purposes) to reclaim equal amounts of farmland, either locally or elsewhere, before projects can begin. There is question, however, about this approach. It is unclear that the net result in productivity of land and in food grain production will be positive, because newly reclaimed land in some border regions simply is not the production equivalent of fertile land lost in economically advanced regions. Moreover, continuing reclamation of land in ecologically fragile regions will do more harm than good to the natural environment.

Given China's recent accession to the World Trade Organization, Chinese agriculture will likely be exposed to the intensified competition of global market forces. The pace of urbanization and industrialization will accelerate as a consequence of economic growth and structural changes. Further reduction of China's cultivated land is, therefore, an inevitable trend that the government will never be able to reverse. In view of these changing circumstances, it may be time to reconsider the conventional wisdom that holds that food security can be safeguarded only by the preservation of a fixed amount of farmland. The revised wisdom will need to consider such factors as changes in diet and comparative advantages in the production of fruits, vegetables and other farm commodities.

Acknowledgments

This research is funded by the International Development Research Centre, Ottawa, Canada and the Hong Kong Research Grant Council. An earlier version of this chapter was published as "China's Land Resources and Land-Use Change: Insights from the 1996 Land Survey," by George C. S. Lin and Samuel P. S. Ho, in *Land Use Policy* volume 20, issue 2 (April 2003): 87–107. The chapter is published in this volume with permission from Elsevier.

Appendix

Preparation work for the 1996 national land survey began from 1981 to 1982, when the Land Use Bureau of the Ministry of Agriculture selected nine counties in different parts of the country as test sites. Based on information gathered at the nine test sites, the Ministry of Agriculture submitted a proposal for a nationwide land survey to the State Council in March 1984. The proposed survey was approved in May 1984, and survey work began seven months later, using the county as the basic operating unit of the survey. The survey work was based on the most recent aerial photos, Landsat images or maps then available. Field surveys were conducted to verify the size, location and uses of land shown on the photographs or existing maps, and to identify any land use changes that had occurred. The results of the field surveys were then converted to land use maps, drawn to a scale of 1:10,000 (1:25,000 or 1:50,000 for forest land and 1:50,000 or 1:100,000 for pasture land). The mapping of approximately 4.73 million square kilometers (or 50 percent) of the land surveyed was based on aerial photos, half of them taken in the 1980s or the early 1990s, and the rest taken in the 1970s or earlier. Mapping of 16 percent (1.55 million square kilometers) of the land surveyed (mainly in Tibet, Qinghai, and parts of Xinjiang) was based on Landsat images, all taken in the 1980s; another 19 percent (1.85 million kilometers) was based on existing topographic maps; and the remaining 15 percent (1.39 million square kilometers) was based on existing plane maps (*pingmiantu*) created from photographs. For further discussion of the 1996 land survey, see Ma 2000.

References

Ash, Robert F. 1988. The evolution of agricultural policy. *The China Quarterly* 116: 529–555.

Ash, Robert F., and Richard Louis Edmonds. 1988. The evolution of agricultural policy. *The China Quarterly* 116:529–555.

———. 1998. China's land resources, environment and agricultural production. *The China Quarterly* 156(Dec.):836–879.

Brown, George P. 1995. Arable land loss in rural China. *Asian Survey* 35(10):922–940.

Brown, Lester. 1995. *Who will feed China?: Wake-up call for a small planet.* New York and London: W. W. Norton & Co.

Buck, J. L. 1937. *Land utilization in China: A study of 16,786 farms in 168 localities, and 32,256 farm families in twenty-two provinces in China, 1929–1933.* Shanghai: Commercial Press.

Byrd, William A., and Qingsong Lin, eds. 1990. *China's rural industry.* New York: Oxford University Press.

Cartier, Carolyn. 2001. "Zone fever," the arable land debate, and real estate speculation: China's evolving land use regime and its geographical contradictions. *Journal of Contemporary China* 10(28):445–469.

Chan, Kam Wing. 1994a. Economic growth strategy and urbanization policies in China, 1949–1982. *International Journal of Urban and Regional Research* (16)2:275–305.

———. 1994b. Urbanization and rural–urban migration in China since 1982. *Modern China* 20(3/July):243–281.

Chen, Jean Jinghan, and David Wills, eds. 1999. *The impact of China's economic reforms upon land, property and construction.* Brookfield, VT: Ashgate.

China State Land Administrative Bureau. 1996. *China land yearbook 1994–1995.* Beijing: People's Publisher.

Chinese Academy of Sciences, Commission for Comprehensive Surveys of Natural Resources. 1989. *A compilation of China's land resource data.* Beijing: n.p.

Crook, Frederick W. 1993. Under-reporting of China's cultivated land area: Implications for world agricultural trade. In *International agriculture and trade reports: China,* U.S. Department of Agriculture, July 1993:33–39. Washington, DC: USDA, Economic Research Service.

Fei, Hsiao-tung. 1986. *Small towns in China: Functions, problems, and prospects.* Beijing: New World Press.

Goldstein, Sidney. 1990. Urbanization in China, 1982–87: Effects of migration and reclassification. *Population and Development Review* 16(4):673–701.

Guo, Xiaolin. 2001. Land expropriation and rural conflicts in China. *The China Quarterly* 166(June):422–439.

Heilig, Gerhard K. 1997. Anthropogenic factors in land-use change in China. *Population and Development Review* 23(1/March):139–168.

Ho, Peter. 2001. Who owns China's land? Policies, property rights and deliberate institutional ambiguity. *The China Quarterly* 166(June):394–421.

Ho, Samuel P. S. 1994. *Rural China in transition.* Oxford, UK: Clarendon Press.

Ho, Samuel P. S., and George C. S. Lin. 2001a. China's evolving land system. Centre for Chinese Research, discussion paper #01-1. Vancouver: University of British Columbia.

———. 2001b. Non-agricultural land use in China's coastal provinces — Evidence from Jiangsu. Centre for Chinese Research, discussion paper #01-4. Vancouver: University of British Columbia.

———. 2003. Emerging land markets in rural and urban China: Policies and practices. *The China Quarterly* 175(Sept.):682–707.

———. 2004. Converting land to non-agricultural use in China's coastal provinces — Evidence from Jiangsu. *Modern China* 30(1):81–112.

Hsu, Mei-Ling. 1994. The expansion of the Chinese urban system, 1953–1990. *Urban Geography* (15)6:516.

Keng, C. W. Kenneth. 1996. China's land disposition system. *Journal of Contemporary China* 5(13):325–345.

Kirkby, Richard J. R. 1985. *Urbanization in China: Town and country in a developing economy, 1949–2000 AD.* New York: Columbia University Press.

Kung, J. K.-S., and S. Liu. 1997. Farmers' preferences regarding ownership and land tenure in Post-Mao China: Unexpected evidence from eight counties. *The China Journal* 38:33–63.

Kung, J. K.-S., and Y.-S. Cai. 2000. Property rights and fertilizing practices in rural China: Evidence from northern Jiangsu. *Modern China* 26(3):276–301.

Li, Hong. 1998. A study of the location and land use pattern of development zones in our country. *China Land Science* 12(3/May):10.

Li, Wen. 1997. *China's land system: Yesterday, today, and tomorrow.* Yanji: Yanbian University Press.

Li, Yuan, ed. 2000. *Land resources of China.* Beijing: China Land Press.

Lin, George C. S. 1997a. *Red capitalism in South China: Growth and development of the Pearl River Delta.* Vancouver, BC: University of British Columbia Press.

———. 1997b. Transformation of a rural economy in the Zhujiang Delta. *The China Quarterly* 149:56–80.

———. 1998. China's industrialization with controlled urbanization: Anti-urbanism or urban-biased? *Issues & Studies* 34(6/June):98–116.

———. 2001. Metropolitan development in a transitional socialist economy: Spatial restructuring in the Pearl River Delta, China. *Urban Studies* 38(3):383–406.

———. 2002. The growth and structural change of Chinese cities: A contextual and geographic analysis. *Cities* 19(5):299–316.

Liu, S., M. R. Carter, and Y. Yao. 1998. Dimensions and diversity of property rights in rural China: Dilemmas on the road to further reform. *World Development* 26(10):1789–1806.

Liu, Yucheng, ed. 2000. *A compilation of China's land resource survey data.* Beijing: Office of the National Survey of Land Resources.

Lo, C. P. 1987. Socialist ideology and urban strategies in China. *Urban Geography* 8(5):440–458.

Logan, J., ed. 2002. *The new Chinese city.* Oxford, UK: Blackwell.

Ma, Kewei. 2000. *The technology of surveying China's land resources*. Beijing: China Land Press.

Ma, Laurence J. C. 1976. Anti-urbanism in China. *Proceedings of the Association of American Geographers* 8:114–118.

Ma, Laurence J. C., and Gonghao Cui. 1987. Administrative changes and urban population in China. *Annals of the Asssociation of American Geographers* 77(3):373–395.

Ma, Laurence J. C., and Chusheng Lin. 1993. Development of towns in China: A case study of Guangdong Province. *Population and Development Review* 19(3):583–606.

Murphey, David. 2001. Just go with the flow. *Far Eastern Economic Review* (July 19):35.

Naughton, Barry. 1988. The third front: Defence industrialization in the Chinese interior. *The China Quarterly* 115:351–386.

Orleans, Leo A. 1991. Loss and misuse of China's cultivated land. In *China's economic dilemmas in the 1990s: The problems of reforms, modernization, and interdependence*, U.S. Congress, Joint Economic Committee, 403–417. Washington, DC: U.S. Government Printing Office.

Pannell, Clifton. 1990. China's urban geography. *Progress in Human Geography* 14(2): 214–236.

Smil, Vaclav. 1984. *The bad Earth: Environmental degradation in China*. Armonk, NY: M. E. Sharpe.

———. 1995. Who will feed China? *The China Quarterly* 143:801–813.

———. 1999. China's agricultural land. *The China Quarterly* 158(June):414–429.

Special Team of Investigation on the Issue of Farmland Protection. 1997. On the serious situation of farmland protection in our country and some policy suggestions. *China Land Science* 11(1/Jan.):3.

State Statistical Bureau. 1994. *China statistical yearbook*. Beijing: China Statistical Publishing House.

———. 1997. *China populations statistical yearbook*. Beijing: China Statistical Publishing House.

———. 1998. *China statistical yearbook*. Beijing: China Statistical Publishing House.

———. 1999. *China statistical yearbook*. Beijing: China Statistical Publishing House.

———. 2000. *China statistical yearbook*. Beijing: China Statistical Publishing House.

State Statistical Bureau, Department of Comprehensive Statistics of the National Economy. 1999. *A compilation of statistical data for New China fifty years*. Beijing: China Statistical Publishing House.

State Statistical Bureau, Team for Urban Social and Economic Surveys. 1999. *Fifty years of cities in New China*. Beijing: Xinhua Press.

———. 2000. *China urban statistical yearbook 1999*. Beijing: China Statistical Publishing House.

Tan, K. C. 1986. Revitalized small towns in China. *Geographical Review* 76(2):138–148.

Verburg, P. H., Y. Chen, and T. A. Veldkamp. 2000. Spatial explorations of land use change and grain production in China. *Agriculture, Ecosystems and Environment* 82(3):333–354.

Wong, K. K, and X. B. Zhao. 1999. The influence of bureaucratic behavior on land appointment in China: The informal process. *Environment and Planning C* 17(1):113–126.

Wu, Chuanchun, and Huangcheng Guo, eds. 1994. *Land use in China.* Beijing: Science Press.

Yang, Chongguan, and Cifang Wu. 1996. *China's land use system: Ten years of reform.* Beijing: China Land Press.

Yang, Hong, and Xiubin Li. 2000. Cultivated land and food supply in China. *Land Use Policy* 17(2/April):73–88.

Yeh, Anthony Gar-on, and Fulong Wu. 1996. The new land development process and urban development in Chinese cities. *International Journal of Urban and Regional Research* 20(2): 330–353.

Yeung, Y.-m., and X. Hu, eds. 1992. *China's coastal cities.* Honolulu, HI: University of Hawaii Press.

Zhang, Li, and Simon X. B. Zhao. 1998. Re-examining China's "urban" concept and the level of urbanization. *The China Quarterly* 154(June):330–381.

Chapter 5

Urban Land Supply in the Chinese Transitional Economy: Case Studies in Beijing and Shenzhen

XIAOCHEN MENG AND YANRU LI

C hina's economy has astonished the world during the past two decades with its double-digit growth rates. This rapid expansion is to some extent attributable to the establishment of "special economic development zones" (SEDZs), particularly in the early 1980s. Establishment of a SEDZ usually involved attractive economic stimulus packages — including tax exemption and abatement, guaranteed loans and access to national assets (such as land use rights) by foreigners — to promote economic development.[1] Indeed, these zones not only contributed to the surge of foreign direct investment, but also gave firsthand experience to government officials in working with emerging market forces. And, as pilot study areas, the development zones provided opportunities to test various policy instruments. The Shangdi Information Technology (IT) industrial zone of Beijing and the city of Shenzhen, two examples of the SEDZ strategy in urban land supply, serve as case studies for our investigation.

Rapid development in China is also evidenced in the pace of urbanization and in unprecedented urban encroachment into rural areas. The vigorous rate of urbanization in China is expected to continue, in part because the government has undertaken gradual but fundamental reforms to develop land and capital markets and to improve labor mobility. These reforms, which have reduced or eliminated barriers to labor and capital movement across both geographic and economic sectors, have pushed the economy forward and resulted in improvements in urban land use efficiency and land price determination of land uses (Ding 2003; 2004). Given that cities generate more than 70 percent of the country's economic output, China's economic success inevitably fuels demand for land at the urban fringes, where economic development activity is most intense. Because land is owned collectively outside

---

1 There is wide policy variation in economic stimulus packages across cities and SEDZs.

cities but is owned by the state in urban areas, urban spatial development that encroaches on rural land requires a conversion of land ownership before capital improvement can take place.

Two government administrative authorities play key roles in urban development: the Land Management Bureau (LMB) and the municipal Urban Planning Bureau (UPB). The former is in charge of land market monitoring and coordination of urban needs, rural development and rural land use planning; the latter is responsible for the determination of urban land use types and intensity of land uses. For urban development, the LMB determines the land supply for development, whereas the UPB determines location and issues construction permits that specify the type and intensity (floor-area ratio) of development.

The administrative village is the basic unit of collective ownership and elects a village committee to conduct routine management duties. The village committee, however, plays a dual role. On one hand, it is at the lowest level of the Chinese administrative system. It functions like a government authority whose roles include implementation of family planning policies and control of migration. On the other hand, it manages the village economy — primarily agricultural farming and small, agriculture-related enterprises. It is difficult for a village committee, as a government body, to disregard regulations, policy, orders and management commands from higher level administrative bureaus, although these regulations often are inconsistent, irrational and ill structured. Conflicts commonly arise when the interests of villagers (farmers) conflict with those of the government.

Since farming is their primary income source, quality of life for farmers depends on the amount and quality of land they own. Land acquisition (for urbanization, for instance) means that villagers lose farmland, which in turn reduces their economic well being. Although both the Chinese Constitution and the Land Administration Law (LAL) mandate that farmers should be compensated during land acquisition, there is no clarity about compensation amounts. The Constitution mandates negotiation between the state government's representatives (from local township, county, city and provincial governments) and farmers as a way to mitigate conflicts resulting from land acquisition.

Because there are no market data that can accurately reflect the price of farmland, compensation does not necessarily reflect market conditions, and varies dramatically from case to case, depending mainly on who plans to develop the land. In many cases, farmers have been forced to accept compensation by local government — a situation possible because of both the power of government and the absence of legal channels through which farmers could appeal government decisions they found objectionable. Thus, governments have overpowered citizens and have been able to prioritize economic development at the expense of farmers and agriculture.

Farmers' resistance to land acquisition has increased dramatically, particularly in the urban fringes, because they have observed windfall gains by developers of rural land, as well as the inconsistency of government compensation.[2] Farmers believe that their compensation will be greater if they hold onto their land for a longer time. Many want to develop the land themselves in order to capture significant profits. This opens wide the door to bribery and corruption of government officials to secure land development rights. Consequently, many illegal and unplanned land developments have taken place. This greatly undermines urban land planning that is intended to consider fully the social, economic, ecological, environmental, historical and cultural values of urban activities.

Land policy reforms have resulted in consequences both positive and negative (see Ding and Knaap, Chapter 1 in this volume). The positive outcomes include housing and real estate development, emerging land markets, improved land use efficiency and an increased role for price in land allocation and use. The negative consequences include inconsistency in land policy and regulations, hidden land markets, illegal development and increasing social injustice. Analyses of the impacts of land acquisition on urban development, though limited in number, are found in the literature. For instance, Dowall (1993), Zhang (1997) and Wu (2001) describe urban land reforms and their impacts on urban development. Zhang and Mao (2000) illustrate the procedure of land transfer. Wang (1987) and Yan and Wang (1995) illustrate the nature, quantity and dynamics of compensation for land transfer. Yang and Liu (2000) and Fang et al. (1999) discuss the institutional issues and policy challenges of land transfer. Du (1999), Jing (1999) and Lin (1999) analyze the village's post-urbanization social, economic, ecological and planning problems.

Despite these resources, there is a lack of comprehensive, comparative studies that identify the policy implications of land acquisition for urban development. This chapter, based on two representative case studies, offers insights into land acquisition and associated problems and issues. A comparison of these cases will show that the Shangdi industrial zone's land acquisition practices are similar to the approach of the pre-reform era (distinguished by central planning and control), whereas Shenzhen utilizes a land acquisition scheme in which farmers are allowed to keep the land use rights on some of their land. By exercising their land use rights, Shenzhen farmers become new landlords who make decisions on land use and allocation. Experience gained in the Shenzhen and Shangdi experiments has provided assistance on further reforms in land acquisition policy. Following a detailed comparison of these approaches, the authors make policy recommendations.

---

2 Compensation increases over time. See Zhang, Chapter 8 in this volume.

The Shangdi IT Industrial Zone: An Old Land Acquisition Approach

The Shangdi IT industrial zone, in a suburb of Beijing, is located about 15 miles northwest of Tiananmen Square (see Map 1). Planned in the early 1990s to promote the development of high-tech industry, the 171.5-hectare site had been farmland for crops and vegetables before the zone was established. A state-owned enterprise, Shichuan Development Company (SDC), was established to manage the entire process of land development in the zone, transfer the land property rights from villages to the government, obtain land use rights from government and sell land use rights

MAP 1
Location of Shangdi Industrial Park

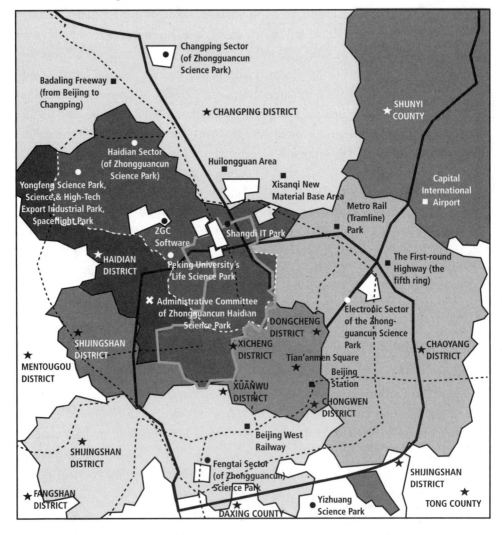

- ■ Transportation Line and Station
- ● Science Park
- ★ Districts and Counties of Beijing
- ✘ Administrative Committee Science Park

to developers. After infrastructure in the zone was established, SDC sold land use rights to developers and IT companies, and kept and developed some lots as residences and office buildings to rent or sell to users. Development work started in 1992 and finished in 1999.

There are several villages in the Shangdi IT industrial zone.[3] One of those surveyed in 1999 had 441 households, 1,189 residents and 67 hectares of land. Because land is used for commericial and industrial development as well as housing provision for people who work in the zone, there is virtually no land left for farming. Indeed, the zone's land development put 796 farmers out of business, causing significant impacts on rural populations that had been kept relatively stable through strict controls on migration (implemented via the hukou, or urban residency permit, system).

Socioeconomic advances in the Shangdi IT zone, brought about by development, have meant significant improvements to housing conditions. Prior to development, land use density was low, residents used public toilets, and basic urban infrastructure was inadequate. The economic improvements associated with development have resulted in urban infrastructure, neighborhoods, open space and community facilities that have been well designed and developed to serve residents. Improvements have also included the demolition of older structures and their replacement by modern buildings that house companies, service and retail activities, entertainment centers and housing.

Problems in the IT zone are related to compensation for land acquisition. The Constitution provides guidelines for compensating farmers during land acquisition rather than specific mandates on the nature and value of that compensation. Villagers and representatives of governments are supposed to negotiate fair compensation in these matters. Since the Shangdi zone is located in the jurisdiction of the Beijing municipal government, municipal representatives worked closely with the SDC to reach compensation agreements. The municipal government's roles in this case included streamlining of land development documents and legal process, conversion of land ownership status, issuance of construction permits, granting of urban hukous for farmers, and job-hunting assistance for those villager-farmers who lose farmland.[4]

After negotiation between the SDC and the villagers, the compensation settlement included agricultural losses, housing, and job provisions for farmers. Those whose livelihoods depended on farming were to be paid 290 RMB for every year they had worked. This meant that a farmer who had worked for 40 years would receive 11,600 RMB in compensation. Younger farmers were paid less as they had worked fewer years; farmers over 49 years of age got a monthly pension of 300 RMB;

---

3 Because the settlement process was the same for all the villages, the authors have reported on one village as representative.

4 See Ding and Knaap, Chapter 1 in this volume.

and farmers under 49 years of age were found jobs by the municipal government. Recognizing the potential issue of social instability, the government provides incentive to firms (usually the state-owned enterprises) to hire these farmers. The government pays 15,000 RMB per job to the hiring firm. Because farmers usually lack the job skills desired by high-tech firms in the zone, they often end up either as janitors for those firms or as workers in labor-intensive manufacturing units (such as food processing) outside the zone.

Economic development in the zone drives up land and housing prices, making housing in the area unaffordable for these minimally skilled farmers. Hence, housing compensation became an essential component in the land acquisition process, and was implemented through two approaches: one that offered a new apartment equivalent in size to the old dwelling, and one that offered cash compensation based on market transaction prices.

In the first option, farmers were granted use rights but no ownership rights. Although farmers were offered the chance to buy ownership at much-lower-than-market prices, few of them chose to do so. The reasons were (1) rents were so trivial that farmers could enjoy the same housing consumption without incurring any costs; (2) farmers were not familiar with the dynamics of real estate markets that can drive up housing prices; and (3) the longtime practice of socialism in China had eroded the concept of private property, so that many farmers felt uncomfortable with it. Thus, housing ownership and use rights were separated: the SDC maintained ownership whereas villagers had rights to live in the housing. Although some farmers never changed their residential locations and did not have an urban job at all (for instance, farmers over 49 years of age), the government granted farmers urban hukous. This may result in overestimation of the urban population even though many of them are not genuinely part of urban life. The desirability of the urban hukou, for farmers, helps keep the cost of land acquisition low.

One of the problems associated with this method of land acquisition is that many state-owned enterprises faced economic problems, and the number of layoffs increased dramatically in the past decade. This obviously made more difficult the government's responsibility of finding (or assigning) jobs for farmers. To ease its charge, the government now pays job-search fees of 20,000 RMB to villagers instead of promising jobs to them. Against the backdrop of rising layoffs and farmers' competitive disadvantage for existing urban jobs (they often lack the skills their urban counterparts possess), the job-search-fee practice results in an inevitable rise in urban unemployment. Some farmers use the cash to set up small businesses such as restaurants, food or retail stores, and other informal enterprises, such as illegal taxi services and streetside vegetable and fruit sales. Thus, one consequence of this land acquisition approach is a proliferation of illegal settlements and unauthorized businesses in the urban fringes.

This approach was distinguished by its severance of farmers' reliance on land and "converting" them to urban residents. Under a planned system, this approach worked very well. Peasants really hoped that the government would take over their land so they could become urban residents and work in state-run factories that offered much better social welfare, including retirement pensions, insurance, subsidies and goods (see Ding and Knaap, Chapter 1 in this volume). But with the establishment of a "socialist market economy with Chinese characteristics," it has become increasingly difficult for farmers to find urban jobs. In addition, more and more villagers, especially in rapidly developing regions, want to keep their land so that they can set up township enterprises or joint ventures. With the presence of demand, especially in suburban areas of large cities, villagers can easily build houses and factory buildings and rent them out. The profit differential between agricultural and non-agricultural enterprises makes this very attractive. Land acquisition in coastal areas, where most development occurs and the price differential can be 10- or even 100-fold, is facing increasing resistance.

Shenzhen: A New Land Acquisition Approach

Shenzhen, in the Pearl River Delta, is one of four SEDZs established in the early 1980s (see Map 2). It was chosen as a SEDZ site because, as the geographic gateway from neighboring Hong Kong to the mainland, there are strong ties between the populations of the two areas, a fact the government sought to optimize.

After the establishment of Shenzhen as one of the SEDZs, manufacturing started moving in from Hong Kong, and the increased demand for labor attracted large numbers of immigrants from the interior regions. Migrant workers currently account for nearly two-thirds of Shenzhen's population. In the 20 years between 1980 and 2000, the Shenzhen SEDZ grew rapidly, with an average annual GDP (gross domestic

MAP 2
Location of Shenzhen Special Economic Development Zone

product) growth rate of 34 percent, an urban population increase from 30,000 to 1.9 million, and expansion of urban built-up area from 3 to more than 120 square kilometers.

With the rapid development of the economy, Shenzhen emerged as a modern city in the late 1980s. Unprecedented demand for land — deriving from enormous success in economic development — pushed the Shenzhen government to annex all land in its jurisdiction into urban areas in 1989. In a span of less than 10 years, all farmers in the jurisdiction were urbanized. Because there were more than 40,000 farmers in 60-plus villages in Shenzhen, it was extremely costly to acquire land from these farmers and resettle them in a satisfactory way. In addition, villagers did not want to accept housing built by the government, mainly because the houses were not large enough to accommodate both living space for a family and enough additional space to use as rental property for additional income.

With the establishment of the Shenzhen SEDZ, the government was committed to reforms that would develop the economy on the basis of the market principles of fair competition, economic efficiency and wealth generation. This economic orientation of development policy made it difficult for the local government to find jobs for villagers whose land was acquired. To provide regional stability and make land acquisition more acceptable, the government needed to find a way to settle newly "freed" farmers. Granting developable land in lieu of the compensation of a job offer became a viable option for the local government. It also appealed to villagers because land became an income-generating asset.

Hence, government took an approach to land conversion different from that used in the Shangdi zone, primarily because of the lack of capital for land acquisition and the government's channeling of any available capital to infrastructure and economic development projects to fuel regional development. The government chose to declare state ownership of land in these new villages, with villagers holding land use rights on their residential land, and the village committee determining land development and use issues within the village boundaries.

Right after the establishment of the Shenzhen SEDZ, the government overcame the cash shortage problem by granting a portion of land to farmers while acquiring the balance of the land. The percentage of a farmer's land parcel acquired depended on both the amount of land owned by a village and the degree of development pressure in the particular location (that is, the size of development projects). Farmers enjoyed complete control of land use decisions on land granted to them: they could choose to build housing for themselves, or to rent, mortgage or sell land and building space.

This worked well for a number of reasons. First, initial cash compensation for farmers was substantially higher than income streams from farming. Second, villages used cash compensation to develop township- or village-owned enterprises that yielded much higher returns than did farming. Farmers could also use their cash compensation to upgrade their housing consumption, as income generated by renting space to industrial firms from Hong Kong could be considerable. Third, farmers enjoyed urban residency status through the granting of urban hukous. Finally, because both population density and demand pressure were low, this approach seemed to work for everyone: government, villages and communes, and farmers.

With unprecedented demand for building space (for both housing needs and economic expansion), farmers greatly increased land use intensity. In the early stage of the Shenzhen development zone, newly constructed houses were 2 or 3 stories high — a reasonable increase compared with the old single-story homes. With a surge of job-seeking migrants from all over the country into the region, housing shortages drove up housing prices dramatically. Farmers immediately recognized this remarkable economic opportunity and capitalized by building larger housing units. Property owners began to tear down their 2- or 3-story buildings and replace them with buildings of 4, 5, 7 and, eventually, even 10 stories. In their effort to keep pace with rapidly rising housing demand, villagers were frequently demolishing and rebuilding their housing units: the average building lifespan in the 1990s was two to three years. Industrial and business uses followed similar patterns.

This redevelopment process is predicted by conventional urban theory, which states that land use intensity increases along with land prices. It also suggests the efficiency of land and capital markets in the sense that land and capital inputs are substituted for each other based on their relative prices.

However, this process generated enormous social and environment problems. The vertical and horizontal expansion of housing construction can endanger public safety, as when the space between buildings is so small that police and fire vehicles cannot pass through. The demand for housing also contributed to the rapid depletion of farmland in urban fringes, which alarmed top leaders in terms of the security of China's food supply.

Recognizing these problems, in the mid-1980s municipal governments issued several executive orders aimed at controlling housing construction by regulating the amount of land that villagers could use and occupy for residential use, determining quotas for grants to villagers of land use rights, and establishing an upper limit for housing land consumption. In doing so, the government hoped to halt village sprawl, preserve cultivated land, coordinate urban development and balance economic development with environmental and ecological protection.

These new orders mandated that a new village should be planned for each existing village. In the new village, boundaries would be drawn, outside of which the primary use would be agricultural, and no land development would be allowed. The amount of land inside these boundaries would depend on the population of the village and the number of households, with each family receiving a lot of 100–160 square meters. The government would take over the land inside the old village when all its families had moved out.

Comparison of the Two Land Acquisition Approaches

The land acquisition approaches exemplified by the Shangdi and Shenzhen SEDZs can inform future land policy reforms. The following evaluation considers property rights, income distribution effects, social structure and organization, and urban planning and development.

Property Rights

Both approaches transferred land ownership from peasants to the state. The Shangdi model didn't have many problems, but it did completely sever the relationship between peasants and the land, and housing dynamics continued to be problematic. When peasants moved into urban residential houses, the development company offered them two alternatives: property rights or use rights. To avoid paying any cash, most families chose the use-rights option, which gives them rights to occupy houses but not the rights to sell them, nor other rights such as mortgaging. The relocated peasant-farmers must pay monthly rents, but resist doing so. It is even difficult for the SDC to collect housing maintenance fees, which may not be problematic in the short term (given that these are new apartments), but in time may pose a serious challenge.

Another problem is that the SDC is ill managed and has not obtained full land use rights from the government, even though land has been developed. As a result, villagers don't have any rights certificates (neither structure ownership nor structure use rights). In the meantime, some households have rented out their apartment flats on the housing market without legal documents.

The Shenzhen approach preserves some tie between land and villagers; thus, villagers are more dependent on land. This model created different kinds of problems related to property rights. Villagers resisted the property rights arrangement: wanting not to give up ownership, they did not go to the government branch office to get their use rights certificates. Their argument was that they had been living on the land for generations and did not need any certificate to continue to do so. According to housing market regulations, however, houses without use rights certificates are not allowed in the housing market. Yet, villagers continue to rent out their dwellings, and there is little the government can do about it. Ironically, the municipal government even collects taxes from these illegally rented apartments, on the basis that the land is owned by the state and private parties ought not to reap windfall wealth from land. This not only causes confusion for government officials, but also encourages villagers to feel justified in renting their properties.

The land acquisition model used in Shenzhen also creates a problem for land management. Urban land users purchase land use rights for a limited period of time, ranging from 30 to 70 years, whereas villagers hold land use rights for recently urbanized land for an infinite period. This implies that land ownership by the state means nothing to urban planning and land management. In fact, many urban planning and land management tools become invalid in the SEDZ. These facts complicate the attempt to use land principles to rationalize land use and land allocation. Indeed, the management ability of the village company is quite limited — it does not hire any managers, but manages the village's business through a social network developed from within the village.

Income Distribution

In the Shangdi approach, peasants lost all of their land and received limited compensation. Since former peasants are not competitive in urban labor markets, their quality of life deteriorated after land acquisition. Most do not have stable jobs, but do temporary work or sell food on the streets. Some families moved out to small, shabby houses and rented their apartment flats to generate extra income. Developers and governments kept windfall gains from land development, whereas farmers shared little, if any, of that revenue. For these farmer-peasants, land was both their main asset and life insurance: when they lost their land, they lost virtually everything. These farmers have not yet benefited from urbanization. Governments should do more to protect the peasants' interests and reduce the increasing resistance to land transfer.

In Shenzhen, former peasants have become very rich from rental income; they now constitute the city's high-income class. Average annual family income is more than 100,000 yuan; a few families earn up to one million yuan per year. Housing rents are the primary income source, whereas industrial and commercial rents are secondary for these villagers, who have benefited enormously from urbanization because renting guarantees their futures.

Social Structure and Organization

In the Shangdi approach, peasants were recreated as urban residents: they were moved into the urban residential area and occupied a few buildings in the community, neighboring with other urban dwellers. The village committee was dismissed and residents elected an urban community committee, which occupies the lowest level of the urban management system. The former peasants were also granted urban hukous and were therefore able to access social welfare programs available only to urban residents.

In the Shenzhen approach, the village committee was changed into a joint stock company and villagers became shareholders, though the company resembles a community organization in terms of structure, common services and products. The head of the company still functions as the community organizer and manager, and villager-members of the company are linked through social networks and cultural background rather than common economic interests. For instance, every village is a clan, all residents in the village have the same family name, and every village has a family ancestral temple that helps maintain community cohesion. Income from rental property has discouraged the socioeconomic ambitions of the younger generation and villages have seen a rise in social problems such as organized crime, gambling and prostitution. The company bears responsibility for these problems.

Urban Planning and Development

In the Shangdi approach, villages have disappeared and been replaced by modern industrial, commercial and residential buildings, thus changing the landscape to that of a modern city. In Shenzhen, however, villages are easily recognized in the landscape. Rural villages have become urban villages. In the mid-1980s, families tended to build 2- or 3-story houses with small yards on the land they were given (as compensation for the transfer of the rights to their land to the government). With the development of the housing rental market, many families reconstructed these modest houses as multi-story buildings (the tallest being 12 stories high).

In this process, both population and structure densities increased dramatically and remained high. Space between these houses was very narrow: some were constructed so close together that they were called "shake hands buildings," the implication being that people in different buildings could shake hands out their windows. In such an environment, urban planning regulations and construction codes cannot be enforced effectively. Streets are too narrow for emergency vehicles, and the density of electrical lines is so extreme that the electricity network looks like a spider's web. Other types of infrastructure are also either absent or inadequate: the sewage system is poor (if there is one in place at all), and greenspace is limited. These urban villages look chaotic and ugly, and housing conditions in them are a legitimate public health concern.

These problems occur because there is no urban planning involved or because the government lacks the tools to carry out such plans. Consequently, there is no coordination among different land users and between land use and basic urban infrastructure such as transportation. Externality is not well recognized and incompatible land use patterns prevail across Chinese cities, even in the new development areas. Land acquisition methods certainly played some role in causing these problems in Shenzhen.

A Recommended Land Acquisition Approach

In summary, problems arising from land acquisition in Shangdi are related to the fact that it cut off the connection between farmers and the land. Resistance to land acquisition became stronger as the market value of land increased and government compensation (for land transfer) could not compete. In general, these problems have more socioeconomic and political than urban planning implications. For instance, land use and infrastructure provision are far less problematic in Shangdi than in Shenzhen.

The impacts of the Shenzhen approach are manifest primarily in aspects of land use efficiency and in coordination between different land uses, including urban infrastructure. Compared with the Shangdi case, the Shenzhen approach has more urban planning implications, though, of course, income from land development in Shenzhen has had major impacts on the socioeconomic life of former farmers. Once land is developed, it becomes extremely expensive to provide basic urban infrastructure such as sewerage and transportation networks.

China's urbanization trend will likely continue for the next 30 to 50 years. It is inevitable that cities will encroach into rural areas, and both urban population and urbanized areas will grow. Recognition of the problems that have accompanied the Shangdi and Shenzhen land acquisition strategies obviates the need for another, innovative approach.

We call our proposed approach "to change peasants into shareholders." In this strategy, land to be converted to urban use is divided into two categories: infrastructure land and development land. For the infrastructure land (including other public use land), government takes over both land ownership and land use rights after giving peasants cash compensation. For the development land, government takes over only the ownership and leaves land use rights to peasants. Development companies can obtain land use rights from farmers, who then become shareholders of these companies. This approach allows farmers to trade their land use rights for stock.

Once all the land is transferred, the village committee is dismissed and villagers move into urban areas developed by companies. The urban planning bureau supervises and regulates land development and coordinates development among different land uses. This approach allows farmers to be full urban residents and to realize dividends from their stock shares, and permits the land management bureau to manage land consistently across geographic areas. This approach should overcome the drawbacks of the Shenzhen approach, and dramatically improve urban land use efficiency.

There are several impacts of this new approach. First, dividend income from stock shares will reduce the fears that farmers face when they move to cities and compete for urban jobs. The continuing bond with villages will provide a sense of security and help to mitigate resistance to land acquisition. An income stream from stock sharing also helps governments reduce land acquisition costs.

Second, the inherent risk in stock investing means there is no lifetime guarantee of income from stock shares. Therefore, the choice of development company becomes extremely important in securing income from land development. This can be an incentive for farmers, who are the shareholders, to seek better education and become involved in business management. The number of landlords will decline and there will be pressure on farmers to look for jobs, perhaps multiple jobs, to earn their livings.

Third, land can be managed according to policy and regulation. Social clans will most likely be dissolved and labor mobility will increase. Fourth, government can control urban land use and land development through urban planning. Zoning and building permits can be used to determine the types and intensity of land development. This approach also makes it easier to enforce building codes and coordinate land use and urban infrastructure. The emerging land markets (or land use rights markets) will help to promote free market transactions and reduce the influence of local governments in land development, as well as in rental-market corruption (Li 1997). This approach should find ready acceptance, as it neither involves private land ownership nor challenges the Constitution.

Conclusions

China is a fascinating country, in part because of its unprecedented development, and in part because of its commitment to socioeconomic reform, including land reform. These realities provide a platform on which many policy-related research questions can be examined. The Chinese government's commitment to reform has not only yielded magnificent outcomes, but also created new challenges and problems (including many negative consequences of land acquisition), which can be better understood in an historical context.

This chapter has illustrated the impacts of land acquisition on urban planning and urban land use. Because the two case studies used provide a limited database, and may be insufficient to a full understanding of the impacts of land policy on urban development and land use, comprehensive empirical studies of those impacts should be conducted. This analysis has taken a first step in the direction of the creative thinking that must be brought to the task of shaping future land policy, and particularly, to issues of land acquisition.

References

Ding, C. 2003. Land use policy reform in China: Assessment and Prospects. *Land Use Policy* 20(2):109–120.

———. 2004. Urban spatial development in the land policy reform era: Evidence from Beijing. *Urban Studies* 41(10/Sept.):1889–1907.

Dowall, David E. 1993. Establishing urban land markets in the People's Republic of China. *Journal of the American Planning Association* 59(2):182–192.

Du, Jie. 1999. The village in city, a survey of the urbanization process in Luohu District, Shenzhen Special Economic Zone. *City Planning Review* 23(9/Sept.).

Fang, Qingdong, Xiangming Ma, and Jinsong Song. 1999. Some strategic choices in urban land use planning. *City Planning Review* 23(9/Sept.).

Jing, Dong. 1999. Policy perspectives for the urbanization process in the developed region. *City Planning Review* 23(9/Sept.).

Li, Ling Hin. 1997. The political economy of the privatisation of the land market in Shanghai. *Urban Studies* 34(2):321–335.

Lin, Geng. 1999. Reform of village and alleviation of antithesis between town and county. Symposium of the International Conference on Urban Development, 27–30 November, Zhongshan, China.

Lin, Zengjie, and Hong Zhang. 1995. *Research on property rights system of real estate in China.* Chinese Renmin University and Hong Kong Association for the Advancement of Real Estate and Construction Technology. Beijing: Chinese Renmin University Press.

Wang, Shuguo. 1987. Master's Degree Thesis. Chinese Agricultural University, Beijing.

Wu, Fulong. 2001. China's recent urban development in the process of land and housing marketisation and economic globalization. *Habitat International* 25:273–289.

Yan, Xing, and Xiaoying Wang. 1995. *Study on land expropriation and acquisition in China.* Chinese Renmin University and Hong Kong Association for the Advancement of Real Estate and Construction Technology. Beijing: Chinese Renmin University Press.

Yang, Hong, and Chuanjiang Liu. 2000. Comparison of systematic arrangement between urbanization from above and urbanization from below in China. *Journal of Middle China University of Technology* 2:77–79.

Zhang, Xingquan. 1997. Urban land reform in China. *Land Use Policy* 14(3):187–199.

Zhang, Anlu, and Hong Mao. 2000. The conversion of rural land into urban land: Channels, patterns and characteristics. *Geography and Territorial Research* 16(2/May).

Zhu, Jieming. 1994. Changing land policy and its impact on local growth: The experience of the Shenzhen Special Economic Zone, China, in the 1980s. *Urban Studies* 31(10): 1611–1623.

Chapter 6

Recycling Contaminated Land: A Potential Strategy for Increasing Land Supply in China

NELSON CHAN

hina's population is immense. The first census after the founding of modern China, conducted in 1953, showed a population of about 583 million people. Nearly 30 years later, the third census (in 1982) registered a jump to about 1.008 billion people (Microsoft Encarta 2001). Despite achievements in family planning, through stringent measures such as the "one-child" policy, the fifth census (in November 2000) demonstrated that the population had exceeded 1.29 billion people (China National Bureau of Statistics 2001).

Both population pressure and economic progress since the introduction of the "open-door" policy in 1978 have contributed to rapid industrialization and urbanization in China. That urbanization is manifested in both the increase in the number of cities and towns, and the enlargement of the boundaries of existing ones (Lo and Yeung 1996). In 1949, for instance, there were 136 cities in China; by the end of 1998 there were 667 cities (State Statistical Bureau 2000). The number of administrative towns had increased from 3,000 in 1980 to more than 19,000 in 2000 (*People's Daily Online* 2000b). The growing pressure for land acquisition for purposes of urbanization often results in the conversion of rural land to urban land uses.

In recent years, agricultural land has disappeared at a rate of hundreds of thousands of hectares per year. The Chinese government has tried various control measures, such as reminders, warnings, legislation and prosecution, to resolve the problem of farmland loss. To reduce encroachments on agricultural land, the government also needs practical strategies for increasing land supply from within urban areas.

Since the founding of the People's Republic of China (PRC) in 1949, a large amount of land has been administratively allocated to government agencies and state-owned enterprises, much of it for industrial uses. A substantial amount of the allocated industrial land has become contaminated for various reasons, and a sizable portion has been left idle. In addition to these industrial areas, considerable acreage has been contaminated by commercial activities and other causes, such as acid rain and contaminated irrigation water or groundwater. Recycling of these contaminated parcels may be a potential means to increase land supply in urban areas. This chapter provides an overview of the current land supply conditions in China and examines the possibilities of such a recycling approach.

Urban Development and Land Supply

The increasing number of new cities and an expansion of existing urban areas are evidence of urbanization in China. Table 1 shows that between 1985 and 1999 total urban area increased by nearly 130 percent, while urban population density increased by slightly more than 76 percent. Such rapid urbanization requires a large amount of land to support the process. Under the land tenure system in China, urban land is owned by the state and farmland is owned by farmer collectives (Chan 1999a). The state has few options for meeting this urban land demand. Although it owns urban land, most of it already has been developed, there are few vacant parcels and the demand far exceeds the state-owned supply. Two methods are commonly used to address the increasing demand for land: urban renewal schemes and compulsory land acquisition.

Urban Renewal Schemes

Living conditions of the Chinese people in the first 30 years after the founding of the PRC were unsatisfactory. There had been inadequate investment in housing development because, during that period, housing was regarded as a "nonproductive" activity in comparison to other, "productive" activities such as manufacturing

TABLE 1

Changes in Urban Areas in China, 1985–1999

Items	1985	1990	1995	1998	1999	% Change 1985–1999
Built-up urban area (sq. km.)	9,386	12,856	19,264	21,380	21,525	129.33
Population density (people/sq. km.)	262	279	322	459	462	76.33
Open space (ha)	159,291	474,613	678,310	745,654	778,161	388.52
Open space (ha/10,000 people)	13.7	32.2	36.7	37.5	38.6	181.75

SOURCE: State Statistical Bureau (2000, Tables 11-5 and 11-11)

TABLE 2

Improvement in Living Conditions in China, 1978–1998

Year	Newly Completed Residential Property in Urban Areas (million sq. m.)	Newly Completed Residential Property in Rural Areas (million sq. m.)	Average Living Area (sq. m./person)	
			Urban Area	Rural Area
1978	38	100	3.60	8.10
1985	188	722	5.20	14.70
1990	173	691	6.70	17.80
1995	375	699	8.10	21.00
1997	405	806	8.80	22.40
1998	477	799	9.30	23.30

SOURCE: State Statistical Bureau (2000, Table 10-26)

and food grain production (Tang 1996). In 1952, the average living area was 4.5 square meters per person. As one result of so little attention on housing, the average living area subsequently dropped to 3.6 square meters per person and remained at that level until 1978 (Chen 1993). There had been various piecemeal attempts to improve living conditions by reforming the housing system, but they failed, primarily because the limited housing development could not keep pace with the rapid population increase.

China began its first comprehensive reform of the housing system in 1978. A target was set in 1983: to increase the average living area to 8 square meters per person by 2000 (Chan 2000a). During the years, considerable progress has been made. Table 2 shows that the target was achieved in 1995, five years ahead of schedule.

Despite that progress, there are still 50 million square meters of unsafe residential buildings in the country, and 60 million square meters of old and substandard properties (built in the 1950s and 1960s) that need to be upgraded. The problems vary from city to city. For example, in Shanghai, there are 20 million square meters of residential properties that are more than 60 years old, of which 4.6 million square meters are damaged and 146,000 square meters are unsafe. In Beijing, there are 8 million square meters of dangerous residential properties scattered around 52 districts (Yu 1998). Schemes to redevelop substandard and unsafe housing stock are either under way or in development.

The reforms begun in 1978 both provided an opportunity to renew miserable sectors of urban areas and released surplus land for other kinds of development. The following example demonstrates the theory of how this can work for the 20 million square meters of old residential properties in Shanghai.

Most residential properties more than 60 years old are low-density, single- or two-story buildings. Some assumptions are necessary: that there is a scheme to redevelop the 20 million square meters of substandard living space; that one-half of that living space is in single-story structures and one-half in two-story buildings; that the modern residential building floor-area ratio is 10:1; and that 40 percent of the cleared land is required for roads, open space and other infrastructure.

The existing single-story buildings, based on assumed site coverage of 100 percent, have an existing floor-area ratio of 1:1 (that is, there is 1 square meter of floor area for every 1 square meter of land). So, 10 million square meters of existing floor space yield 10 million square meters of land for redevelopment. The existing two-story buildings, based on assumed site coverage of 100 percent, have an existing floor-area ratio of 2:1 (that is, for every 2 square meters of floor area, 1 square meter of land area is required). So, 10 million square meters of existing floor space yield 5 million square meters of land for redevelopment.

Because the floor-area ratios of the existing buildings are lower than the floor-area ratios of modern buildings, there exists a potential for redevelopment. The estimated new floor area from the massive urban renewal scheme is calculated on the chart below.

	Million sq. m.	Million sq. m.
A. Single-story properties		
Land area	10	
Less 40% for roads and open space	4	
Net land area for redevelopment	6	
Floor-area ratio	10	
New floor area		60
B. Two-story properties		
Land area	5	
Less 40% for roads and open space	2	
Net land area for redevelopment	3	
Floor-area ratio	10	
New floor area		30
Total new floor area		**90**

Based on the old average living area of 3.6 square meters per person, the original 20 million square meters of poor living space could house about 5.5 million people. Based on the new average living area of 8 square meters per person, the new floor space of 90 million square meters can house about 11 million people in much-improved conditions. In addition, there are 6 million square meters of spare land for roads, open space and other infrastructure. No doubt this example provides an overly optimistic picture. In real life, urban renewal is difficult, lengthy and uncertain because it depends on the ability of government to solve a number of socioeconomic conflicts. While the urban renewal process helps release land for urbanization, other sources of land supply are important, as well.

Compulsory Land Acquisition

Another way to increase land supply for urban development is through compulsory land acquisition, as authorized by the Constitution of the People's Republic of China 1978. Article 10 of the Constitution states that "the State, for public interest, may acquire land according to the provisions of legal requirements." Farmland may be compulsorily acquired for construction purposes under the Land Administration Law (LAL) of 1998. Before any acquisition of farmland can occur, approval for converting the land to construction use has to be obtained. Buildings on land covered by a city plan also may be acquired under the Urban Buildings Demolition Removal Management Regulation 1991 for urban development or renewal schemes. Given the important role compulsory land acquisition plays in supplying land for urbanization, the State Council has issued Order No. 15, which requires local governments (with the necessary resources) to establish a land acquisition-reserve system. As of 2001, 241 cities in 12 provinces had established a land acquisition-reserve agency (China Ministry of Land and Resources 2001a).

Figure 1 shows the amount of land compulsorily acquired from 1995 to 1999. The statistics do not indicate whether the acquired land was from farmland only, or from a combination of farm and urban lands. Land acquisition peaked in 1996, the year in which an amount of land equivalent to the size of Hong Kong was acquired for urban development. The decline in the amount of land acquired since then may be due to the government's attempt to control acquisition and conversion of farmland to urban development, and to the considerable expense of compulsory land acquisition.

To acquire farmland, the land acquisition unit (authority) has to pay compensation for the land taken, crops, resettlement of affected farmers and improvements on land, as well as a farmland occupation tax, agricultural facilities compensation, a farming rehabilitation fund fee, a vegetable-fields establishment fee, etc. (Bi 1994). For the acquisition of urban land, equivalent replacement accommodation and relocation fees have to be paid to the dispossessed occupants (Chan 2000b). The total compensation amounts can be very substantial.

The cost of increasing land supply through compulsory land acquisi-

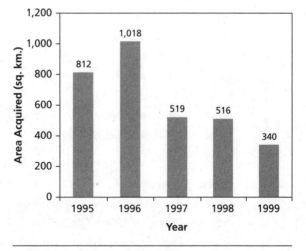

FIGURE 1

Land Acquisition in China, 1995–1999

SOURCES: State Statistical Bureau (1996–2000)

tion is one of several reasons it has become less favored as a strategy. In recent years there has been increasing resistance to this approach, in part because dispossessed people feel that the compensation is unjust. For example, in April 2001 a group of dispossessed households in Nanjing protested against the low compensation payment because the acquiring authority had ignored the fact that the acquired properties were within the busy city-center district (The Sun News Publisher Ltd. 2001a).

The lack of transparency in determination of compensation can easily lead to corruption. Conversion of farmland for development can be done either legally, under the LAL, or illegally. Because farmland must be acquired prior to conversion, its conversion may be regarded as an extension of the compulsory land acquisition process. While it is not a secret that the regulated farmland conversion system is subject to abuse, it is the illegal conversion of farmland that is most problematic.

In the so-called "development zone craze" of 1993, a large amount of land was occupied and zoned by various levels of government for development. Approximately 80 percent of such land encroached on farmland (Bi 1994), and many of the development zones had not gone through the legal process. The U.S. Embassy in China disclosed that "satellite photos from NASA's [National Aeronautic and Space Administration's] Landsat-5 for 1987, 1991 and 1995 for 17 large Chinese urban areas showed that the rate of conversion of agricultural land to nonagricultural use was two-and-one-half times greater than official statistics" (U.S. Embassy in China 1997, 1). Even in recent years, farmland in China has continued to decrease at an alarming rate: the China Ministry of Land and Resources (CMLR 2000) reported the loss at hundreds of thousands of hectares per year. Figure 2 shows the reduction in farmland from 1997 to 1999.

To control these problems, Section (Sec.) 342 of the Criminal Law of the People's Republic of China 1979 was revised in March 1997 to punish offenders (involved in unlawful conversion of large areas of farmland and severe damage to farmland) by imprisonment of up to five years, a fine or both. Sec. 45 of the 1998 LAL mandates that any acquisition of farmland must have prior approval (under Sec. 44) for conversion of farmland to nonagricultural uses. In addition, acquisition of farmland in the following categories needs the prior approval of the State Council:

- basic farmland;
- arable land, other than basic farmland, of more than 35 hectares; and
- all other land exceeding 70 hectares.

Furthermore, the 1998 LAL and the Basic Farmland Protection Regulation of 1998 aim to control more stringently the acquisition and conversion of farmland, thus ensuring that the nation's agricultural land aggregates to not less than 1.28 billion hectares (*People's Daily Online* 2001). Although these measures may not eliminate unauthorized conversion of farmland, the supply of land from both legal and illegal conversion should be greatly reduced. (This trend is noticeable in Figure 2.)

FIGURE 2
Reduction of Farmland in China, 1997–2000

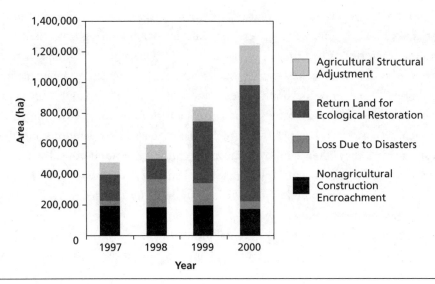

SOURCE: CMLR (2000, 2001b)

Under the broad principle of protecting farmland, land for urban development needs to be made available differently — through urban renewal schemes, higher-density development, rezoning of permitted uses, etc.

Contaminated Land — A New Land Source to Accommodate Urban Growth

To balance the increasing (and ongoing) demand for land for urbanization and the considerable pressure to preserve farmland, brownfield redevelopment becomes a viable solution, even if at a higher cost. The U.S. Environmental Protection Agency (USEPA) defines brownfields as "abandoned, idle, or under-used industrial and commercial facilities where expansion or redevelopment is complicated by real or perceived environmental contamination" (USEPA 2001a). The following sections examine China's brownfields and explore the possibility of recycling contaminated land.

Causes and Extent of Land Contamination in China

As in other countries, in China land may become contaminated for a number of reasons, but industrialization is the primary cause. And, though industrialization is relatively recent, the environmental problems are already very serious. Contributing factors are the lack of understanding by the population and by industry of the importance of environmental protection; relatively undeveloped management skills; inadequate equipment and production technology; and unsatisfactory pollution prevention and control measures (State Council 1996a).

The rise of rural industries (*xiang zhen qi ye*), which are regarded as a significant source of income and employment opportunities for peasants (Chang and Kwok 1990), further aggravates the situation. These industries are established and run by farmers who have gained knowledge and skills in manufacturing from their work in urban factories. When they return to their home village to set up their own factories, considerations such as social costs, environmental impacts and management techniques are generally beyond their education and skills. The manufacturing processes these industries use often produce substantial amounts of environmentally unfriendly waste, and because these are generally small-scale operations and thus, cost sensitive, they often employ primitive technology without consideration for environmental impacts. The situation was so bad that the State Council (1996b) ordered a number of these low-tech or low-productivity industries to close down before the end of September 1996.

Other sources of these environmental problems are environmentally hazardous industries established in, or transferred to, China by foreign firms, and the shipment of hazardous waste for disposal from developed countries to China (Zhang 1992). For example, *Reuters News Service* (2002) reported that as much as 80 percent of electronics waste collected for recycling in the U.S. is shipped to countries such as India, Pakistan and China.

China now has 8 of the 10 most polluted cities in the world (The Sun News Publisher Ltd. 2001b). Environmental problems in China are so serious that they were among the concerns of the International Olympic Committee when considering China's bid for the Olympic Games in Beijing in 2008. In response, China has pledged to spend US$12.2 billion for environmental protection and improvement projects in Beijing from 1998 to 2007 (Preparatory Office Organizing Committee 2001). A large number of "dirty" industries will be closed down or removed in preparation for the 2008 Olympic Games, including Capital Iron and Steel (the largest heavy industrial enterprise in Beijing), which will leave two million square meters of spare land for other development (*South China Morning Post* 2001). The industrial layout in Beijing will be restructured so that industrial enterprises occupying, in the aggregate, a total of more than six million square meters of land will be relocated to areas outside the downtown district or to other cities (Commercial Service China 2001).

There are no specific statistical data about contaminated land in China; the magnitude of the problem must be inferred from a variety of information sources. Airborne, liquid and solid pollutants may pollute land, each causing different degrees of contamination. Coal supplies 75 percent of China's industrial fuel, 76 percent of its power-generating fuel and 80 percent of its residential- and commercial-use fuel (*China Environment News* 2000). The annual use of millions of tons of coal has caused significant land contamination and the release of a huge amount of soot, smoke, fumes and sulphur dioxide into the atmosphere during the burning process.

The latest figures show that China discharges about 20 million tons of sulphur dioxide each year, leading to the formation of significant amounts of acid rain that affect nearly one-third of the country, including the Sichuan Basin, areas south of the Yangtze River and areas east of the Qinghai-Tibet Plateau (Xinhua Net 2002).

Given the area affected by acid rain, the cumulative damages are tremendous. Zhang (1997) reported that the average annual pH value of acid rain in Central China was below 4.0 and that more than 80 percent of the time, rain was acidic. The *People's Daily* (2002) reported that Tongling, in Anhui Province, has been affected since 1980 by acid rain with a pH value of 4.5 to 5.0, and that more than 7,000 hectares of farmland have been contaminated by acid rain. The damage done includes not only soil contamination but also damage to metal and cement. Because elevated soil acidity affects concrete foundations, it will likely increase total project costs to allow for either neutralizing the soil or providing acid-resistant foundations in redevelopment of land contaminated by acid rain.

At present, one-half of the seven major river systems in China are heavily polluted. In particular, one-half of the 200 branches of the Huai River have lost their riverine functions. Chao Lake (Chaohu), one of China's five largest freshwater lakes, has become a notorious wastewater collector due to the indiscriminate discharge of municipal and industrial wastewater into it (Min 1999). As a result, Chaohu is one of the three lakes (Chaohu, Taihu and Dianchi) targeted for remediation under the "3321 Project" (National Environmental Protection Administration [NEPA] 2000).[1] Due to water scarcity in some areas, water from polluted river systems is used for irrigation and household uses, and has caused serious health risks to people (Min 1999). A large amount of land has become contaminated from irrigation with polluted water or percolation of polluted groundwater.

There are no statistics about the annual amount of solid waste produced by the burning of coal fuel in China, but the annual coal production and consumption figures may suggest the magnitude of the waste. In 1999, China's coal production totaled 1,050 million tons. In 2000, the figure dropped to 950 million tons, due to regulation of the coal industry by the government (Mbendi 2002). Coal consumption figures in recent years are shown in Figure 3. Apart from the small portion of solid wastes that are recycled for other uses (such as manufacturing of brick and other construction materials), the rest goes to solid waste stockpiles. Given that there is currently no alternative to coal as a cheap fuel, it will likely continue to be the main fuel source in China. Land contamination by the resultant acid rain will continue until there are technological changes that can significantly reduce the amount of sulphur dioxide discharged.

---

1 The "3321 Project" aims to remediate three rivers (Huai River, Lio River and Hai River), three lakes (Tai Lake [Taihu], Chao Lake [Chaohu] and Dian Lake [Dianchi]), and two zones (Sulphur Dioxide Pollution Control Zone and Acid Rain Pollution Control Zone), and to enhance environmental protection in one city (Beijing). It is thus known as the 3-3-2-1 or "3321" project. It also aims to reduce atmospheric air pollution by controlling the quantities of major pollutants and implementing the cross-century green project; to enforce vigorously environmental protection laws; and to promote environmental protection investment, technology and education.

FIGURE 3

Coal Consumption in China by Use, 1980–1997

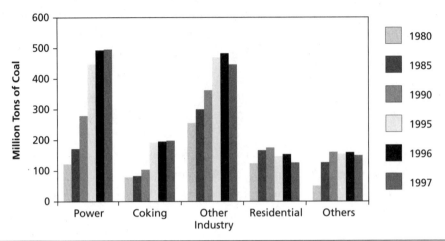

SOURCE: China E-news (2000)

Increased industrial activity also creates large amounts of solid waste every year. Table 3 shows the creation, discharge and stockpile of solid waste from 1990 to 1999, and the increase in the amount of land required for stockpiling that waste since 1990. The statistical figures do not indicate how much of this land is farmland, but at present, solid waste landfills have already swallowed more than 134,000 hectares of farmland nationwide (China Online 2001). In addition, there are numerous industrial sites in the nation with varying degrees of contamination and extensive areas of land contaminated by acid rain and/or percolated contaminated groundwater. Although the exact number of sites and the precise acreage involved are not known, the magnitude of the damage is considerable.

A substantial number of state-owned enterprises have had a role by virtue of their fiscal failures. The central government used to subsidize and finance these concerns, which have operated at a deficit for decades, but now recognizes that it cannot continue to support these inefficient and uncompetitive enterprises. Since 1995 a

TABLE 3

Creation, Discharge and Stockpile of Solid Waste in China, 1990–1999

Year	Solid Waste Created (million tons)	Solid Waste Discharged (million tons)	Solid Waste Stockpile Area (ha)
1990	577.97	47.67	58,390
1995	644.74	22.42	55,440
1998	800.43	70.48	64,756
1999	784.42	38.80	62,808

SOURCES: State Statistical Bureau (1996, 1997, 1999 and 2000)

series of economic measures, including the introduction of bankruptcy law, has been implemented to mobilize economic resources and introduce market mechanisms to guide and rationalize resource use (Fang 1999). As of the end of 1999, more than 6,400 large- and medium-sized state-owned enterprises had reduced the sizes of their operations (*People's Daily Online* 2000a). Given the long-standing practice of industry-oriented national economic policy (in which the industrial sector was overallocated land), the streamlining of state-owned concerns frees up a substantial amount of land, a good portion of which is contaminated. Thus, redevelopment of these brownfields will likely significantly increase land supply for urban development.

Although the total area of contaminated land in China is not known, this analysis shows that the scale of damage is considerable. Depending on the location, site characteristics, underlying market conditions and seriousness of contamination, these sites may be remediated for reuse at varying costs. Recycling of these sites for other beneficial uses will not only ease the short supply of land for urban development, but also help relieve the adverse environmental impacts. Before any contaminated land can be put to alternate uses, it must be remediated to the satisfaction of the environmental protection authority and rezoned for the intended uses. Therefore, it is important to establish health and environmental standards to guide the remediation and redevelopment of contaminated land.

Urban Planning Encourages Recycling of Contaminated Land

Urban planning aims to balance economic development and protect the environment through prudent planning and control of development. The latter is achieved by managing land use through zoning and rezoning processes, which separate incompatible land uses in order to minimize negative externalities. Another objective of urban planning is to ensure a decent environment in which people can live and work. An implicit goal is the reduction of contaminated land in the community and reuse of that land for beneficial purposes. In the seminal English court case *Donoghue v Stevenson* [1932] AC 562 (HL), the principle of "duty of care to one's neighbors" was introduced.[2] Lord Atkin (a presiding judge in the case) considered neighbors as "persons who are so closely and directly affected by my act." Accordingly, there is a social and legal obligation (duty of care of one's neighbors) of landowners to remediate contaminated sites.

Cost is always the challenge in redeveloping contaminated land, particularly in developing countries that are typically short of capital. While the environmental protection authority may require remediation of the sites by enforcing the relevant

---

2 In this case, a female customer was sick after drinking a bottle of ginger beer, which contained the decomposed body of a snail. Although there was no direct contractual relationship between the plaintiff customer and the defendant brewery, the court found that the defendant owed the plaintiff a "duty of care" based on the principles of foreseeability and proximity. The defendant was held liable for the physical damages suffered by the plaintiff.

environmental laws, landowners or other responsible persons may not be able to afford the cost of carrying out the necessary remediation. In Western countries, the reluctance to clean up often leads to a challenge of the cleanup order through lengthy litigation. Even if the contaminated land is eventually remediated, there is no guarantee that the land will be used to the benefit of the community afterward. A better approach is the use of urban planning to achieve the goal because litigation about cleanup orders can be avoided (Chan 1999b).

Where redevelopment of contaminated land is supported by other factors, such as location and market demand, the planning authority may plan the beneficial uses of the land and accordingly rezone it to higher-value uses (such as commercial or residential) to encourage redevelopment. While rezoning alone does not change the land use, when coupled with economic forces, it effectively adds value to the sites and increases their redevelopment potential. When redevelopment proceeds, a site will be cleaned up according to the sensitivity of the alternative uses, and the result is an end use that is acceptable to the community. If the contaminated land is in a desirable location and there is overwhelming market demand, the land value is unlikely to suffer from any stigma impact from the contamination history.

Environmental Protection and Planning Control in China

Environmental protection was officially considered for the first time in China when the State Council called for the first national environmental protection conference in August 1973. Provisions for environmental protection were subsequently included in the Constitution of the People's Republic of China in 1978. Article 26 stipulates that "[t]he state protects and improves the living environment and the ecological environment, and prevents and remedies pollution and other public hazards." The Constitution thus provides a foundation for environmental protection in the nation.

The Environmental Protection Law of 1989 subsequently replaced a 1979 temporary law, and is now the principal environmental protection law. Currently, there are 28 national laws, more than 70 administrative decrees, and more than 900 local laws related to environmental protection (NEPA 2000). The laws aim, primarily, to control and prevent the "three wastes" problems: airborne, liquid and solid wastes. At present, there is no specific law on land contamination. Nevertheless, the principles of "polluter pays," "user pays," "developer protects" and "destroyer restores" are enforced, and China has committed one percent of its gross domestic product (GDP) annually to halt the growth of environmental problems (China Embassy in the U.S. 1997).

The U.S. takes a "carrot-and-stick" approach to tackling land contamination problems. The stick is in the form of penalties under environmental laws, in particular, The Comprehensive Environmental Response, Compensation, and Liability Act of 1980 (CERCLA). The law introduced "joint and several" liability for land contamination. A Superfund program was also set up under CERCLA to clean up contaminated sites at a national level (Chan, Jefferies, and Simons 1998). The Superfund is a trust fund financed through a special tax on the chemical and petroleum industries. This trust fund may be used for site remediation when no viable, potentially responsible parties are identified or when those parties fail to take necessary response actions (USEPA 1988). At a state level, "[m]ore than 35 States now have voluntary cleanup programs under which private parties that voluntarily agree to clean up a contaminated site are offered some protection from future State enforcement action at the site, often in the form of a 'no further action' letter or 'certificate of completion' from the State" (USEPA 2001b).

The carrot is in the form of a brownfield tax-incentive scheme to assist and encourage landowners in remediating contaminated land and to spur redevelopment. Under this scheme, "environmental cleanup costs are fully deductible in the year they are incurred, rather than having to be capitalized. The government estimates that while the tax incentive costs approximately $300 million in annual tax revenue, the tax incentive is expected to leverage $3.4 billion in private investment and return 8,000 brownfields to productive use. This ability to spur investment in blighted properties and revitalize communities makes the tax incentive a valuable tool for restoring brownfields" (USEPA 2001c).

No one owns the environment. For this reason, it is regarded as a public good that is "not depleted by an additional user" and that it is "difficult or impossible to exclude people from its benefit" (Baumol et al. 1992, 688). Because property rights of the environment are poorly defined, there is no incentive to conserve the environment (Gowdy and Olsen 1994). Before the economic reforms of 1978, individuals had little private property. Under the ideology of communism, many people had the impression that nearly all resources, including the environment, were a public good, and there was little incentive to care about them. The introduction of the open-door policy helped loosen the government's grip on everything and revitalize the concept of private property rights. However, the environment is still generally regarded as no one's property. Despite the government's one percent GDP commitment for environmental protection, and the passing of a large number of environmental laws and decrees, environmental problems, including land contamination, are still serious in China. At present, there are neither a national program to clean up contaminated sites nor voluntary cleanup programs to encourage remediation by private parties.

Current environmental laws contain mainly sticks, with very few carrots. Financial incentives to remediate contaminated land are minimal. Under Sec. 28 of the Environmental Protection Law, the environmental protection authority in an administrative region may levy a pollutant-discharge fee on any enterprise that has exceeded the allowable pollutant-discharge limit. Environment Protection Grants are created from collected pollutant-discharge fees, and major polluters may apply for grants to help finance remediation. However, the grants are limited to 80 percent of the fees a particular enterprise has previously paid.

In addition, the State Council has authorized a Pollution Source Remediation Fund, which is financed by 20–30 percent of the pollutant-discharge fees levied. Major polluting enterprises may borrow money from the fund for remediation work, to a maximum of 40 percent of the total remediation cost and with repayment within three years. The tight controls will likely severely affect the amount and quality of remediation that enterprises undertake. At present, there is no tax incentive or other financial aid to encourage polluters to carry out remediation work. It is apparent that the number of carrots is insufficient to the enormous task of remediating and recycling the country's contaminated land.

Although China has a series of environmental protection standards covering environmental quality, pollutant discharge and environmental protection basics, a standard for remediation of land contamination is not yet available. Of the various standards, the following are commonly used.

(1) **Environmental Quality Standard for Surface Water** (GB3838-88)

It establishes thresholds for water quality for rivers, streams, lakes and reservoirs. It divides water into five categories according to the location of the water, such as national science protection areas, domestic areas, industrial areas, rural areas, etc.

(2) **Integrated Wastewater Discharge Standard** (GB8978-1996)

It divides pollutants into two categories and specifies the maximum discharge concentration according to the destination of the discharge. It also specifies the point of sampling according to the category of pollutants.

(3) **Ambient Air Quality Standard** (GB3095-1996)

It categorizes ambient air into three classes according to location, and specifies the concentration of pollutants in the air, and the sampling and analysis methods.

(4) **Integrated Emission Standard of Air Pollutants** (GB6297-1996)

It specifies the maximum discharge limit of 33 pollutants, the discharge speed, the height of flues and distance between them, and the monitoring, sampling and analysis procedures.

(5) **Standard of Environmental Noise of Urban Area** (GB3096-93)

It divides urban areas into five categories (0–4), ranging from areas of sanatoriums or high-class villas to areas bisected by major roads. It also specifies maximum noise limits in the categorized urban areas.

(6) **Standard of Noise at Boundary of Industrial Enterprises** (12348-90)

It divides areas bordering industrial enterprises into four categories (1–4), ranging from residential and educational sites to areas bisected by major roads. It also specifies the peak value of noise during daytime and nighttime.

7) **Noise Limits for Construction Sites** (GB12523-90)

It sets limits for construction work sites in urban areas, specifying the maximum value of noise (during both daytime and nighttime) from bulldozers, excavators, loaders, piling machine, concrete mixers, vibrators, electric saws, hoists, lifts, etc. (NEPA 2000).

These environmental protection standards do not directly relate to remediation or recycling of contaminated land for alternative uses. Nevertheless, if remediation or recycling of contaminated land is to be carried out, compliance with these standards does indirectly increase development costs.

Urban planning and development in China are governed by the City Planning Law of the People's Republic of China 1989 (CPL). The law empowers city government to prepare a master plan for the city, which has to conform to the master land use plan prepared by the State Council under Sec. 17 of the LAL. Sec. 14 of the CPL requires that the master city plan include the designation of a planning authority to oversee details of protecting and improving the city's ecological environment and preventing pollution and other public hazards. Under Sec. 32 of the CPL, a system of planning permission and development approval is created.

The requirement to carry out an environmental impact assessment for environmentally sensitive development projects has been established in China, as it has in many countries. In addition, such a project in China needs to comply with the "three-at-the-same-time" system promulgated by the State Council (1996b). This system has been incorporated into Clause 4 of the Construction Projects Environmental Protection Management Measures 1986. It applies to new projects, expansions, alterations and technological improvement projects. The three elements — design, construction and operation — are shorthand for the aim of the law, which is to ensure that the environmental protection features of a project are designed, constructed, and implemented simultaneously with the primary production project. The goal is to ensure that environmental protection features are closely integrated and operating concurrently with the main project.

The U.S. Cleanup Experience

Table 4 outlines some successful cleanup experiences in the U.S., showing that recycling contaminated land is a practical way to release more land for development and has a number of benefits. Apart from increasing land supply, it helps revitalize the habitat of fauna and flora, removes eyesores and sources of health risks, increases job opportunities, rejuvenates deserted areas, improves the economy and increases property values.

In China, there are ample opportunities to reclaim contaminated land. Increasing numbers of bankrupt state-owned enterprises have left behind numerous brownfield sites. It is also likely that a considerable number of these sites lie idle and underutilized by inefficient and uncompetitive state-owned enterprises. Recycling this sleeping land resource is a potential way to increase land supply. It is worthwhile for the government to consider making a comprehensive policy on recycling contaminated land an integral part of urban planning. The U.S. experience is a good reference for this purpose. One could predict diminishing resistance to environmental protection policies in China as the government exercises greater control over the population and the land. But, strict enforcement of those policies would still constitute a challenge.

TABLE 4

Successful U.S. Cleanup Experiences

Location	Property	Cleanup Year	Before	After	Impact
Pickaway County, Ohio	Bowers Landfill	1991	Hazardous waste landfill with municipal, chemical, and industrial waste	Wetlands home for plants, wildlife, and migratory birds	Productive use of land as an ecological sanctuary
Richland, Washington	Hanford 1100 Area	1993	Distribution center for U.S. nuclear weapons arsenal	Rehabilitated rail hub and locomotive repair facility	Local jobs; magnet for business development
Anaconda, Montana Smelter	East Anaconda	1994	500 acres contaminated from copper smelting	An award-winning golf course and hiking trail	New jobs; increased public revenues; revitalized town
Stratford, Connecticut	Raymark Industries	1995	Hazardous waste site resulting from 70 years of automotive parts and products manufacturing	Future shopping center and restaurants	Local jobs and income; increased spending and public revenues; catalyst for economic activity
Clear Creek, Colorado	Central City	1998	Contaminated waste rock piles, tailings piles and mine tunnels as a result of nearly 100 years of mining	Casinos, hotels, restaurants and other amenities	Revitalization of Black Hawk and Central City with local jobs and income; increased property values and public revenues

SOURCE: USEPA (2001d)

Conclusions and Recommendations

The modernization process in China has brought unprecedented urbanization, which in turn requires a large amount of land to support the development of new cities and the expansion of existing ones. At present, land supply for urban development comes primarily from land owned by the government, land from urban renewal schemes, compulsory land acquisition and conversion of farmland. As previously identified, land supply from these sources is not guaranteed. The balance between farmland protection and adequate land supply for urban development has become a serious challenge to government officials. Redevelopment of contaminated land certainly helps mitigate the pressure of this land demand.

The exact amount of contaminated land in China is not known, but our previous discussion indicates that it may be substantial. The U.S. experience shows that recycling contaminated land can increase land supply for redevelopment and offers socioeconomic benefits. There is no reason for China not to adopt this strategy. At present there are no specific laws and remediation standards governing contaminated land in the nation. The current legislation provides the sticks to control and prevent land contamination, but fails to provide sufficient carrots to encourage cleanup and redevelopment of brownfield sites. To unlock this potential land supply resource, China needs to consider the following recommendations.

(1) Formulate a suitable carrot-and-stick policy to clean up contaminated sites, and make specific contaminated land laws and remediation standards to clarify the legal positions of the stakeholders.

(2) Provide financial subsidies and/or incentives for site remediation.

(3) Carry out voluntary remediation of orphan sites (sites with ownership complications).

(4) Reduce red tape and require environmental protection and planning authorities to play a proactive role in helping stakeholders clean up and redevelop contaminated land.

(5) Relax control of disposal of administratively allocated (contaminated) land to increase its marketability.

Contaminated land affects human health and may impose financial and legal liabilities on the owner. Recycling contaminated sites for alternative uses is a win-win solution: the landowners reap financial benefit; the community gets a more healthful and pleasant living environment; and it provides another source of land for urban development. Recycling of contaminated land will not, by itself, eliminate all contaminated sites in the nation. However, it does help reduce the number of sites, improves environmental quality of life and increases land supply. The Chinese government should seriously consider this winning strategy.

References

Baumol, W. J., A. S. Blinder, A. W. Gunther, and J. R. L. Hicks. 1992. *Economics Principles and Policy*, 2nd Australian ed. Australia: Harcourt Brace Jovanovich.

Bi, B. D. 1994. *China Real Estate Market Studies*. Beijing: China People's University Press.

Chan, N. 1999a. Land-use rights in mainland China: Problems and recommendation for improvement. *Journal of Real Estate Literature* 7(1):53–63.

———. 1999b. The impact of environmental planning on the value of contaminated land. *Australian Land Economics Review* 5(1):8–20.

———. 2000a. Housing system reform in China. *Australian Property Journal* 36(1):37–42.

———. 2000b. Compulsory acquisition compensation of the Three Gorges project. *The Hong Kong Institute of Surveyors Journal* 11(2):41–51.

Chan, N., R. L. Jefferies, and R. A. Simons. 1998. Government regulation of contamination land — a tale of three cities. *Environmental and Planning Law Journal* 15(5):321–337.

Chang, S. D., and R. Y. Kwok. 1990. *The urbanisation of rural China*. In *Chinese urban reform: What model now?* R. Kwok, W. Parish, A. Yeh, and Xueqiang Xu, eds. Armonk, NY: M. E. Sharpe. Cited in F. C. Lo and Y. M. Yeung, eds., *Emerging world cities in Pacific Asia* (Tokyo, New York, and Paris: United Nations University Press, 1996).

Chen, Jia Lou. 1993. *Residence Sociology*. Beijing: China Construction Materials Industry Press.

China Embassy in the U.S. 1997. China to spend 1% of GDP to halt pollution growth. http://www.china-embassy.org/Cgi-Bin/Press.pl?266.

China E-news. 2000. Energy efficiency, environment, economy. http://www.pnl.gov/china/coalcons.htm.

China Environment News. 2000. Clean coal technology: Remediation via burning. Issue 6, 4 January. http://www.envir.online.sh.cn/info/index.asp.

China Ministry of Land and Resources (CMLR). 2000. China's management and legal systems for land resources. http://www.mlr.gov.cn/english/Pland%20Management.html.

———. 2001a. Increase in land banks. http://www.mlr.gov.cn/information/info/querying/gettingInfoRecord.asp?infoIdx=2113.

———. 2001b. Net farmland reduction area 14,435,000 mu in year 2000 in our country. http://www.mlr.gov.cn/information/info/querying/gettingInfoRecord.asp?infoIdx=2116.

China National Bureau of Statistics. 2001. Communique on major figures of the 5th national census in year 2000. http://www.p2000.gov.cn/02fix/02pcgg/gg200101.htm.

———. 2001. Key data of the 5th national census. http://www.stats.gov.cn/sjjw/pcsj/rkpc-5/rk0501.htm.

China Online. 2001. Pollution, landfills devouring agriculture. http://65.161.182.24/industry/agriculture/currentnews/secure/c00060803.asp.

Commercial Service China. 2001. 2008 Olympic Games — Beijing. http://www.usembassy-china.org.cn/english/commercial/english/olympics/.

Fang, X. M. 1999. The difficulties of China's state-owned enterprises and the reform measures ahead. *Economic reform today*. Working paper #7. http://www.cipe.org/wp/prc.html.

Gowdy, J. M., and P. R. Olsen. 1994. Further problems with neoclassical environmental economics. *Environmental Ethics* 16(Summer).

Liu, T. C., Z. X. Lin, and Y. N. Liu, eds. 1982. *An overview of environmental protection.* Beijing: Advanced Education Press.

Lo, F. C., and Y. M. Yeung, eds. 1996. *Emerging world cities in Pacific Asia.* Tokyo, New York and Paris: United Nations University Press.

Mbendi. 2002. China: Mining: Coal mining. http://www.mbendi.co.za/indy/ming/ coal/ as/cj/p0005.htm.

Microsoft Encarta. 2001. China: Population. http://www.encarta.msn.com/find/concise .asp?ti=761573055&sid=106#s106.

Min, K. C. 1999. Wastewater pollution in China. http://Darwin.bio.uci.edu/~sustain /sustain/suscoasts/hrismin.html.

National Environmental Protection Administration of China (NEPA). 2000. China envi-ronmental policy, laws, regulations and system establishment. http://www. nepa.unep.net /po-law/law/jianshe.htm.

People's Daily. 2002. Acid rain causes substantial damages: Anhui carries out integrated remediation. 10 January. http://search.envir.com.cn/tppmsgs/msgs10.htm#1076.

People's Daily Online. 2001. China to guarantee cultivated land no less than 1.92 mu. 1 February. http://english.peopledaily.com.cn/20010201/print20010201_61417.html.

————. 2000a. China reaches "turning point" in revamping SOEs. 8 January. http:// english.peopledaily.com.cn/200001/08/eng20000108X105.html.

————. 2000b. Speed of urbanization in China's countryside above world average. 28 September. http://english.peopledaily.com.cn/200009/28/eng20000928_51463.html.

Preparatory Office Organizing Committee of the 2008 Olympic Games. 2001. New Beijing. http://www.beijing-olympic.org.cn/eolympic/xbj/lsbj/lsbj.htm.

Reuters New Service. 2002. China's poor pick profits from toxic tech trash. 15 March. http:// www.planetark.org/dailynewsstory.cfm/newsid/15028/story.htm.

South China Morning Post. 2001. Capital to slash output due to environmental pressure. 26 June. http://special.scmp.com/beijingolympicbid/doingbiz/ZZZSYWQ7EOC.html.

State Council of the People's Republic of China. 1996a. White paper: Environmental pro-tection in China. http://www.china-embassy.org/Press/wpenvi.htm.

————. 1996b. State Council's decisions about certain environmental protection problems. http://www.zhb.gov.cn/sepa/.

State Statistical Bureau. 1996. *China statistical yearbook.* Beijing: China Statistical Publishing House. http://stats.gov.cn/yearbook/.

————. 1997. *China statistical yearbook.* Beijing: China Statistical Publishing House.

————. 1998. *China statistical yearbook.* Beijing: China Statistical Publishing House.

————. 1999. *China statistical yearbook.* Beijing: China Statistical Publishing House.

————. 2000. *China statistical yearbook.* Beijing: China Statistical Publishing House.

Tang, W. F. 1996. Slow shifts from egalitarianism to the market: Public housing in urban China. *China Rights Forum* (Summer). http://www.hrichina.org/crf/English/96summer /et.html.

The Sun News Publisher Ltd. 2001a. Thousands of dispossessed households in Nanjing protest with roadblock. 23 April. http://www.the-sun.com.hk/channels/news/20010423 /20010423020157_0001.html.

———. 2001b. China has 8 of the 10 most polluted cities in the world. 15 May. http:// the-sun.com.hk/channels/news/20010515/.

U.S. Embassy in China. 1997. China's farmland loss rings alarm — satellite photographs reveal serious problem. http://www.usembassy-china.org.cn/sandt/remotesensing-maps.html.

U.S. Environmental Protection Agency (USEPA). 1988. *The superfund enforcement process: How it works.* Washington, DC: USEPA.

———. 2001a. Brownfields glossary of terms. http://www.epa.gov/swerosps/bf/glossary .htm#Brow.

———. 2001b. Brownfields-related law and regulations: State voluntary cleanup programs. http://www.epa.gov/swerosps/bf/gdc.htm#vc.

———. 2001c. Brownfields tax incentive. http://www.epa.gov/swerosps/bf/bftaxinc.htm.

———. 2001d. Case studies. http://www.epa.gov/superfund/programs/recycle/success /casestud/index.htm.

Xinhua Net. 2002. The discharge of sulphur dioxide in our country will be reduced annually — as much as 10%. 19 February. http://search.envir.com.cn/tppmsgs/msgs10.htm.

Yu, S. Y., ed. 1998. *Real estate — housing reform operation manual.* Beijing: China Construction Materials Industry Press.

Zhang, H. 1997. China 2000: Addressing pollution and ecological damage in China. http://www.china2thou.com/9704p5.htm.

Zhang, K. H. 1992. *Enterprise environmental economics.* Beijing: China Environmental Science Press.

Housing Policy Reform

Chapter 7

Housing Policy in the People's Republic of China: An Historical Review

YAN SONG, GERRIT KNAAP AND CHENGRI DING

ousing policy in the People's Republic of China (PRC) has changed dramatically in recent years.[1] Not long ago, residential space was extremely scarce, most dwellings were owned by the central government and Chinese households paid nominal rent. Today, rents reflect the cost of construction and maintenance, many Chinese own their own homes and an aggressive commercial sector dominates construction activities. There are still many problems in Chinese housing markets that can be understood only in an historical context. This chapter provides a brief review of urban housing policy during the last 50 years, illustrating the country's progress in developing fully functional housing markets and extracting, from this remarkable experience, lessons for China and for other countries around the world.

This discussion considers the history of housing policy in China in four periods. From 1949 to 1956, between the founding of the PRC and the end of the first five-year plan, urban housing was provided within a controlled market in which private ownership and speculative building were effectively eliminated and most housing resources were systematically brought under the control of the central government. From 1957 to 1976, urban housing was provided as a fundamental element of socialist welfare and ideology. From 1978 to 1989, following the adoption of the National Plan for Housing Reform, a promarket approach was introduced to encourage private ownership and relax government control. From 1990 to the present, since the revision of the National Plan, full commodification of urban housing has become the official policy, and China has made significant steps toward a market-oriented housing system.

---

1 Though specific references are cited throughout this chapter, much of the structure and content of this review is taken from Lu, Rowe, and Zhang 2001; Wang and Murie 1999; and Zhang 1996.

A Controlled Urban Housing Market: 1949–1956

Before 1949, most Chinese people lived in self-provided housing without assistance from the government. Housing conditions were poor — overcrowded, unsanitary, dark, damp and poorly ventilated conditions were common — but housing was not viewed as the responsibility of the central government (World Bank 1992). When the PRC was founded in 1949, a socialist system was established and the state systematically assumed ownership of all major economic assets, including housing. This socialist transformation shaped the principal features of urban housing policies for the next 30 years.

TABLE 1

Proportion of Private Housing in Some Major Cities, 1955

City	Private Housing (as % of Total Housing Stock)
Beijing	53.9
Harbin	42.0
Jinan	78.0
Nanjing	61.3
Qindao	37.0
Shanghai	66.0
Shenyang	36.0
Tianjin	54.0
Wuxi	80.3

SOURCE: Chinese Communist Party Central Committee (1956)

Although eager to establish a socialist system, the Chinese Communist Party intervened in urban housing markets very slowly, for a number of reasons. First, the central government had limited administrative capacity. It could not immediately implement a new system of central planning because it lacked experience in managing urban affairs. Second, the government still relied heavily on the private sector, and, for the sake of the national economy, was not eager to antagonize private business interests. Thus, the gradual approach to housing reform, during the period from 1949 to 1956, can be characterized as a "controlled market" (Zhang 1996). Rents were set by the government to eliminate the so-called exploitative behavior of landlords, but it was still a market in the sense that legal transactions involving private property were protected. In fact, as shown in Table 1, private ownership was still the dominant form of housing tenure in Chinese cities in the mid-1950s, and renting from private individuals was still allowed (Wang and Murie 1999).

Despite government efforts toward reform, housing conditions actually deteriorated in many cities (Lu, Rowe and Zhang 2001). Explosive demand resulting from rapid population growth far exceeded the limited housing supply. The housing policy of this era, which was guided more by politics than by housing demand, compounded the problem (Zhang 1996). Human needs often were neglected because China committed most of its limited resources to heavy industry and military production (Shaw 1997; Lu, Rowe, and Zhang 2001). In response to poor housing conditions, the government proposed several policies to resolve the contradictions between private ownership of housing and the socialist system. One distinctive change that occurred during this period was the emergence of work-unit, or *danwei*, housing (Kirby 1985).

A work unit, or danwei, is an economic institution in the context of state socialism. Workers depend on the work unit for many aspects of their economic, political and social lives. Danwei workers acquire housing units through the danwei housing allocation system "according to his work." According to this fundamental socialist allocation principle, an individual's social status and length of employment, rather than price and income, determine housing allocation (Li 1997).

The danwei housing system operated within a centrally planned economy in which financial resources were planned with all sectors (such as industrial, educational, health care, etc.) considered in combination. Housing projects, therefore, were mere elements of larger industrial projects, such as the construction of a factory or an educational institution (Wu 1996; Lu, Rowe, and Zhang 2001). Housing might be constructed if economic development projects or educational institutions needed workers and those workers needed housing. Investment in housing and other infrastructure, such as elementary and middle schools (if the project was large), canteens, and simple, daily-use grocery stores, was made in conjunction with the overall project. Entire communities were thus built all at once, enabling workers to live close to their work.

The distinctive role of the danwei in urban China has had a profound impact on the morphology of cities and has complicated housing policy reforms ever since its inception. According to Wang and Murie (1999, 70):

> Although this initial period is very short in the history of the People's Republic, it occupied a very important time in relation to contemporary Chinese housing policy. The pattern and style of housing construction, distribution, management and the rent system have since become the basis of all subsequent policies and practice. Recent housing developments and housing reforms must be examined against this historical background.

The Danwei Housing System: 1957–1976

The transition from private to public ownership was gradually accomplished through the introduction of the danwei housing system (Wu 1995). In the process, by 1966 the private housing market was eradicated and the government gained control over housing investments, rent pricing, property tax payments, repairs, maintenance and management. Housing began to be regarded not as a commodity but as an element of the welfare state.

A few key statistics illustrate this transition. Between 1949 and 1956, the share of housing in the private sector had fallen from almost 100 percent to 52 percent as a result of the expansion of the public sector. It then fell to 23 percent in 1958 and to 15 percent in 1977. After 1956, new housing construction consisted almost entirely of state-provided danwei housing units (Zhang 1996). Although the government did not prevent private housing production explicitly, privately developed and owned housing became almost nonexistent because acquiring land for housing became nearly impossible and rent controls made private housing unprofitable. By eliminating the potential for profit, these policies effectively stopped private housing construction and left the full responsibility for housing to the central government.

Objectives of the Danwei System

Within a short period, the danwei became a central and distinctive feature in Chinese society. In addition to serving as a vehicle for housing allocation, the danwei became the dominant institution for allocation of many other human necessities, such as education, health care and even the right to travel. As the central institution for allocating housing resources, the danwei had several implicit objectives (Zhang 1996).

- **To improve living standards with a policy of low rents.** The government adopted a rent standard based on the principle that rent should cover only the cost of housing maintenance. This policy insulated rents from market forces and responded only to political concerns, such as demonstrating the superiority of socialism over capitalism. The low-rent housing policy was also one of the means of stimulating productivity in the workers of urban industrial enterprises.

- **To control urban population growth**. To foster the development of the national economy, the government considered control of the urban population essential. A population registration system was introduced in 1950 and legally enforced beginning in 1958. The system aimed to control population movement and prevent unauthorized rural–urban migration by dividing the entire population into two social classes — those with urban residence (*chengshi hukou*) and those having rural residence (*nongcun hukou*). The state-controlled danwei housing system provided housing only to officially registered urban residents, which discouraged unplanned, rural–urban migration and served to limit urban population growth. The enforcement of this registration system may be a primary reason that the industrialization and urbanization process in China did not generate shanty areas around large cities, as is often the case in other rapidly developing countries. It may also help explain why Chinese industrialization was achieved, during a 40-year span, with limited urban population growth and urban migration compared with other countries.

- **To stabilize the labor force for the danwei system.** The danwei system tied the welfare of urban residents to their workplaces, providing stability for both workers and workplaces, but also greatly reducing labor mobility.

The Form of Housing in the Danwei System

The government promoted standardized housing to accelerate housing construction (thereby mitigating housing shortages) and to reduce costs. Not surprisingly, the danwei system strongly influenced the style and character of that housing, primarily comprising groups of multistory dwellings. These clusters of residences helped to further the principle of a collective spirit in a socialist society. Several such clusters formed a neighborhood unit, for which basic communal facilities such as schools, nurseries, grocery stores, entertainment venues and social service facilities were provided. Resources available to any danwei enterprise were limited by the allocation criteria set by the government and shaped by the social status and political or professional qualifications of the danwei's employees.

Financing of the State-Controlled Danwei System

Because private investment was almost nonexistent, the state had to fund all urban housing investment. There were two kinds of financing strategies: direct government provision of housing and state investment via the danwei system. Before 1978 the Central Government Planning Commission controlled all public housing investments according to the National General Construction Investment Scheme. Although investment through the danwei system was classified as public investment, it was budgeted by the government based on that same scheme. The government did not directly provide housing construction funds to work units; danweis had to fund housing investment with their own surpluses. Therefore, the general welfare of Chinese citizens, including the quality of housing, health care and social services, was directly linked to the economic performance of the danweis to which they belonged.

The Impact of Housing Policy in the Era of Mao Zedong (1949–1978)

The state-controlled danwei housing system removed the influence of market forces in shaping China's housing supply. Housing was treated not as a commodity, subject to the forces of supply and demand, but as a reward for work and the achievement of social status. Housing supply was determined by administrative planning rather than as a response to consumer demand. The danwei housing policy also has had direct impacts on popular perception, as in the longing of many citizens for the low rents of the old system — perhaps one reason for the failure of privatization policies to gain rapid popular acceptance.

Disadvantages of the State-Controlled Danwei System

While offering great potential for cost minimization and social control, the danwei system had several disadvantages.

- **Technical inefficiency.** Every work unit had to provide housing for its workforce; this forced the management of every danwei to attend to housing affairs, whether or not those individuals had particular expertise in housing management or construction. This placed additional human resource burdens on every danwei enterprise and imposed obstacles to capturing economies of scale in housing construction and management.

- **Inequity.** Despite its socialist foundations, the system created considerable inequities. For example, people who worked in different danwei systems, though performing similar tasks, received different levels of housing services, and danweis of different sizes provided different levels of housing quality to their employees. Housing investment tended to be very modest in small danwei systems, particularly for small enterprises in the urban collective sector and for some nonprofit organizations, such as schools. Large danwei systems, meanwhile, were able to make more generous housing investments for their employees. Employees of municipal institutions often enjoyed better housing than did workers in other settings. And, because danweis had the authority to set allocation policies, corruption in the distribution of housing was widespread.

  Additional inequities, by gender and marital status, occurred and undermined women's independence. In most cases, policy allowed housing allocation to married males, and most wives lived in their husband's danwei system. The linkage between housing and workplace in the danwei system made it difficult to provide housing in a location convenient to both husband and wife. Furthermore, divorced and single people (irrespective of gender or age) were generally excluded from danwei housing assignments.

- **Allocative inefficiency.** In the danwei, workers lived in housing provided by their employer. To utilize economies of scale, employers often provided housing limited in style, location, size, and tenure, precluding worker choice over housing attributes.

A Promarket Approach: 1978–1989

Beginning in 1978, China launched a series of economic reforms that introduced market forces and allowed private enterprise an increasing role in the production and consumption of goods and services. Important structural changes in the economy occurred, such as the relaxation of government control over investment, and over the production and distribution of goods; the emergence of a small private sector; and the promotion of a considerably larger collective sector that behaves much like private enterprise (Zhou and Logan 1996). In the context of such structural change, evolution in housing policy produced a similar promarket approach. Further, by the end of the 1970s, the government recognized a need to address many housing problems.

Lingering Problems Under the Danwei System

- **Housing shortage and overcrowding.** Under the danwei housing system, supply remained well below demand. In 1978, the government revealed that the housing shortage across all major cities had reached one billion square meters, and that it would require the investment of 80–100 billion yuan and a large-scale building program coordinated between central and local governments, and between individual institutions and enterprises.

- **Distorted demand.** The welfare system distorted the structure of demand by stimulating excessive housing demand and separating it from ability to pay. This combination of negligible rents and excessive housing demand placed heavy financial and production burdens on the state.

- **Paucity of housing investment.** The state alone could not afford the burgeoning expenditure on public housing. To reduce the burden and increase return from housing investment, the state attempted to privatize public housing and raise housing rents.

- **Housing inequity.** Allocation of housing investment differed between central and local governments, and between large and small work units, creating housing inequity. Unequal distribution of housing to individuals occurred because the allocations were based on criteria such as occupation, administrative rank, job performance, loyalty and political connections.

- **Distorted supply.** Inadequate revenue generation from rent diminished the quality of housing management and maintenance in the public sector. The low-rent policy also discouraged the construction of private rental housing or owner-occupied housing by private developers (Chen 1996).

The Seeds of Market Reform

In response to these housing problems, the government began to view the welfare approach as the major cause of China's housing problems. Deng Xiaoping, who came to power in 1978, indirectly attacked the state-controlled public housing system and introduced market forces into the housing policy arena. Arguing that the provision of housing should not depend on the state alone, Deng proposed a diversified set of policies for housing investment in which the central government, the danwei system and individuals would all play a role (Chen and Gao 1993).

In 1980 Deng pushed housing reform further toward privatization by stating that housing should be commercialized through private ownership and the sale of public housing, rather than treated as a nonproductive sector. In April of that year, Deng gave a speech on urban housing to central government leaders.

> With regard to the housing problem, we should consider policies concerning housing construction and housing allocation. Individual urban citizens can buy or build houses for themselves. Not only can new housing be sold, but old housing can be sold

as well. People can buy their houses outright or by installments over a period of 10 or 15 years. Once the sale of housing starts, rent might also need to be adjusted. The adjustment of rent should consider the relationship between purchasing price and rent, and make people feel that buying a house is more worthwhile than renting (Wang and Murie 1999, 143).

In response to Deng's speech, policy makers began to incorporate market concepts into socialist policies (Shaw 1997). The government adopted new urban housing policies and initiated a reform program whose main objective was to change the public housing system to a market system, with privatization as a major component. The privatization of the state-controlled housing sector included several elements (Zhang 1996):

- rent increases to market levels;
- sale of public housing to private individuals;
- encouragement of private and foreign investment in housing;
- less construction of new public housing;
- encouragement and protection of private home ownership;
- promotion of commercial housing by profit-making developers; and
- promotion of self-build housing in cities.

As in the period between 1949 and 1956, the transformation of the housing sector was, for several reasons, implemented gradually. First, it takes time for residents to adjust to rents set by market forces. Second, housing commercialization was not an isolated reform, but part of a larger, comprehensive reform effort. Without progress toward broader political and economic reform, housing reform could not go forward. A system committed to low salaries, for example, is inconsistent with market-determined rents. Thus, changes in rent policy could not occur without concurrent changes in policies that governed salaries.

Because of these factors, privatization policies were fragmented and even self-conflicting, and no objectives were clearly defined in the early stage (Gu 1988). The reform process was, as Deng Xiaoping said, "to cross the river by feeling the stones" with your feet. Another important dimension brought into the reform effort was Deng's argument that the choice of approach was not critical — both socialist and capitalist development approaches were valid. Policy makers adopted a trial-and-error approach that resulted in ambiguity and frequent changes of emphasis at different stages in the privatization process. Frequent shifts in housing policy caused confusion among city residents and officials. Various policies on rent increases and preferential sales were tried, changed and in some cases terminated. For example, from 1979 to 1982 housing reform focused on selling new houses at full cost; from 1982 to 1985 on selling new homes at subsidized prices; and from 1986 to 1988 on rent reform (Chen and Gao 1993; Wang and Murie 1996, 1999).

The First Housing Reform Experiment:
The Sale of New Houses, 1979–1982

The first housing reform experiment was initiated in 1979 despite widespread public resistance (Zhou and Logan 1996). In selected cities, new housing was offered for sale at the cost of construction (Chen and Gao 1993). For example, one million yuan were allocated by the central government to the city of Xian to build houses for sale to local urban families. The selling price (per square meter) was set at 150 yuan, making a mid-sized, three-room flat (about 60 square meters) available at an average price of approximately 9,000 yuan (Wang and Murie 1999). The government then extended the experiment to the national level. The response to this program was disappointing, for a number of reasons. The price per unit was much higher than most average-income households could afford, and rents for public housing remained extremely low. Further, the housing finance system had not been reformed to support housing sales, and methods of payment were too inflexible. The experiment was formally abandoned in 1982.

The Second Housing Reform Experiment:
Subsidized Sale, 1982–1985

Because of the failure of the first strategy — to sell houses at construction cost to individual purchasers — a new, subsidized sales experiment was initiated in June 1982. Under this program, municipal governments and danweis would each contribute one-third of the total housing price and the individual buyer would pay only the remaining one-third (State Economic Reform Commission 1983). The subsidized price scheme applied only to danwei employees; the self-employed or unemployed were not entitled to any discounts. Even with these subsidies, however, only a small number of residents could afford to buy. Further, both the state and the danweis were severely burdened by the cost of the subsidies. This experiment worked against the goal of privatization, because it meant continuation of the state-controlled public housing system and was abandoned in 1985, when policy makers concluded that a more comprehensive approach was required.

The Third Housing Reform Experiment:
Rent Reform to Promote Sales, 1986–1988

In response to the failure of the subsidized program, the government announced a scheme to limit subsidies and again sell public housing at full cost. In February 1986 the State Council established a Housing Reform Steering Group, which aimed to raise rents to market-clearing levels and achieve financial equality between renters and owners by means of comprehensive and innovative reform measures (Chen and Gao 1993; Tong and Hays 1996). The program expanded nationwide in 1988 to encourage privatization by making rental housing a less attractive option. In addition, the government provided housing vouchers to offset rising rent burdens under

TABLE 2
The Direction of Chinese Housing Reform, 1949 Onward

	Pre-Reform	Reform Direction
Nature of housing	Welfare service	Consumable commodity
Distribution	Secondary; material; free	Primary; monetary; through market
Ownership and tenure	Public	Private
Rent	Subsidized minimum rent	Market rent
Source of investment	State	State, local government, danwei and individual

SOURCE: Wang and Murie (1999, 162)

the low-salary system. The housing subsidy was to have been phased out gradually when salaries increased sufficiently to meet family housing costs.

The reform was designed to change the processes of housing production and distribution by relieving the state and danwei systems of any direct distribution functions. Distribution would become "monetarily based" rather than "materially based." Finally, to promote the sale of both existing and new public housing, the price of new housing was based on market price but was exempted from construction and property taxes, and from development fees (Zhang 1996). Implementation of the new policy was very successful — long-standing patterns of housing tenure changed as the costs of renting rose relative to the costs of home ownership.

The National Housing Reform Plan and Preferential Housing Sales: 1988–1990

After these housing policy experiments, the objectives of privatization were stated clearly for the first time in the 1988 National Housing Reform Plan (see Table 2). The plan included several elements:

- a decrease in government control and in dependence on the state for housing;
- a decrease in the government's economic burden through a mandate that housing investment must yield a balanced financial return;
- continuation of the policy to increase housing rents;
- further transformation of the allocation system from in-kind to cash subsidy;
- an expanded effort to promote housing ownership; and
- the transformation of both existing housing stock and newly built housing into market commodities.

Following the issuance by the State Council of the Implementation Plan for a Gradual Housing System Reform in Cities and Towns, the sale of public housing was introduced nationwide in 1988 (State Council 1988; World Bank 1992). Its intent was to sell public housing according to the following principles.

- New housing distribution should follow the principle of "sale first and rent second."
- Sale prices for new housing should reflect building costs and land compensation costs, with no other subsidy involved.
- The individual should pay more than 30 percent of the price at the outset and the remainder should be paid over a period of 10–20 years.

Further Housing Commodification: 1990 Onward

After a period of experimentation from the late 1970s to the late 1980s, consensus emerged that the socialist housing system was too complex to be reformed by an all-inclusive package, and that a variety of initiatives were needed to revitalize the housing market.

The Urban Housing Reform Resolution: Diversification of the Housing Provision

In 1991 a new resolution, On Comprehensive Reform of the Urban Housing System, was issued at the second National Housing Reform Conference (General Office of the State Council 1991). This document updated the 1988 housing reform resolution which, in the long term, aimed to "rationalize rents to the market level, to take into account the costs of building, repair, management, investment interest, property tax, land use fees, insurance and profit, to provide every family with a reasonable standard apartment, and to replace state housing provision through commercialization and socialization" (ibid.). After this conference, large-scale housing reforms were carried out in many cities. In Beijing, for example, 140,000 units of public-sector housing were sold between 1990 and 1993, generating an income of 1,700 million yuan (Wang and Murie 1999). In an effort to realize the full potential of market reforms, several additional programs were put forward.

- **Commercial Housing Development.** To reduce significantly the role of danweis in the housing market, the government enacted policies designed to stimulate a commercial housing sector. Commercial housing, which included state-owned, foreign and joint development companies, soon began to dominate the market. Whereas in January 1981 there was only one real estate company in the country, by the end of 1992 the number had risen to 17,000 (Zhou and Logan 1996). In 1992 Deng toured the Shenzhen special economic development zone (SEDZ), calling for faster economic development and welcoming foreign investment. That year, foreign investment became the largest portion of total basic construction investment in the Shenzhen SEDZ, accounting for 30 percent of all investment. Foreign or joint companies could be more profitable because their pricing did not require government approval and they were eligible for tax abatements. Foreign developers not only provided financial benefits, but also brought much-needed real estate development skills and experience, thus helping to create a market environment that had never before existed in the Chinese real estate sector (Zhang 1996).

- **Compulsory Housing Savings Program.** As part of the comprehensive housing reform program, in 1991 a compulsory housing savings program was established, in which a certain proportion of an employee's income was put aside as savings that could be used only for housing purchases. Combined with mandatory contributions on the part of the danwei, the cumulative total from danwei contributions plus employee housing savings varied from approximately 5 to 25 percent of wages (Zax 1999).

- **Self-Build Housing Program.** Self-build housing was encouraged in some small cities or towns to solve severe housing shortages (Zax 1997). Developments of this type appear quite successful as an alternative housing type. Though the self-build approach provided access to housing for households with weak or no claims to allocated housing, it is unlikely to represent any significant portion of the aggregate housing stock (Zax 1999).

A New Approach: Deepening Urban Housing Reform, Post-1994

In 1993, The Decision on Deepening Urban Housing Reform was issued at the third National Housing Reform conference. This plan extended the reform process by further increasing rents to cover depreciation, repairs, management costs, interest and property tax. In addition, several new elements were added to the reform package (Housing Reform Steering Group of the State Council 1994). One changed the housing investment system to make urban citizens responsible for more of their housing costs. Another involved changing the housing management system by outsourcing management functions to specialized, nongovernmental entities such as property development and management companies. These companies were able to develop advanced management techniques and capture economies of scale.

A third element of the 1994 reform package involved the housing distribution system. The in-kind housing allocation of the danwei system, wherein salaries were insufficient to cover housing costs, gave way to a cash-based distribution system, which required increases in both rents and wages. The reforms also sought to establish a dual housing system, aimed at providing middle- and low-income households with public housing and to provide high-income families with commercial housing (*People's Daily* 1995, 2). Finally, the reforms sought to establish a standardized and regulated market system of property exchange, repair and management.

The 1994 reforms included a number of features designed to establish systems of housing insurance and finance for both public and commercial developments. Before the reforms were enacted, financing of new construction depended solely on state budget allocations. The reforms generated a wide range of financial institutions and resources. Banks were one type: the Construction Bank and the Industrial and Commercial Bank, for example, established housing credit departments to provide mortgage services to individual house buyers. By 1993 the Construction Bank had issued mortgages to 198,000 home buyers, and mortgage loans issued by the Industrial and Commercial Bank totaled 390 million yuan (*People's Daily* 1993, 2). By 1994 there were more than 4,000 housing credit departments around the country.

Additional funds for housing development were made available both from municipal government collections from the transfer of land use rights and the sale of existing housing, and from the retained profits of work units. Whereas in the past danweis depended on the central government to allocate funds for housing investment, after the reforms danweis were given the flexibility to make their own housing investment decisions, and to buy and sell in the housing market. Finally, funds were also made available from the private savings of individual workers and from foreign corporations (Zhou and Logan 1996).

Conclusion: Assessment of Chinese Housing Reform

The long-term objective of Chinese housing reform has been the introduction of a market system through privatization. The process has been painfully slow and fitful, but significant progress has been made. Chinese households are no longer dependent exclusively on the government or on their danwei to provide them with a place to live (see Table 3). Chinese residents can and do own their own homes. A vibrant commercial sector is rapidly increasing aggregate housing supply (see Table 4), but progress is incomplete, and a number of problems have yet to be addressed.

Remaining Problems

Many remaining problems are contextual. Housing privatization was an integral part of the overall privatization program in the national economy. Thus, progress in housing reform is necessarily linked to changes in other sectors. For example, since the adoption and implementation of comprehensive privatization programs in other areas of China's economy, such as the health and education sectors, the economic burden on households has increased and disposable income (available for housing investment) has decreased (Zhang 1996; Zhou and Logan 1996).

Progress is impeded by the lack of an appropriate legal framework, as well. China's privatization has emphasized deregulation and decentralization, but a comprehensive legal framework for regulation of economic behavior in the emerging housing market has not yet formed. This has led to serious speculative activities in

TABLE 3

Proportion of Privately Purchased Floor Space
to Total Floor Space of Sold Commercial Housing, 1987–1998

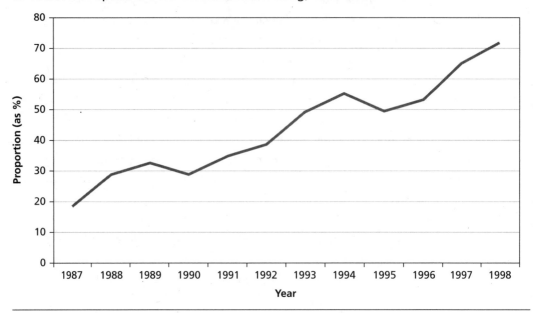

SOURCE: State Statistical Bureau (2000)

TABLE 4

Total Floor Space of Sold Commercial Housing, 1987–1998

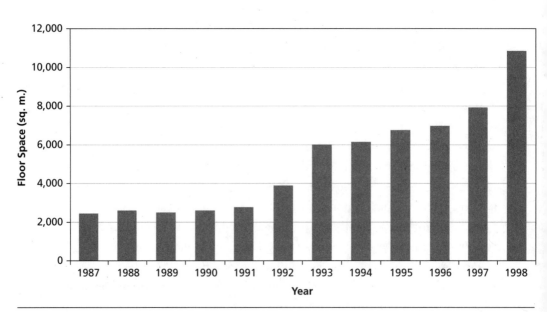

SOURCE: State Statistical Bureau (2000)

the housing market (Zhang 1996). In addition, China's version of privatization differs from the concept of privatization in most Western nations, in that Chinese reform grants most house purchasers *user* rights, not *property* rights. Homeowners are thus restricted in their ability to resell and exchange property, which in turn limits their mobility.

The confusion in housing administration remains another important cause of distortions in the housing sector. After privatization many housing administration agencies appeared, creating duplication of administrative activities in some areas, but a vacuum in others, and resulting in inconsistent policies across different departments (Wang and Murie 1999).

These problems are exacerbated by the segregation between land and housing management. The complicated and time-consuming task of land acquisition plays a critical part in the housing development process. Because land and housing development are managed under different agencies that seldom communicate with each other, problems in housing construction are only too common (Zhang 1996).

To lessen its burden and to increase returns from housing investment, the state attempted to privatize public housing and to raise housing rents. But the low salaries of many workers continue to contribute to the problem of housing affordability. This situation stands in sharp contrast to the opportunities recently created for those with higher salaries. There is a surplus of privately provided housing units for higher-income families, but an undersupply of low-cost housing to accommodate low-income and unemployed families. These problems are compounded by the fact that higher-ranking and profitable danwei systems are able either to build new housing or to purchase commodified housing for their workers, while the lower-ranking danweis cannot (Logan and Bian 1999). These remaining imbalances could result in urban social unrest and instability if they are not addressed (Lai 1998).

Finally, though housing reform has led to some significant changes, the process of commercialization or privatization of public housing stock is far from complete. On the production side, the danwei system has withdrawn from direct involvement in housing construction (see Table 5). However, on the consumption side, the low incomes of state workers have forced the danwei system to maintain in-kind housing subsidies (Wu 1996). Housing reform has not fully relieved the danwei system of its historical housing provision function (Wu 1996; Lai 1998).

Although so-called commercial housing is developing through market mechanisms, these apartments are not necessarily allocated to final users through market allocation. Instead, most commercial housing is sold to danweis at market prices and then resold to their employees at below-market value. Housing built or purchased by work units is usually sold to workers at further discounts, the most common of which include:

TABLE 5
Proportion of Total Floor Space Constructed by Danweis, 1981–1998

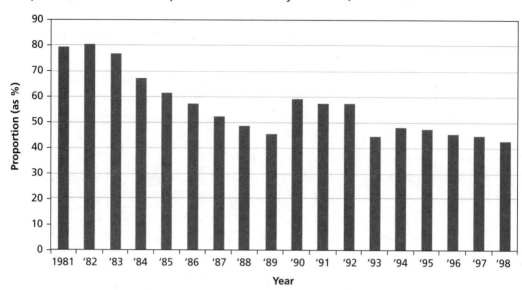

SOURCE: China Planning Research Institute (2000)

- 20 percent discounts off the standard price in return for cancellation of the purchaser's monthly cash subsidy from the work unit;
- seniority discounts;
- pay-up discounts if paid in full at the time of purchase; and
- waiver of property taxes and land use fees.

Commercial housing transactions thus continue to be conducted largely between state-owned parties within the public sector — hardly the goal of the government's reform efforts. The situation undermines many of the virtues of market allocation (Zhou and Logan 1996; Lai 1998).

To tackle this problem, the government has set minimum housing prices for the danwei system and warned local organizations against setting low prices. In SEDZs and other areas with more market-oriented policies, there is a higher percentage of individual purchasers because of greater market orientation, higher income and, sometimes, a higher percentage of overseas relatives. Therefore, it can be argued that the international opening of a city remains an important factor in its commercial housing development and in the sale of commercial housing (Zhang 1996; Wang and Murie 1999).

The Future of China's Housing Policy

China's housing reform program has been implemented within the Communist framework, with the government continuing to justify each reform policy on the basis of principles of a Chinese-style, socialist, planned economy. Innovations in macroeconomic planning and regulation are needed to ensure the functioning of this mixed market economy (Zhou and Logan 1996).

There is no doubt that urban housing development will continue to be an important growth sector in the Chinese economy in the current economic and political climates. The reform process may, however, never be fully complete by Western standards. Many scholars argue that what is being created is a privatized housing system, rather than a fully functioning market (Xu 1993; Wu 1995; Wang and Murie 1999). A Western-style housing market exists only among high-income people employed by prestigious, private-sector enterprises.

To control inflation and maintain social stability, the government still controls salaries. Therefore, the incomes of most urban residents remain low, making the purchase of commercial housing out of reach, but the buying of a highly subsidized small flat possible. Government housing policies thus focus on providing housing for the salary-earner class, that is, the middle- or low-income groups. The goal of a comprehensive market-oriented housing sector — under the restraint of economic reforms and as an integral part of the social context — faces many challenges and remains a considerable distance off.

References

Badcock, B. 1986. Land and housing policy in Chinese urban development. *Planning Perspectives* 1(2):147–170.

Carlson, E. 1987. Housing finance: Affordability problems and options. *Building in China* 4:25–29. Beijing: China Building Technology Development Center.

Castells, M. 1988. *Economic development and housing policy in the Asian Pacific rim: A comparative study of Hong Kong, Singapore, and Shenzhen special economic zone.* Institute of Urban and Regional Development, Monograph #37. Berkeley, CA: University of California Press.

Chao, K. 1986. Industrialization and urban housing in Communist China. *Journal of Asian Studies* 25(3):381–396.

Chen, A. 1996. China urban housing reform — Price-rent ratio and market equilibrium. *Urban Studies* 33(7):1077–1092.

Chen, K. 1993. From providing to supporting: An alternative approach to state housing provision in China. *Open House International* 18(4):35–40.

Chen, X. M., and X. Y. Gao. 1993. Urban economic reform and public housing investment in China. *Urban Affairs Quarterly* 29(1):117–145.

China Planning Research Institute. 2000. *Residential planning.* Beijing: China Construction Industry Publishing House.

Chinese Communist Party Central Committee. 1956. The current private housing condition in cities and recommendations to transform private housing in the socialist framework.

Gao, Y. 1989. Housing commercialization as affected by housing development and design. *Building in China* 2(2):36–41. Beijing: China Building Technology Development Center.

General Office of the State Council. 1991. On comprehensive reform of the urban housing system. *Housing reform handbook.* Xian: Xian Housing Reform Office.

Gu, Y. 1988. China's on-going housing reform. *Building in China* 1(3):36–41. Beijing: China Building Technology Development Center.

Housing Reform Steering Group of the State Council. 1994. The decision on deepening urban housing reform. *Urban housing system reform.* Beijing: Reform Press.

Kim, J. 1987. Shelter policy and planning in developing countries: China's current housing issues and policies. *Journal of the American Planning Association* 53(2):171–226.

Kirby, R. 1985. *Urban conditions in the aftermath of Mao — Housing, urbanization in China: Town and country in a developing economy 1949–2000 AD.* London, New York: Columbia University Press.

Lai, O. 1998. Governance and the housing question in a transitional economy: The political economy of housing policy in China reconsidered. *Habitat International* 22(3/Sept.): 231–243.

Li, Y. 1997. *Survival and development: Research and thinking on agricultural land preservation in China.* Beijing: China Land Press.

Li, Z. 1996. Deepening reform to realize two fundamental transformations. Speech by Vice Minister Li Zhengdong on Urban Housing Development. *Housing Science* 4:3–5. Shanghai Real Estate Management Department.

Lim, G. C., and M. H. Lee. 1993. Housing consumption in urban China. *Journal of Real Estate Finance and Economics* 6(1):89–102.

Logan, J., and F. Bian. 1999. Housing inequality in urban China in the 1990s. *International Journal of Urban and Regional Research* 23(March):7–25.

Lu, J., P. G. Rowe, and J. Zhang. 2001. *Modern urban housing in China: 1840–2000.* New York: Prestel Verlag.

People's Daily. 1993. Overseas edition, 2. 16 December.

People's Daily, 1995. Overseas edition, 6. 12 January.

Phillips, D. R., and A. G. O. Yeh. 1987. The provision of housing and social services in China's special economic zone. *Environment and Planning C: Government and Policy* 5:447–468.

Pudney, S., and L. M. Wang. 1995. Housing reform in urban China — Efficiency, distribution and the implications for social security. *Economica* 62(246):141–159.

Shaw, Victor N. 1997. Urban housing reform in China. *Habitat International* 21(2/June): 199–212.

State Council. 1988. Implementation plan for a gradual housing system reform in cities and towns. *References on urban housing system reform in Xian city.* Xian: Xian Housing Reform Office.

State Economic Reform Commission. 1983. *Urban housing problems and reform proposals.* News Bulletin of the State Economic Reform Commission, #46. Beijing.

State Statistical Bureau. 2000. *China statistical yearbook.* Beijing: China Statistical Publishing House.

Steinberg, F. 1989. Self-help and step-by-step housing in China. *Building in China* 1(2): 30–38. Beijing: China Building Technology Development Center.

Tong, Z. Y., and R. A. Hays. 1996. The transformation of the urban housing system in China. *Urban Affairs Review* 31(5):625–628.

Walser, A. G. 1993. Urban housing reform in China — An economic analysis. *The China Quarterly* 135:611–612. London: School of Oriental and African Studies.

Wang, Y. 1989. The dynamics of housing finance in China. *Building in China* 2(1):9–13. Beijing: China Building Technology Development Center.

Wang, Y. P., and A. Murie. 1996. The process of commercialization of urban housing in China. *Urban Studies* 33(6):971–989.

———. 1999. *Housing policy and practice in China.* New York: St. Martin's Press.

World Bank. 1992. *China: Implementation options for urban housing reform.* Washington, DC: World Bank.

Wu, F. 1995. Urban processes in the face of China's transition to a socialist market economy. *Environment and Planning* C 13(2):159–177.

———. 1996. Changes in the structure of public housing provision in urban China. *Urban Studies* 33(9/Nov.):1601–1627.

Xu, X. Y. 1993. Policy evaluation in China housing reform. *Evaluation and Program Planning* 16(1):39–47.

Xue, Q., and E. R. Scoffham. 1993. China's housing in transition: A case study of Shanghai. *International Journal for Housing Science and Its Applications* 17(4):219–232.

Zax, J. S. 1997. Latent demand for urban housing in the People's Republic of China. *Journal of Urban Economics* 42(3/Nov.):377–401.

———. 1999. Housing reform in urban China. Working paper #65. Center for Research on Economic Development and Policy Reform. Palo Alto, CA: Stanford University.

Zhang, X. Q. 1996. *A study of housing policy in urban China*. Commack, NY: Nova Science Publishers, Inc.

Zhou, M., and J. R. Logan. 1996. Market transition and the commodification of housing in urban China. *International Journal of Urban and Regional Research* 20(3/Sept.): 400–421.

Zhu, Y. 1987. Reform of China's urban housing system. *Building in China* 4:13–16. Beijing: China Building Technology Development Center.

Chapter 8

Development of the Chinese Housing Market

XING QUAN ZHANG

The transformation of the housing sector from a planned system to a market system has come to be one of the dominant themes in contemporary housing research (Clapham 1995; Pickvance 1994; Renaud 1995; Turner et al. 1992; Walker and Li 1994). In China, the post-Mao reforms of the past two decades have transformed the fundamental nature and structure of the housing system, with market mechanisms gradually replacing the welfare orientation. The emergence of the housing market has played a major role in improving overall housing conditions and has stimulated housing investment, which has enjoyed rapid growth. For example, total housing investment in Shanghai in 1997 was more than 190 times that in 1978; during the same period, per capita living space increased from 4.5 to 9.3 square meters (Shanghai Statistics Bureau 1998).

This chapter discusses the characteristics and recent development of the Chinese housing market. It also identifies new problems resulting from that development, particularly those arising after the mid-1990s, such as housing affordability, inappropriate housing subsidies, high rates of vacancy, high housing prices and inflated housing standards.

Characteristics of the Chinese Housing Market

The Role of the State in Development of the Housing Market

The state plays an important role in the development of the Chinese housing market by formulating a regulatory environment, and through its direct involvement as both the largest developer and the largest buyer (through work units, or danweis), of commercial housing. To increase the role of the market in housing development, the government introduced a series of initiatives in the early 1980s to decentralize power to local governments and work units. It increased the power of local governments and work units to invest, thereby allowing them to retain more financial resources. As a result, expenditures by local governments grew rapidly, while the share of total central government expenditure decreased by comparison (see Figure 1).

FIGURE 1

Changes in Local and Central Government Expenditures in China, 1975–1999
(in 100 million RMB)

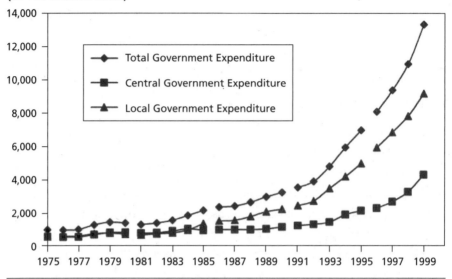

SOURCE: State Statistical Bureau (2000)

FIGURE 2

Investment in Fixed Assets in China, 1980–2000
(in 100 million RMB)

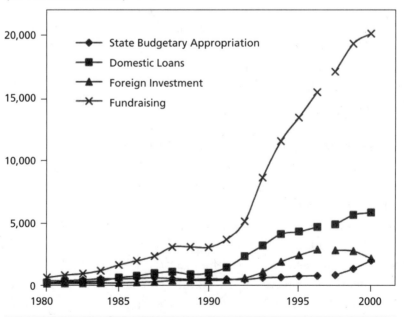

SOURCE: State Statistical Bureau (2000)

In addition to this devolution of power to local governments, the state increased the autonomy of work units, particularly in housing finance. Before reform, virtually all urban housing was financed by the state through state budgeted funding. Since reform, the ratio of state funding to total housing investment has decreased substantially. Figure 2 shows that the proportion of state budgeted funding in the total investment in fixed assets in China decreased to only 6.2 percent (or 33 billion RMB in 1980), which is lower than the figure for foreign investment (6.7 percent, or 34 billion RMB in 1980). Most investment (67 percent of total investment, or 2,000 billion RMB in 1999) came from work units' self-raised funds. The profits retained by work units increased substantially from 7.9 percent in 1979 to 43.2 percent in 1987. Work units were freed from state control over their investment in housing and other welfare expenditures. This freedom has paved the way for danweis to buy commercial housing on the market when work units are no longer allowed to build housing in order to promote housing privatization (Zhang 2001).

Rapid Expansion of Commercial Housing Development

Before the 1980s there was no market in the housing sector: all housing was developed either by work units or by residents themselves. The development of commercial housing is regarded as an important step in fostering a housing market in China, and has gained in importance. In January 1981 the first real estate company (the state-owned China Real Estate Development Company) was founded. Since then, commercial housing production has experienced rapid growth — the fastest development occurring in 1993, a year after Deng Xiaoping toured Shenzhen and called for accelerated economic development (see Figure 3). By 1993, the

FIGURE 3

vestment in Capital Construction in China, 1957–1999
1 100 million RMB)

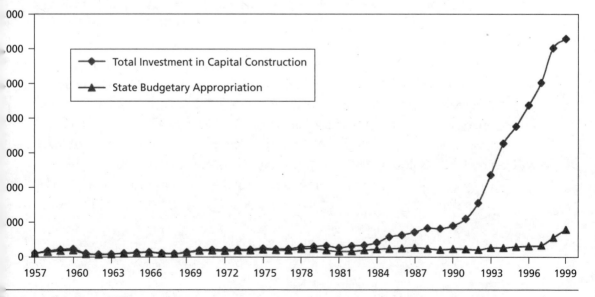

RCE: State Statistical Bureau (2000)

TABLE 1

Development of Real Estate Companies in China, 1997–1999

Enterprise Type by Funding/Ownership	Number of Enterprises			Average Employment (in 10,000 persons)		
	1997	1998	1999	1997	1998	1999
Total	21,286	24,378	25,762	68.32	82.59	88.03
Domestically funded, state-owned		7,958	7,370		33.28	31.22
Collectively owned		4,538	4,127		13.49	12.74
Funded by entrepreneurs from Hong Kong, Macao and Taiwan	1,989	3,214	3,167	5.00	8.38	8.02
Foreign-funded	2,095	1,204	1,173	5.43	3.34	3.29

SOURCE: State Statistical Bureau (2000)

number of real estate companies grew to an incredible 19,000 (State Statistical Bureau 1997). Annual commercial housing investment increased by 296 percent from 1992 to 1993 (China Real Estate and Housing Research Association 1994).

Since then, commercial housing has begun to dominate housing provision in China. The number of real estate companies reached 25,762 by 1999. Many of them are state-owned or collectively owned enterprises. There is also a substantial presence of companies owned by citizens of Hong Kong, Macao and Taiwan, and by foreign countries. In 1999, 880,300 people worked in real estate companies, though the average size of a real estate company is very small and shrinking. On average, a state-owned real estate company employed 31 people, a collectively owned company 13 people and a foreign-owned company only 3 staff members (see Table 1).

Commercial housing development grew dramatically in the 1990s. Urban housing completions reached 3.1 billion square meters and 44.3 million housing units from 1996 to 2000 (*China Construction Newspaper* 2001). The sale of commercial housing increased from 27.45 million square meters in 1991 to 129.98 million square meters in 1999 (see Figure 4). The government required the termination of the provision of welfare housing by work units; virtually all housing is now developed by developers or self-built. Figure 5 shows that most income from real estate development in China comes from the sale of real estate. Since 1996 the average operating surplus of real estate development concerns has remained low, possibly a result of the increasing amount of property that does not sell after its completion. Many projects even stop halfway through construction due to lack of funding.

FIGURE 4

Total Sales of Property and Commercial Housing in China, 1991–1999 (in 100 million RMB)

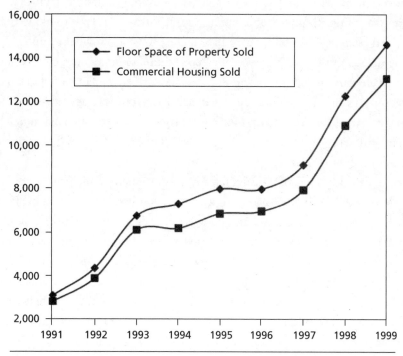

SOURCE: State Statistical Bureau (2000)

FIGURE 5

Real Estate Development in China, 1990–2000 (in 100 million RMB)

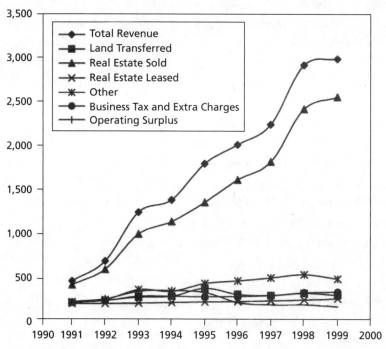

SOURCE: Constructed from data in State Statistical Bureau (2000)

Institutional Reform

The 1990s saw rapid development of market institutions in the housing sector. The government initiated a series of policies to overcome the difficulties of personal mortgage financing for home purchasers. It introduced laws to guide the practice of real estate agents and intermediates. The Housing Provident Fund — to which the state, work units and workers all contribute, so as to amass the capital needed to accelerate housing construction — has been widely implemented in China. More recently, the government began to seek securities for mortgage financing of housing and to establish a secondary housing mortgage market. The government also has removed many of the obstacles for purchasers of privatized public housing trying to enter the housing market.

In the early stage of housing reform, work units were the primary purchasers of commercial housing. The housing consumption behavior of state-owned entitites (which had enormous purchasing power) was problematic: housing dwelling units purchased by these work units not only increased housing prices but also boosted housing standards. Table 2 shows the increasing size standards of commercial housing in Shanghai. In the 1990s the government realized that it was almost impossible to have a functional housing market without eliminating the connection between housing allocation and work units; in 1998 it completely severed that connection. Meanwhile, the majority of Chinese households still cannot afford high-quality housing.

Suburbanization Drives the Development of Commercial Housing

The mismatch of demand and supply between submarkets was due largely to the high prices and standards of commercial housing and to low per capita incomes. Lower prices in suburban areas created hope for the dream of more spacious housing. Suburban areas experienced very rapid development in the mid- and late 1990s. For example, Shanghai housing stock located in the central urban area decreased from 16.23 percent (of total Shanghai housing stock) in 1993 to 10.86 percent in 1998. Housing stock located in the suburban areas increased from 27.25 percent (of total Shanghai housing stock) to 34.36 percent during the same period (Jiang 2001). Suburban areas became particularly active in commercial housing development, with more than 70 percent of Shanghai's 1997 housing transactions occurring in suburban areas (see Table 3).

TABLE 2

Commercial Housing Size Standards in Shanghai, 1990–1999

Year	Size of an Average Flat (in sq. m.)
1990	54
1991	54
1992	60
1993	60
1994	60
1995	70
1996	75
1997	80
1998	85
1999	90

SOURCE: Wang (2001)

TABLE 3

Housing Transactions in Shanghai by Area Type, 1997

	Housing Transactions							
	Area Type						Total	
	Urban Central		Fringe		Suburban			
	in sq. m.	as %	in sq. m.	as %	in sq. m.	as %	in sq. m.	as %
Advance sales of commercial housing	300,774	2.32	3,234,493	24.93	9,438,033	72.75	12,973,300	100
Transactions of commercial housing	40,194	1.23	724,350	22.14	2,507,199	76.63	3,271,746	100
Transactions in secondary housing market	7,251	1.22	146,426	20.55	558,789	78.43	712,466	100

SOURCE: Jiang (2001)

Emerging Housing Problems

Housing Affordability

Under the welfare housing system, housing costs to households were nominal and accounted for about one percent of household income. Increasingly, affordability is an issue as the market process intensifies. Since the introduction of nationwide housing privatization in 1988, the public housing stock has been shrinking quickly. For example, by 1996, 52 percent of public housing was sold out. In some cities, such as Jiangsu, Guangdong, Shanxi, Guangxi and Yunnan, the proportion of public housing sold to individuals reached 70–80 percent (*Housing and Real Estate* 1997). This trend has created difficulties for the improvement of housing conditions for most low-ranking and low-income employees. Improvement of housing status used to happen through the housing filtering process, in which middle-income households move into houses formerly occupied by high-income households that have moved to newly constructed units. However, privatization leads to a situation in which the larger and better housing units are sold to higher-ranking, higher-income workers. Most of the better housing units are now permanently occupied by these higher-ranking employees, thereby confounding the filtering process (Brink 1993).

At the same time, public housing production has decreased rapidly. More and more housing demand must be met on the open market. For example, in Shanghai in 1997 profit-oriented, commercial housing built by developers constituted 70 percent of total housing completions. The government's decision to stop all in-kind subsidies in public housing allocation after 1998 further stimulated the development of the housing market. Between January and April 1998, 409,000 square meters were sold in Beijing for a total price of 2.07 billion RMB. Compared with the same period of the previous year, housing construction increased by 61.6 percent, while housing prices increased by 130 percent.

The fast growth of the housing market has also changed the tenure structure of the housing sector. Public rental housing has declined. According to a survey in Chinese cities, 90 percent of households lived in public rental housing in 1978. By 1998 only 49 percent of households continued to live in public rental houses. Amazingly, 33 percent of households owned dwelling units by then, a striking increase from the 10 percent ownership of 20 years earlier (Xia 1999).

The rapid expansion of the housing market has also contributed to the affordability issue. Between 1985 and 1997, average annual total household expenditure increased by 654 percent (from 802 RMB to 6,048 RMB) — an annual increase of nearly 17 percent. In the same period, the average annual expenditure on housing increased by 1,019 percent — an annual increase of more than 21 percent (State Statistical Bureau 2000). The ratio of average annual housing expenditure to average annual total household expenditure rose by 50 percent for that period. However, this figure represents an increase of the national average housing expenditure for urban residents as a whole. Because about half of urban residents live in public housing, much of the increase comes from households that obtain housing units from the housing market. Their housing expenditure, therefore, is much higher than is represented by the average figure.

Another frequently used indicator of affordability is the ratio of housing cost to annual household income. The average ratio from 52 countries surveyed by Lin (1993) was 5:1. But the ratio reached 25.4:1 in China in 1998, making it more than 5 times the average of those 52 countries. Compared with ratios in market economies like the UK (2.4:1 in 1985), France (2.8:1 in 1982) and the U.S. (2.8:1 in 1988), the Chinese ratio is almost 10 times greater (Lin 1993). This fact is all the more grave considering that China's rate of economic growth is slowing down, many state enterprises are in economic difficulty, and a large number of workers have been laid off since the onset of reform efforts — all of which affect China's capacity to boost household income. Furthermore, these housing cost-to-income ratios refer to averages; some households (particularly those whose workers have been laid off by their work units due to state-owned enterprise reform) are paying a much larger share of their incomes for housing.

Inappropriate Housing Subsidies

In theory, the affordability problem can be alleviated to some extent by government housing subsidies (Malpass 1993). However, the distribution of newly introduced housing subsidies is based not on income but on employee status: people with higher rank receive larger subsidies (see Table 4).

Public housing rents are set at a constant price per square meter. The social reward system is institutionalized through this differential subsidy that is based on status

TABLE 4

Distribution of Housing Subsidies in Guangzhou, 1998

Rank by Position	Monthly Subsidy (in yuan/ person)	Total Subsidy in 25-Year Period (in 10,000 yuan)		Floor Space That Can Be Purchased (in sq. m.)	
		One Person	Two People	One Person	Two People
Clerk	233	6.99	13.98	25	50
Executive Officer	280	8.40	16.80	30	60
Deputy Section Head	327	9.81	19.62	35	70
Section Head	373	11.19	22.38	40	80
Deputy Dept. Head	420	12.60	25.20	45	· 90
Dept. Head	467	14.01	28.02	50	100
Deputy Bureau Director	543	16.29	32.58	55	110
Bureau Director	607	18.21	36.42	65	130
Deputy Mayor	747	22.41	44.82	80	160
Mayor	933	27.99	55.98	100	200

SOURCE: Xia (1999)

rather than on income and wages, as is commonly the case in free market economies. Low-status employees receive fewer subsidies but have to pay the same rent rate as do higher-income households that receive larger subsidies. Public housing rents suddenly increased from 0.27 RMB per square meter in 1997 to 2 RMB per square meter in 1998 (Xia 1999). Furthermore, the government housing subsidy schemes cover only a small share of urban households. Only those employees who work in central, budget funded work units (mainly government organizations) are eligible for housing subsidies. In a time of economic uncertainty, the households already bearing severe hardships are working in non-central, budget-funded work units and therefore are unable to receive housing subsidies. Housing affordability becomes increasingly problematic for these households. They should be the prime target group for subsidies, but in fact they are not.

High Vacancy Rates

Two contrasting phenomena have appeared in the Chinese housing sector since 1994. On one hand, millions of urban residents are homeless or live in poor and overcrowded conditions, with less than 4 square meters of floor space per person. On the other hand, there has been a steep increase in vacancy rates for newly developed property, particularly in housing and commercial/office space. In 1994, the floor space of vacant real estate was 32.9 million square meters, increasing to 50.5 million square meters in 1995, 66.2 million square meters in 1996 and 70.4

FIGURE 6
Increase in Vacant Real Estate in China, 1994–1997

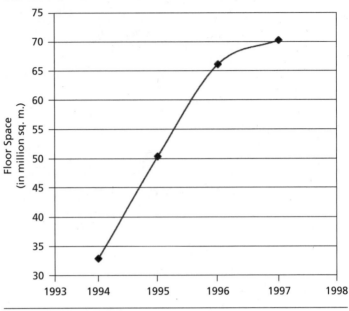

SOURCE: Xia (1999)

million square meters in 1997 (see Figure 6). The trend continued in 1998 when, for example, the floor space of vacant real estate in Shenzhen totaled 3.3 million square meters, an increase of 28.5 percent over the previous year's figures. In some cities, such as Zhuhai and Shenzhen, the vacancy rates for new properties were as high as 70+ percent in 1995 (Fong 1997). Housing vacancies represent the biggest share, by far, among the categories of real estate vacancies (see Table 5 for 1998 figures). For example, 77 percent of vacant real estate in China in 1995 was housing. The main reason for such high vacancy rates is the high price of commercial housing.

TABLE 5
Distribution of Vacant Property in China, 1998

Type of Property	Vacant Floor Space (in million sq. m.)	% of Total Vacant Property
Housing	48.3	69
Office	8.19	11.70
Commercial building	9.38	13.40
Other	4.06	5.80

SOURCE: Liang (1999)

However, the vacancy rate for government-subsidized, low-cost commercial housing, such as *aiju* (comfortable) housing projects, also remains high. For example, in 1997 the vacancy rate for aiju housing was 46 percent in Dalian and 60 percent in Guanlin. Of the 600,000 square meters of aiju housing in Beijing, only 50,000 square meters were sold in 1997 (Xia 1999). Because aiju housing is particularly designed for the promotion of home ownership for low- and medium-income households, the extremely high vacancy rates indicate that these households cannot afford even "low-cost" housing. Therefore, it is almost impossible for them to afford housing offered on the open market. This leads to an increasing mismatch of demand and supply between submarkets: the housing market for high-income households is heavily oversupplied whereas the housing market for low-income households is seriously undersupplied.

High Housing Prices and Inflated Housing Standards

The task of transforming a socialist system to a market system is more complicated and wide-ranging than are the development issues facing a developing country. A socialist system lacks even basic institutions that are transferable to a market system, and has little acquaintance or experience with its concepts and operations (Rana and Paz 1994; Renaud 1995; Zhang 1999). These realities lead to distortions in the housing market, such as unreasonable housing prices and speculative activities.

Compared with housing markets elsewhere in the world, the Chinese example has some unique features, such as the extensive involvement of work units (danweis). The continuing role of work units as mediators between producers and consumers in the housing market has distorted the price mechanism. In fact, since the introduction of the market mechanism in the Chinese housing sector, 70–75 percent of commercial housing has been bought by state-owned enterprises and then resold to their employees at rates far below market prices. Because corporate purchasing power is always greater than that of individuals, the involvement of work units has inflated housing prices and housing standards. The ratio of housing price to income in China rose from 14.8:1 in 1993 to 25.4:1 in 1998 (Lin 1993). Figure 7 shows average housing prices in Shenzhen's five urban districts in 1998. The average housing price in the city center (Luohu) was 8,302 RMB per square meter, though the average annual salary per capita in Shenzhen was 18,381 RMB (Shenzhen Real Estate Yearbook Editorial Committee 1999). Thus, the average annual salary could purchase a little more than two square meters of commercial housing floor space. The rule of thumb in housing markets is that households buy houses priced at approximately three times their annual household income. In the U.S., most commercial banks provide home loans based on an expectation that a household's monthly mortgage payment would represent 32–38 percent of monthly income.

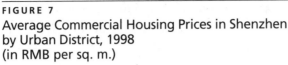

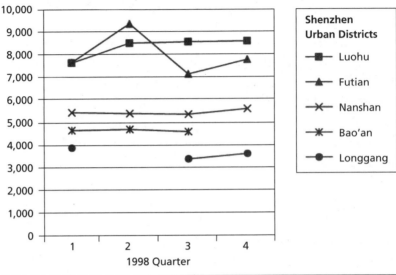

FIGURE 7
Average Commercial Housing Prices in Shenzhen
by Urban District, 1998
(in RMB per sq. m.)

SOURCE: Chan and Wang (1999)

The relationship between housing supply and demand explains, in part, the high housing prices. Steep land prices make most housing unaffordable for average urban residents. For instance, the average land cost in 1998 was 2,292 RMB per square meter — 45 percent higher than the average construction cost for housing units (1,576 RMB per square meter). Extensive taxes and charges levied on developers, along with land costs, contribute to the high price of housing. There are between 50 and 80 types of taxes and charges that can be levied, 48 of which the government has found to be unreasonable (Xia 1999). Though these taxes may help to reduce housing investment for the sake of speculative and profiteering activities, they also share the responsibility for high housing prices.

Meanwhile, developers have tended to build larger housing units. For example, in the first quarter of 1998, the average floor space per unit in Shenzhen was 128 square meters for high-rise commercial housing, 133 square meters for medium-height commercial housing and 117 square meters for multistory walk-ups (Chan and Wang 1999). This standard of commercial housing is highly inflated, considering that, nationally and on average, units with less than 30 square meters of floor space are occupied by approximately 17 percent of households; those with 31–40 square meters by 17 percent; those with 41–50 square meters by 21 percent; and those with 61–80 square meters by 17 percent. Only 8 percent of households have floor space of more than 81 square meters (Xia 1999). These inflated standards, in terms of housing size, have boosted per-unit housing prices.

Summary and Conclusions

During the last two decades, the housing sector has undergone fundamental changes, with market mechanisms playing a predominant role. Housing used to be treated as a social good, but now is treated not only as an economic asset, but also as a growth axis for the whole economy. This shift has pushed China to reallocate a larger share of its resources to housing, thereby significantly improving housing conditions for urban residents. However, the emergence of the housing market also has created many unprecedented problems. This chapter has discussed issues such as affordability, inappropriate housing subsidies, high vacancy rates, high prices and inflated standards. All of these features reflect the distorted nature and volatility of the Chinese housing market.

The extensive involvement of work units in the housing market has altered the direct relationship between producers and consumers, and therefore distorted the price mechanism. Speculation, profiteering activities, and unreasonable taxes and charges on commercial housing development are primary contributors to high housing prices, which in turn affect affordability. Because work units purchase most of the high-priced commercial housing (and resell it to their employees far below market prices), the economic burden on work units has increased at a time when many danweis are losing money. This dynamic, in turn, affects the ability of work units to continue buying housing for their employees. The increasing economic instability of the danweis has forced them to withdraw from the housing market since the mid-1990s.

Further, most individuals are unable to afford the high housing prices that were previously driven by the danweis' purchasing power. This is a major reason for the high vacancy rates since the mid-1990s, and for the relatively sudden change in the Chinese housing market from boom to something of a bust.

There are other factors that contribute to the distortion of the housing market. One is the continued bureaucratic behavior of many real estate developers. Because most of the development companies are state owned, they are not accustomed to making decisions based on market signals. When there is a high rate of vacancy in newly developed housing, the market prices should be adjusted to encourage buyers. But developers reduce neither their housing prices nor the scale of their new housing investment, because managers of state-owned development companies regard investment as power over the use of resources, regardless of market signals. They are more interested in exercising this power than in making rational investment decisions on economic grounds. This explains why, when the market indicates that high-standard commercial housing is oversupplied and investment in that sector should be reduced, managers simply ignore the fact. Such irrational behavior has worsened the imbalanced relationship between producers and consumers. The Asian financial crisis and the poor performance of China's state-owned enterprises are additional factors that have increased people's sense of uncertainty and have created a negative psychological environment for the further development of the Chinese housing market.

Perhaps one of the most challenging issues that housing providers and policy makers will face is related to housing affordability in light of the massive urbanization expected in the coming years. Currently, 39 percent of the total Chinese population is urbanized — slightly more than 500 million (of a total of 1.3 billion) people live in cities. The government's socioeconomic goal is a 55 percent urbanized population by 2020. Assuming that the current population remains constant — an unlikely outcome, based on demographic composition and population growth trends — there will be more than 13 million people migrating to cities from rural areas during the next 15 years. The striking differences between rural and urban residents suggest that the majority of these new urban residents will be poor and will lack skills with which to compete for high-income jobs. Even with their enormous impact on urban economic growth, the provision of affordable housing for these low-income residents and their households will be very challenging for years to come. Therefore, housing affordability should be a focus for scholars and policy makers during this period of rapid urbanization.

References

Brink, S. 1993. Policy strategies for affordable housing in cities. In *Housing policies and housing programmes: Orientations, strategies and evaluation,* CIB, ed. Publication #158. Lisbon: CIB.

Chan, M. Y., and L. Wang. 1999. Report on real estate development in Shenzhen in 1998. *Shenzhen Real Estate Market Analysis* 1:1–15.

China Construction Newspaper. 2001. The human settlement report of China 1996–2000. 5 June. China Ministry of Construction.

China Real Estate and Housing Research Association. 1994. *Real Estate and Housing Research Information,* #129.

Clapham, D. 1995. Privatization and the East European housing model. *Urban Studies* 32:679–694.

Fong, J. L. 1997. The reasons and solutions for high vacancy rates of property. *City* 4:24–26.

Housing and Real Estate. 1997. Report on China's housing reform work. *Housing and Real Estate* 1:14–21.

Jiang, J. 2001. Spatial distribution of housing in China. *Shanghai Housing and Land* 4:27–30.

Liang, J. Y. 1999. Vacant property in mainland China. *Hong Kong Economic Daily* 11(March):32.

Lin, Z. Q. 1993. *Comprehensive housing indicators.* Working paper #137. Beijing: China Academy of Urban Planning and Design.

Malpass, P. 1993. Housing tenure and affordability: The British disease. In *The new housing shortage: Housing affordability in Europe and the USA,* G. Hallett, ed. London: Routledge.

Pickvance, C. G. 1994. Housing privatization and housing protest in the transition from state socialism: A comparative study of Budapest and Moscow. *International Journal of Urban and Regional Research* 18:433–450.

Rana, P. B., and W. Paz. 1994. Economies in transition: The Asian experience. In *From reform to growth: China and other countries in transition in Asia and central Europe,* C. H. Lee and H. Reisen, eds., 119–141. Paris: OECD.

Renaud, B. 1995. The real estate economy and the design of Russian housing reform: Part 1. *Urban Studies* 32(8):1247–1264.

Shanghai Statistics Bureau. 1998. *Statistical yearbook of Shanghai 1998.* Beijing: China Statistical Publishing House.

Shenzhen Real Estate Yearbook Editorial Committee. 1999. *Shenzhen real estate yearbook 1999.* Shenzhen: Haitian Press.

State Statistical Bureau. 1997. *Statistics yearbook of China real estate 1997.* Beijing: China Statistical Publishing House.

———. 2000. *China statistical yearbook 1998.* Beijing: China Statistical Publishing House.

Turner, B., J. Hegedus, and I. Tosics, eds. 1992. *The reform of housing in Eastern Europe and the Soviet Union.* London: Routledge.

Walker, A., and L. H. Li. 1994. Land use rights reform and the real estate market in China. *Journal of Real Estate Literature* 2:199–211.

Wang, J. 2001. The problems of price-to-income ratio and rent-to-income ratio in Shanghai. *China Real Estate Studies* 1:41–57.

Xia, Z. Q. 1999. *China's housing reform movement.* Beijing: Social Science Books Press.

Zhang, X. Q. 1999. The impact of housing privatization in China. *Environment and Planning B* 26(4):593–604.

———. 2001. Redefining state and market: Urban housing reform in China. *Housing, Theory and Society* 18:67–78.

Chapter 9

Property Developers and Speculative Development in China

BO-SIN TANG AND SING-CHEONG LIU

Since the launch of open economic policies and market-based reforms in the late 1970s, socialist China has experienced an unprecedented restructuring of its economy and society. Between 1979 and 1999 China's gross domestic product (GDP) grew at an enviable average annual rate of more than 9 percent, from US$175.6 billion to US$996.3 billion (World Bank 2000). The country also has become the largest recipient of foreign direct investment (FDI) in the emerging markets. In 1997, for instance, China received net FDI inflows of US$44.2 billion (12 times the 1990 amount), ranking second only to the U.S. and representing some 72 percent of all net FDI inflows in the East Asia and Pacific area (World Bank 1999).

TABLE 1

Per Capita Living Space in China, 1978–2000

Year	Rural/Village (in sq. m.)	Urban (in sq. m.)
1978	8.1	3.6
1980	9.4	3.9
1985	14.7	5.2
1990	17.8	6.7
1995	21	8.1
1997	22.4	8.8
1998	23.7	9.3
1999	24.4	9.8
2000	24.8	10.3

SOURCES: State Statistical Bureau (1998, 1999); and China INFOBANK (2001)

Concomitant with such economic momentum, many Chinese cities have witnessed enormous building booms during the past two decades. Housing investment, for instance, has increased tremendously since the early 1980s, resulting in considerable improvement in housing conditions.[1] Per capita living space increased approximately threefold between 1978 and 2000 (see Table 1). Many Chinese cities, especially those in the coastal regions, have faced not only a rapid transformation of the urban landscape (Gaubatz 1995), but also the endemic problems of land speculation and building oversupply (Cartier 2001). The bursting

---

1 According to a ministerial report, more than 640 million square meters of new housing floor space were completed within a five-year period (1981–1985, inclusive), representing 47.7 percent of the total housing stock developed since 1949 (Ye 1986). From 1980 to 1990, investment in housing construction totaled more than 260 billion yuan — 4.6 times the investment made during the 31 years from 1949 to 1980 (Zhang 1991, 19).

of property bubbles was held responsible, in part, for the Asian financial turmoil (Mera and Renaud 2000). Despite its property glut, however, China has largely escaped the backlash of the Asian crisis because of its protected economy, nonconvertible currency and high foreign-exchange reserves (Sum 1999; Tse 2000).

Pre-reform socialist China had no property development sector. Before 1978 the state was dominant in directing land development, and central economic planning determined the use of urban space. The urbanization strategy was dictated by the hard-line socialist ideology that aimed to achieve egalitarianism, classlessness and uniformity (Fisher 1962; Lo 1987). Collectivization of all resources and elimination of market relations sustained the supremacy of the socialist state's goal of steering the country toward collective industrialization. Irrespective of their competitive advantages, Chinese cities were all transformed into industrial production centers. The backwardness of the national economy encouraged the socialist state to invest disproportionately in industry at the expense of "nonproductive" items such as housing (Xu 1999).

In the cities, production and consumption were organized mainly through a top-down administrative hierarchy: work units supervised by departments in various sectors of the central government (Yeh and Wu 1999). These self-contained state work units were responsible for organizing economic production, housing, social welfare and education for their employees. The central government was responsible for extraction of all the economic surpluses from these work units and subsequent redistribution in accordance with the national economic plan. The municipal governments played a limited role in organizing urban development within their territories (Wu 1995b; Yeh and Wu 1996).

However, gradual reforms since the early 1980s have engendered power shifts from the central to the provincial or local governments, and from governments to local markets in influencing urban spatial transformation (World Bank 1990, 1993). The constitutional amendments of 1988 that allowed paid transfer of land use rights have further fueled the growth of a property development industry and have revitalized the land and property markets (Wu 1999a, 1999b; Zhu 1999a, 1999b). These developers have local as well as external origins. Due to ethnic ties, cultural affinities and locational proximity, Chinese property developers from the former British colony of Hong Kong are among the dominant investors in Chinese property markets (Ross and Rosen 1992). On the other hand, recent years have witnessed the emergence of some successful local mainland developers. While possessing fewer financial resources and less experience than their Hong Kong counterparts, they are capable of sustaining attractive returns from their land development projects.[2]

---

2 For instance, based on Year 2000 annual reports (released by the end of March 2000), 18 local developers (out of 43 in total) listed on China's stock exchanges achieved, on average, an increase of ROEs from 12.4 percent in 1999 to 13.6 percent in 2000 (*GD-HK Information Daily* 2001).

This chapter examines market structure, behavior and performance of property developers in mainland China through exploration of the competitive strategies of these developers, examination of their operational constraints and explanation of their behavioral outcomes. This study discusses three categories of developers in the Chinese market: state-owned developers, Hong Kong-based developers and locally originated private developers. The classification is based on the differences in corporate background, development scale, resources, expertise and business strategy.

A major finding from the initial study is that Hong Kong developers, despite their financial strength and business competence, have been less successful in securing attractive returns from their projects in mainland China than from projects in Hong Kong (Tang and Liu 2001). The mainland China property sector has undergone significant transformations after more than two decades of market-based reforms orchestrated by the state. An emerging phenomenon is the rise of local private capital that is gradually challenging the dominance of the state-owned developers. This chapter examines the factors leading to this shift from state to market in the property development industry, and discusses its relationships with land speculation, property development and urban spatial changes.

The subsequent sections of this discussion review the historical evolution of the property development industry in China; summarize the key forces causing the emergence of property developers in the post-reform era; examine the competition and performance of the different categories of property developers in China's property market; explain these outcomes in terms of the transitional socialist market structure and the strategies of the developers; and offer concluding observations.

The Property Development Industry: An Historical Review

The evolution of the property development industry in China has been closely linked with the open economic policies and market reforms instigated by Deng Xiaoping since 1978. In contrast with many Eastern European countries, China did not pursue full-prong privatization or "shock therapy" in its reform process. Instead, it pursued incremental changes, thereby decreasing the likelihood of major social instability. Economic reforms were first introduced in the rural agricultural sectors and then gradually extended to the industrial and urban sectors. Furthermore, experiments were initially carried out in a few selected geographic regions before they were generally implemented over a wider area. Despite spasmodic changes in the pace of reform, success in agricultural-sector reforms helped to sustain dynamism in the momentum for reforms in other areas. Throughout the 1980s, strong export-led growth and an influx of external investment caused enormous development pressure on Chinese cities.

Cities have become the loci of economic activity and population concentration since economic reform. In the late 1970s, however, Chinese cities were plagued by numerous inefficiencies and problems, which were all legacies of the authoritarian socialist planning of the Maoist era. Capital investment in urban infrastructure, housing and community facilities was extremely deficient. For instance, with growing urban populations, the supply of fresh water became a major problem for many cities. Most urban roads were substandard and highly congested.[3] Housing space was highly insufficient, leading to tremendous overcrowding. The average living space of urban dwellers was far less than that in many developing countries at the time (Shi 1998, 5). The urban environment was poor, pollution was pandemic under a chronic mix of incompatible land uses, and the urban physical layout was irrational, inefficient and fragmented as a result of uncoordinated, project-specific developments by separate work units within a city. And, municipal governments were generally short of funds to improve urban conditions.[4]

Property development was designated by Chinese leaders as a potential solution to these urban problems. Four key forces, resulting from the economic reforms initiated by the state, supported the emergence and growth of property developers in China: land leasing, the commodification of housing, enterprise reform and municipality-based comprehensive urban development (Zhang 1991; Yang and He 1998; Ding 1999; Wu 1999b; Zhu 1999a).

Land Leasing

Land reforms in China provided a strong impetus to the emergence of the property development industry. During the pre-reform period, allocation of land to the end users was administratively decided by the socialist state in accordance with the priorities of the national economic plans. Land was allocated without charge and for an infinite period. The users, primarily the state work units, were ultimately responsible for the use and development of the land — they became the builders as well as the de facto landowners of the land parcels. Abolition of the land markets in the pre-reform period eliminated the transfer of land between users, even when the land was subsequently found to be underused by the original users. All these features contributed to overconsumption of and underinvestment in urban land. Land resources failed to provide value appreciation and capital accumulation for the users; thus, there was no role for a profit-making property development industry. Further, the state could not extract any revenue from the productive use of this national resource.

Land market reforms since the early 1980s worked to reinstate economic value in land use. Land is no longer a free commodity in China — its use requires monetary compensation by the users. Urban space has become a revenue-generating

---

3 Only about 20 percent of the roads in the country were completed with asphalt; the average vehicular speed was only 30 km per hour (Li 1986).

4 As an example, according to the Guangzhou Municipal Board of Urban and Rural Construction, the estimated funding requirement for urban capital construction in 1981 exceeded 4 billion yuan; however, only about 50 million yuan were designated in the local government annual budget for such purposes.

asset to local governments. Many localities have levied land use fees (*tudi shiyongfei*) on users based on site location, land use type and size of land parcel. These fees, replaced by land use taxes since 1988, provide a stable income source to support urban construction. Land use fees were initially imposed on enterprises involving foreign investment in the "open" cities, and were gradually introduced to local enterprises in other parts of China.[5] In 1988 the National People's Congress formally approved the paid transfer of land use rights, and the constitution was amended to support the separation of land use rights from land ownership. Since then, a number of regulations have been promulgated to formalize land transfer and provide an avenue for foreign capital investment in urban land.[6] In many cities, the legal framework expedited urban land reform.

Hence, urban land reforms support the state's monopolistic control of all urban land supply and legalize land leasing through the payment of land premiums. Municipal land administration authorities, as representatives of the state, manage the transfer of land use rights. Local governments can now sell urban land through competitive auction, tender and negotiation. This facilitates the shift from isolated, project-specific development by work units to comprehensive planning and development by municipal governments. Establishment of land markets supports the growth of property developers, who can acquire large pieces of land from peasants, level the sites, provide the infrastructure and sell the land or property back to the end users.[7] Urban land development is thus better coordinated, reducing the problems of duplication and waste.

Commodification of Housing

The housing market was eliminated during the pre-reform era because housing property was treated as a welfare product to be provided by the state through the various state work units. Completed housing properties were allocated to employees according to administrative criteria other than affordability. Housing rents were kept extremely low because of state subsidies. Households were forced to wait for

5 Shenzhen, Fuzhun and Guangzhou were among the first few cities that introduced the land use fees in the early 1980s. In 1982 Shenzhen's land use fees ranged between 1 and 21 yuan per square meter, contributing an annual total fee revenue of more than 10 million yuan. In 1984 Fushun's classification of urban land into four categories established land use fees, ranging between 0.2 and 0.6 yuan per square meter, that provided total annual fee revenues of approximately 13 million yuan. On the other hand, in 1984 Guangzhou began collecting land use fees based upon a classification of urban land into seven categories, ranging from 0.5 to 4 yuan per square meter; the total revenue collection amounted to approximately 20 million yuan (Bi 1994, 35).

6 Two important regulations were promulgated in 1990: The Provisional Regulation on the Granting and Transferring of the Land Use Rights over State Owned Land in Cities and Towns, and Provisional Measures for the Administration of Foreign Investors to Develop and Operate Plots of Land. In 1992 the Regulation of Implementing Land Administrative Law and Limits of the Authority on Land Management governed the practices of land leasing and urban land administration. In 1994 the promulgation of the Urban Real Estate Management Act further formalized the comprehensive legal provisions in governing urban land leasing, property development, transactions, mortgages, title registration, property rental and agency services.

7 In 1991 approximately 409.6 square kilometers of rural land were acquired; land use rights were transferred for 36 square kilometers of that land (Yeh and Wu 1999, 221).

centralized housing allocation as there was no outside market for individual purchase. Investment in housing by the work units constituted part of the national budget for capital investment and was subject to the final approval of the central government. Its status as a nonproductive, welfare item meant that housing investment was accorded a lower priority than other kinds of investment. Between 1950 and 1978 housing investment comprised approximately 0.9 percent of the gross national product (GNP) and 6.6 percent of capital investment (Zhang 1991, 12). By the late 1970s this meager level of investment led to a severe shortage of living space for the growing urban population.

In solving urban housing problems, the central government proposed to examine imaginative housing reforms, including permission for private housing, public housing subsidies and housing loans, self-help (or self-build) housing and market adjustment of public housing rents. Various measures, including pension fund schemes, rental subsidy increases and the sale of welfare housing, were tried in different cities. All these proposals aimed at replacing the socialist centralized system of housing provision with a decentralized housing market.[8] Housing investment began to rely less and less upon national capital budget allocations that restricted housing supply in the cities. Local governments, enterprises and individuals were encouraged to build and invest in housing property for sale and for individual use. This policy has significantly expanded the sources of housing investment from one to multiple sources. Individual investment in housing, for instance, increased dramatically from 2 percent of total housing investment in 1979 to approximately 20 percent in 1990 (Zhang 1991, 24–25).

Commodification of housing led to the emergence of a monetized housing market and, thus, the demand for property developers. It resuscitated the exchange value of housing property. Now, existing and new housing units are sold to urban dwellers, mortgages are extended to home buyers, and public housing rents are gradually being increased to reduce the level of state subsidy in housing provision.[9] All these reform measures have successfully revitalized the housing sector. Housing

---

8 In 1986 the State Council set up a task force to coordinate national housing reforms. In 1987 the State Planning Commission, the Ministry of Urban and Rural Construction and the State Statistical Bureau promulgated the Provisional Regulations for Strengthening the Planning and Management of Commodified Properties, which symbolized a major step forward in promoting private housing production. These regulations sought to separate property investment from capital investment. Since then, investment in commodity housing and real property production has been identified as a separate item under national planning (Zhang and Zhang 1993, 12). In 1994 the State Council approved the Resolution for Enhancing Housing Reforms. According to Yang and He (1998, 20–21), this resolution comprised "three changes" and "four establishments" *(sangai sijian)* in the Chinese housing market. The "three changes" included (1) a shift from state subsidy in housing investment to shared contributions by the state, enterprise and individual; (2) a shift of responsibility from the work units to professional companies for housing construction, allocation, repair and management; and (3) a change from welfare distribution of housing to an affordability-based, monetized system. The "four establishments" included (1) establishing the social housing system for poor households and private, commodified housing for wealthier families, respectively; (2) establishing a housing pension scheme; (3) establishing housing mortgage and insurance institutions; and (4) establishing the necessary market provisions to facilitate proper housing transactions, maintenance and repair.

9 Housing rents in some new housing units, for instance, may be three to four times the rents for existing properties.

development has become a profitable business for land developers: they can now recoup their investments through the sale and lease of completed units. This possibility attracts capital from various sources to housing production, thereby increasing the urban housing supply and helping to ameliorate the acute housing shortage in many Chinese cities.[10] Expansion of the private housing sector has also stimulated the growth of a full range of property-related businesses such as mortgage banking, property agency, property management and maintenance, and interior decoration, among others.

Enterprise Reforms

Urban enterprise reform lies at the heart of the successful modernization of the Chinese economy. During the pre-reform era, all production was organized by state-owned enterprises that also shouldered responsibility for providing employment and welfare to urban dwellers. Due to state protection and lack of competition, most state-owned enterprises operated inefficiently. Soft budget constraints and a closed market environment kept these concerns from bankruptcy. However, with the influx of competing foreign enterprises after more open economic policies were instituted, companies' problems were increasingly exposed. Many encountered financial difficulties and required ongoing subsidies from the government to survive. The Chinese leadership was quick to realize that this situation was not viable in the long run, and that decentralization of management authority was a potential means of promoting rational corporate governance.

Enterprise reforms aimed to encourage greater operational autonomy and financial incentives for these firms (Jefferson and Rawski 1994; Perkins 1994). These reforms allowed the companies to retain some portion of certain profits and output (after planned production goals were realized), and established dual pricing and contract responsibility systems. Dual pricing allowed enterprises to sell their surplus outputs in the marketplace. Contract responsibility systems encouraged organizations to determine their production goals and have greater control of their business operations. In addition, incentives such as salary increases and additional bonuses were provided to management and labor. Relaxation of price controls pushed state-owned enterprises to procure their resource supply from the free markets. Reductions in state funding support and encouragement of credit finance imposed more severe budget constraints.

Many state-owned enterprises had secured excessive amounts of urban land through administrative allocation. The increased autonomy of these enterprises encouraged rationalization of their use of existing land resources (Wang 1995,

---

10 Even so, the problem of overcrowding has not been completely solved. In Guangzhou, for instance, the average living space for urban dwellers amounted to about 8.7 square meters in 1991. However, more than 15,800 families — approximately 3.2 percent of the total number of urban households — had less than 2 square meters of living space per person (Qiu and Shi 1993, 33).

9–10). Some turned into property development businesses and some entered into joint ventures with developers to develop their land assets. Factories were relocated and obsolete urban land uses were replaced by new developments. Local governments often encouraged ailing state-owned enterprises to make profitable use of their land stock (Wu 1999b). Property development was treated as a cash cow for these Chinese enterprises.

Municipality-Based Comprehensive Urban Development

Chinese leaders regarded comprehensive urban development (which was equivalent to comprehensive property development) as an appropriate means to achieving social, economic and environmental improvements in the cities.[11] Comprehensive development is often defined to include several key elements: unified planning (*tongyi guihua*), rational layout (*heli buju*), and supportive infrastructure (*peitao jianshe*), all by local government. Comprehensive land development and the extraction of land use fees from users constituted the twin economic pillars of urban management reform. These measures were intended to implement efficient urban land use under a rational master plan, increase local government income and resolve the problems of funding urban development.

The central government, in an effort to contain the expansion of large cities, specifically encouraged the establishment of development companies to take responsibility for developing new cities and urban development zones and revitalizing old urban districts. These companies were expected to be profit-oriented and free from intervention by superior administrative departments in their daily operations.[12] The funding for these companies was initially derived from three sources: advances from urban capital construction investments of the central and local governments, loans from construction banks and deposits from the property buyers.

The role of local governments was strengthened through this strategy, in which they designated, managed and acquired urban development land. Development companies then acted as their development executive arms, acquiring projects either

---

11 The idea of comprehensive urban development evolved from the earlier concept of unified construction (*tongjian*). This concept was proposed by the central government as early as 1963 to tackle the urban problems of duplicated construction, fragmented planning and waste of investment from multiple sources in many Chinese cities. It proposed that new and expanded facilities of work units, such as housing, schools and other municipal facilities, should be the responsibility of the local city governments that took up the role of "unified construction and unified management" or "decentralized management under unified planning." However, such a proposal did not make much headway at that time, given that local governments had limited power vis-à-vis the strong governing regime of the central state. In 1978 the central government further proposed the policy of six unified actions (*liu tongyi*). This policy required local governments to take up the task of unifying six separate areas of urban development: planning, investment, design, construction, distribution and management.

12 In 1984 the State Planning Commission and the Ministry of Urban and Rural Construction promulgated the Provisional Regulations for Comprehensive Urban Construction and Development Companies. These regulations required the development companies to be autonomously run, separately audited and self-financed.

through competitive tender or direct government appointment. Based on the master plan of the city, these development companies prepared detailed development plans for the sites. Their mission was to service the sites and/or develop all the buildings and ancillary facilities; serviced land and completed properties were then sold to the work units. To promote competition, the policy encouraged municipalities to establish several development companies.

In 1990 the National Congress of the Chinese Communist Party approved a 10-year national economic and social development plan that aimed to increase the production value of property development to 10 percent of GNP by the turn of the century. With central policy support, the property development industry in mainland China grew tremendously during the 1980s and 1990s. According to the State Statistical Bureau (1998, 234), China had more than 21,280 registered property development companies in 1997. Between 1981 and 1990, for instance, more than 1.3 billion square meters of housing space were completed and inhabited, representing an 80 percent increase over the analogous figure from the period between 1949 and 1980 (Zhou et al. 1992, 2). The urban landscape of many Chinese cities has been transformed. In recent years, the real estate sector has become an engine of national economic growth: between 1998 and 2000, for instance, its contribution to fixed asset investment rose some 35.6 percent, from 361.4 billion yuan to 490.2 billion yuan (*Zhongguo Jingyingbao* 2001).

The Property Development Industry:
Structure, Competition and Performance
Registration of Real Estate Development Companies

In mainland China, property development companies must register with the government before they can engage in the land and property development business. To register, an enterprise must fulfill certain conditions regarding company management structure, personnel requirements and financial capability. Because property development is regarded as capital- and technology-intensive, the central government implements a grading system to prevent companies from taking on projects beyond their financial and technical capabilities[13] (see Table 2). The different grades correspond to specific project parameters; companies are eligible to adopt projects that correspond to their assigned grades.[14] However, these grading criteria are

---

13 In 1989 there were four grades. Substantial amendments were made to the grading criteria in 1989: financial requirements were made more stringent while requirements for skilled personnel were relaxed. According to criteria laid down by the Ministry of Construction in 1993, property development companies were henceforth classified into five different grades.

14 For instance, Grade 1 property developers can undertake housing projects of more than 200,000 square meters of floor area, or other similar development works. Grade 2 developers, however, can only develop housing projects of less than 200,000 square meters of floor area, and other equivalent works. Moreover, they cannot take on projects requiring specialized and complicated technical skills. Grade 3 developers can undertake housing projects of less than 120,000 square meters, or similar works; they are not allowed to build structures exceeding 12 stories and a span of 24 meters.

TABLE 2

Classification of Specialized Property Development Companies in China, 1993

Grade	Capital (in million yuan)	Personnel	Levels of Personnel	Years of Experience	Track Record
1	Liquid capital > 20 Mn Reg. capital ≥ 20 Mn	Professional staff ≥ 40 Middle-to-top mgmt. ≥ 20	Chief engineers, accountants and economists at senior levels; other key responsible staff at middle professional levels	5 years	completed more than 300,000 sq. m. housing floor area (or equivalent venture) in last 3 years; 100% "pass" and 20% "good" ratings in building quality check during 4 consecutive years
2	Liquid capital > 10 Mn Reg. capital ≥ 10 Mn	Professional staff ≥ 20 Middle-to-top mgmt. ≥10	Key staff in civil engineering, accounting, finance and economics at middle professional levels	3 years	completed more than 150,000 sq. m. housing floor area (or equivalent venture) in last 3 years; 100% "pass" and 10% "good" ratings in building quality check during 3 consecutive years
3	Liquid capital > 5 Mn Reg. capital ≥ 5 Mn	Professional staff ≥ 10 Middle-to-top mgmt. ≥ 5	Key staff in engineering and finance at middle professional levels; other key staff at assistant professional levels and supported by junior bookkeeping staff	2 years	completed more than 50,000 sq. m. housing floor area (or equivalent venture) in last 3 years; 100% "pass" ratings in building quality check
4	Liquid capital > 2 Mn Reg. capital ≥ 2 Mn	Professional staff ≥ 5	Key staff in engineering at middle professional levels; finance staff at junior professional levels supported by bookkeeping staff	No requirements	No requirements
5	Liquid capital > 3 Mn	Allowed to develop land only in local districts Detailed controls to be set by relevant provinces and municipalities			

NOTE:
Newly established companies that meet the criteria for financial and personnel standards for Grades 1–3 but lack sufficient years of experience and track records will be accredited at one grade lower.

SOURCE: Summarized and translated from Shen (2000, 115–116)

applicable only to "specialized" property development companies (*zhuanying gongsi*) — those that engage in the property development sector as their core business and, typically, are better endowed in finance, technology and personnel.

There are two other types of property development companies: branch companies (*jianying gongsi*) and project companies (*xiangmu gongsi*). In accordance with government policy, these two categories of companies can embark on property development projects only on serviced land. Branch companies are permitted to diversify into other real estate sectors, such as investment, construction and consolidated business. Although they are waived from the grading system, they face more stringent financial requirements.[15] Alternatively, project companies are set up specifically for particular land development projects. Their establishment requires a one-off company registration with authorities local to the site of the projects, and the grading system is waived. Once the projects are completed, the company is dissolved. The majority of the existing real estate development companies in mainland China belong to this category, resulting in an extremely pluralistic market. In Guangzhou in 2000, for example, only approximately 300 of the 1,500 development companies were "graded developers." Only 10 of the 300 were classified as Grade 1 developers; the remainder were mostly project-specific companies (Zhao and Chen 2000).

Corporate Background of Property Developers

Corporate background and structure are highly correlated with the conduct and performance of property development companies. This analysis distinguishes between three different categories of property development company in mainland China: state-owned real estate development enterprises; property developers originating from Hong Kong; and privately run property development companies.

State-owned real estate development enterprises evolved largely from the government bureaucracy and from public organizations. Some emerged from the city- and district-based unified urban construction offices (*tongjian bangongshi*) responsible for comprehensive planning and land management within their respective jurisdictions. These development companies are often regarded as "administrative work units managed in the form of enterprises" (*shiye danwei qiyehua guanli*). Such a corporate model implies that, though corporate mission and personnel arrangements

---

15 Branch property development companies' requirements are as follows.

- Consolidated enterprises and investment and trust companies must have a minimum equity capital base of 0.2 billion yuan and liquid capital of at least 0.1 billion yuan.
- Grade 1 (construction quality standard) construction companies that belong to the ministries of the central government must have a minimum equity capital base of 0.1 billion yuan and liquid capital of at least 50 million yuan.
- Local construction companies with Grade 1 (construction quality standard) must have a minimum capital base of 50 million yuan and liquid capital of at least 30 million yuan.

are still subject to the bureaucratic control of the government, these companies are required to be self-financing in their operations. Some are quasi-governmental enterprises (*banguanfang qiye*) and subordinate organizations set up by the central government ministries, local government bureaus and construction enterprises.

These various forms were among the earliest property developers established by local authorities to manage comprehensive urban development. They have strong connections with the government bureaucracy, although they all have attained independent legal status. These enterprises often operate with a large corporate structure (see Figure 1), and constitute the major force in the real estate development sector. In many cities, one or two of these enterprises act as the "backbone" (*gugan*) or primary builders under the direction of local authorities. Often, favorable policy support, such as tax waivers for the first three years of business, was provided to these companies. They could obtain development rights from local authorities for huge tracts of land within the planned development areas and inner cities. During the 1980s these companies were primarily responsible for providing mass housing for the state work units.

The second category refers to the external, Hong Kong-based investors who were the pioneers in investment in China's housing market. Initially, their investment was concentrated in the manufacturing sector but subsequently spread to real estate. The influx of Hong Kong developers was particularly euphoric after Deng Xiaoping's 1992 southern tour that helped speed up economic reforms. These Hong Kong developers comprised the neophytes and the experienced, exhibiting a wide range of expertise and financial capability. Some were industrialists who had relocated to

FIGURE 1
Company Structure of Large-Scale, State-Owned Developers: An Example

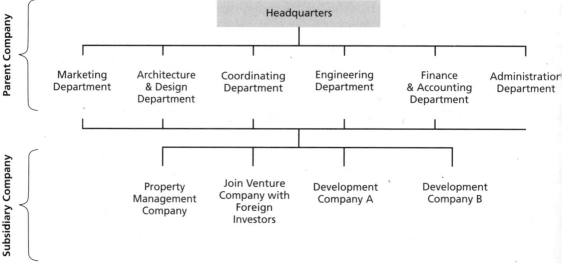

SOURCE: Modified from Shi (1998, 23)

the mainland and wished to jump on the property bandwagon with a view to capturing quick profits (*Asian Wall Street Journal* 1992). Some were dominant, brand-name Hong Kong developers who sought to diversify their property business into the mainland (Tang and Liu 2001). These Hong Kong companies were required to form joint ventures with local enterprises in undertaking land development projects on the mainland.[16] Local authorities encouraged the Hong Kong-based investors, for they brought new capital and imported new technology and management skills into the Chinese market. In general, these developers have focused their efforts on the development of up-market properties in the key cities for well-off buyers in China and abroad.

The last category refers to the numerous mainland Chinese property development companies funded by nonstate capital. In various forms and emerging from diverse backgrounds, they included collectively owned enterprises (*jiti qiye*), private companies (*siren qiye*), shareholding companies (*gufenzhi gongsi*) and publicly listed companies (*shangshi gongsi*). Some evolved from state-owned enterprises and successfully detached from the state bureaucracy and its control. Some belong to collectively owned work units that have decided to enter the real estate market. Others are established by the emerging capitalist class and by local entrepreneurs. These companies could be specialized property developers, project companies or property development branches of business conglomerates. The defining feature is that these real estate companies are entirely economically independent and self-financing. Their business objective is to maximize return on investment for owners and shareholders. In general, these companies are much smaller in scale, staffing and operation than the state-owned development companies (see Figure 2).

Developer Performance

Property development has been a highly profitable business in China, especially during the 1980s, when property floor space was in acute shortage and there were few developers in the market. Profitability of development developers has generally decreased with the rising number of developers entering the industry and the resultant intensified competition. There are complex methodological issues in

---

16 There are several corporate forms of involvement of external capital in real estate development in mainland China. First, Sino-foreign, equity joint-venture (*hezi qiye*) real estate development enterprises are set up by equity contributions from foreign, and local Chinese, partners. The ratios of equity injection, profit distribution and management authority are determined in accordance with the relative share contributions of the two parties. This form of joint venture normally represents a long-term commitment of the foreign partners. Second, Sino-foreign, contractual joint-venture (*hezuo qiye*) real estate development enterprises are set up by contracts between the foreign and local Chinese partners, and represent short-term, project-specific arrangements. The shares of investment, profit distribution and management responsibility are determined in accordance with the terms of the contracts. Third, wholly foreign-owned real estate development enterprises are companies wholly funded, owned and managed by foreign investors; these constitute an insignificant portion of the industry.

FIGURE 2

Company Structure of Smaller-Scale, Private Developers: An Example

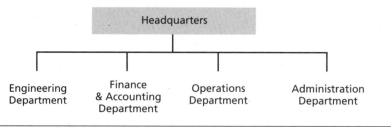

SOURCE: Modified from Shi (1998, 23)

---

determining precisely the profitability of property developers.[17] In 2000 an examination of the general performance of these mainland developers used returns on equity (ROEs) as an indicator of profitability.[18] Table 3 illustrates the findings for the mainland Chinese developers then listed in China's Shenzhen and Shanghai stock exchanges.[19] A review of the corporate performance of these publicly listed mainland developers reveals the following general picture.

First, the ROEs of the mainland developers in 2000 ranged between 0.13 percent and 52.9 percent, excluding those developers whose earnings were negative. The wide range of investment returns reveals that strong competition has led to polarization and differentiation within the real estate development industry. In a more competitive market environment, the performance gap of developers is expanding. Second, three listed developers were found to be losing money. They were small-to-medium-scale developers with total asset values between 1.1 billion yuan and 2.6 billion yuan.

Third, some small-to-medium-scale property developers tended to achieve higher ROEs (see Figure 3). Three companies newly listed in 2001, including Beijing Tianhong Baoye, Goldfield Industries and Guangzhou Donghua, attained incredibly attractive returns that surpassed those of many of the incumbent firms. These companies were small in scale with total assets ranging between about 540 million yuan and slightly more than 1 billion yuan.

Fourth, the long-established developers generally were larger in scale. For instance, the first developer listed in Table 3, China Vanke at Shenzhen (with total

---

17 For example, profits are private data for companies that are not publicly listed. For diversified companies, investment returns come from various sources in addition to property development, and it is difficult to separate real estate profits from other types. For developers, only state-owned property developers were allowed a public listing at the stock exchanges during the early reform era. Mainland developers now represent a variety of complicated ownership structures ranging from state-owned to privately owned. It is hard to identify the nature of ownership of these companies and to trace any subsequent changes in status.

18 The return on equity (ROE) of a company is defined as the ratio of net profit divided by the value of shareholder equity. For instance, if the net profit is $1 million and shareholder equity amounts to $10 million, the ROE will be 10 percent.

19 According to the regulation of China's stock exchanges, the listed company will be classified as a property development company when operating income from its real estate business equals or exceeds 50 percent of the company's total income.

FIGURE 3

Performance of Mainland Chinese Developers, 2000

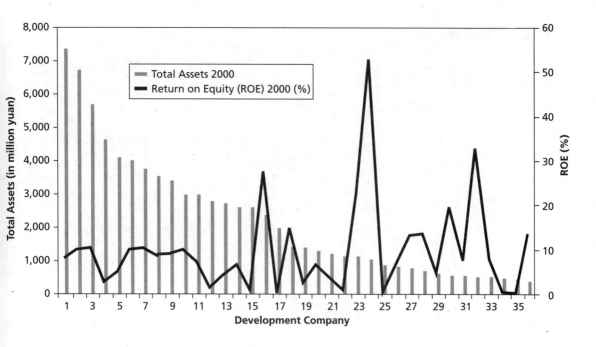

assets exceeding 5.6 billion yuan), achieved a net profit of some 301 million yuan, the second-highest profit figure on the list. The largest developer, Shanghai Lujiazui Finance and Trade Zone Development (with total assets nearing 7.4 billion yuan), earned a net profit of about 350 million yuan.[20]

However, incumbents did register a broad range of investment performance. Century Zhongtian and Cosco Development were among the best-performing developers, attaining a return of some 52.9 percent and 27.9 percent, respectively. China Vanke, on the other hand, achieved a return of approximately 11 percent, and Shanghai New Huangpu managed a return of only some 3.3 percent (already an increase of some 28.8 percent over the previous year's figure). Beijing Urban Construction Co. Ltd., which was the second-largest developer on the list (with total assets exceeding 6.7 billion yuan), logged a return of 10.23 percent.[21]

Though in terms of asset value many Hong Kong developers were giants compared with their mainland counterparts, they appear to have been outperformed by mainland competitors in the China market.[22] A survey of their ROEs yields the

---

20 The company was first established in 1990.

21 Although this company was listed in 1999, it was, notably, the first comprehensive development company set up in the early 1980s in response to policy initiatives of the central government.

22 Our interviews with many senior professionals working in and with these development companies have confirmed that most of these projects have not attained satisfactory returns.

TABLE 3
Publicly Listed Mainland Chinese Property Development Companies, 2000

Company	Registered Headquarters	Year Listed	Net Profit 2000 (in million yuan)	Total Assets 2000 (in million yuan)	Return on Equity (ROE) 2000 (%)	Return on Equity (ROE) 1999 (for comparison) (%)
China Vanke Real Estate Co. Ltd.	Shenzhen	1988	301.2	5,622.25	10.37	10.95
Shenzhen Fountain Holding Co. Ltd.	Shenzhen	1994	1.1	2,020.67	0.13	11.84
Shenzhen Zhenye (Group) Co. Ltd.	Shenzhen	1992	118.4	3,787.81	10.55	8.84
Shenzhen Baoan Enterprises (Group) Co. Ltd.	Shenzhen	1991	37.2	4,664.23	2.85	2.49
Shenzhen Properties & Resources Development (Group) Co. Ltd.	Shenzhen	1992	-14.2	2,606.37	—	25.67
Shenzhen Universe (Group) Co. Ltd.	Shenzhen	1993	17.8	828.55	6.60	9.92
Shezhen Special Economic Zone Real Estate & Property (Group) Co. Ltd.	Shenzhen	1993	76.6	4,113.91	4.78	6.71
Shenzhen Bao Heng Co. Ltd.	Shenzhen	1993	20.4	1,406.70	2.29	-12.02
Shenzhen Changcheng Estate (Group) Holding Co. Ltd.	Shenzhen	1994	111.8	3,448.56	9.14	9.38
Shenzhen Nanguang (Group) Plc.	Shenzhen	1994	16.5	1,241.92	3.77	3.82
Guangcai Construction Co. Ltd.	Shenzhen	1994	37.8	1,304.62	6.82	17.95
Shenzhen Over Globe Development Co. Ltd.	Shenzhen	1994	-120.7	1,371.65	-1433.30	-103.69
Shenzhen Worldsun Enterprise Co. Ltd.	Shenzhen	1995	0.4	460.88	0.21	8.65
Shenzhen Tonge (Group) Co. Ltd.	Shenzhen	1999	97.1	3,007.68	9.95	11.42
Financial Street Holding Co. Ltd.	Beijing	1996	40.1	599.75	19.90	6.97
Hainan New Energy Co. Ltd.	Haikou	1992	36.0	428.85	13.84	15.83
Hainan Pearl River Enterprise Holdings Co. Ltd.	Haikou	1992	62.7	804.01	13.20	6.65
Chongqing Real Estate Development Co. Ltd.	Chongqing	1993	0.5	497.66	0.29	6.75
Century Zhongtian Inv. Joint Stock Co. Ltd.	Guiyang	1994	229.5	1,082.51	52.90	12.03
Shenyang Fangtian Co. Ltd.	Shenyang	1994	13.3	531.81	8.12	6.62

Company	Registered Headquarters	Year Listed	Net Profit 2000 (in million yuan)	Total Assets 2000 (in million yuan)	Return on Equity (ROE) 2000 (%)	Return on Equity (ROE) 1999 (for comparison) (%)
Hainan Jinpan Enterprise Co. Ltd.	Haikou	1994	0.9	913.26	0.36	0.53
Hainan Baohua Industry Share Co. Ltd.	Haikou	1999	18.9	648.33	4.49	8.21
Zhongheng Group	Wuzhou	2000	27.9	584.27	7.57	21.93
Beijing Urban Construction Co. Ltd.	Beijing	1999	147.3	6,739.38	10.23	11.21
Beijing Tianhong Baoye Real Estate Co. Ltd.	Beijing	2001	72.8	537.42	32.96	17.91
Goldfield Industries Inc. Co. Ltd.	Shenzhen	2001	84.2	1,132.51	22.71	14.35
Guangzhou Donghua Enterprise Co. Ltd.	Guangzhou	2001	52.3	711.69	13.60	14.66
Shanghai Xingye Real Estate Co. Ltd.	Shanghai	1992	4.0	1,146.18	1.07	7.24
Shanghai New Huangpu Real Estate Co. Ltd.	Shanghai	1993	123.0	2,986.28	7.33	6.16
Jinqiao Export	Shanghai	1993	70.3	2,740.91	4.14	2.93
Cosco Development Co. Ltd.	Shanghai	1993	281.4	2,410.75	27.91	27.59
Shanghai AJ Corp	Shanghai	1993	135.5	2,611.08	6.62	6.30
Shanghai Wai Gaoqiao Free Trade Zone Development Co. Ltd.	Shanghai	1993	23.8	2,797.41	1.65	2.16
Shanghai Lujiazui Finance & Trade Zone Development Co. Ltd.	Shanghai	1993	350.0	7,384.60	8.13	0.64
China Enterprises Co. Ltd.	Shanghai	1993	108.1	3,578.35	8.92	10.01
Guangzhou Pearl River Industrial Development Co. Ltd.	Guangzhou	1993	-102.0	1,060.05	-17.73	3.00
Jilin Yatai Group Co. Ltd.	Jilin	1995	174.3	4,033.22	10.11	10.44
Shanghai Zhangjiang Hi-tech Park Development Co. Ltd.	Shanghai	1996	127.9	1,430.46	15.07	8.60

SOURCE: China Yahoo Finance (2000)

TABLE 4

Investment Performance of Selected Hong Kong Developers

Company	Month/Year Reported	Return on Equity (ROE) (%)
Cheung Kong (Holdings) Ltd.	12/1999	41.89
Sun Hung Kai Properties Ltd.	06/2000	8.95
Henderson Land Development Co. Ltd.	06/2000	10.03
Henderson China Holdings Ltd.	06/2000	2.02
New World Development Co.Ltd.	06/1999	2.23
New World China Land Ltd.	06/1999	1.07
Lai Sun Development Co. Ltd.	07/2000	-43.21
Lai Fung Holdings Ltd.	07/2000	0.23
Sino Land Company Ltd.	06/2000	5.02
Kerry Properties Ltd.	12/1999	4.99
Great Eagle Holdings Ltd.	12/1999	4.08
China Overseas Land & Investment Ltd.	12/1999	-5.98
New Asia Realty & Trust Co. Ltd.	03/2000	5.77
Top Glory International Holdings Co. Ltd.	12/1999	1.16
SEA Holdings Ltd.	12/1999	4.57
Tern Properties Co. Ltd.	03/2000	2.05
Hon Kwok Land Investment Co. Ltd.	03/2000	3.02
Prestige Properties Holdings Ltd.	12/1999	6.79
Hopson Development Holdings Ltd.	12/1999	17.20

SOURCE: E-finet.com (2001)

following findings (see Table 4). First, Cheung Kong achieved an outstanding ROE of 41.89 percent, far surpassing that of its counterparts. We attribute this result to its successful management, its globally diversified business and some recent profitable deals.

Second, Hong Kong developers whose businesses were less concentrated on the Chinese property market tended to achieve higher ROEs, as is obvious when the returns of parent companies and Chinese subsidiaries are compared. For instance, Henderson China, which is 57.65 percent owned by the Henderson Land Group, recorded an ROE of 2.02 percent, a rate much lower than the parent company's 10.03 percent. Similarly, New World China, with market capitalization of approximately HK$4.6 billion as of March 2001, attained an ROE of 1.07 percent, compared with the 2.23 percent earned by its parent corporation (with market capitalization of approximately HK$22 billion for the same period). The only exception was the case of Lai Sun and its China subsidiary, Lai Fung. Lai Sun was known to have been adversely affected by the Taiwan lawsuits against its founder and its losing real estate and media investments in Hong Kong. It recorded ROEs of -78.45 percent in 1999 and -43.21 percent in 2000. For the same periods, Lai Fung experienced ROEs of 0.21 percent and 0.23 percent, respectively.

Third, investment returns of all the surveyed China subsidiaries of these major Hong Kong developers were much lower than those of the listed mainland Chinese counterparts. In 2000 the weighted average ROEs of the 35 mainland Chinese developers listed in Table 3, excluding the three losing ones, amounted to approximately 8.94 percent. Performance of Hong Kong developers in the China market appears to have been lackluster.

Fourth, Hopson Development was an interesting exception to these trends. A publicly listed, medium-scale firm in Hong Kong, this company specialized in housing development in Guangzhou and was regarded by many as a mainland Chinese developer. It achieved remarkably attractive ROEs of 17.2 percent in 1999 and 25.3 percent in 1998 — much higher returns than those secured by the mainland subsidiaries of the dominant developers in Hong Kong.

Discussion

The following discussion of the pattern of developer profitability relates it to the changing market environment and business strategies, and focuses on three emerging phenomena. First, the state-owned property developers, although typically more long-standing and larger, are losing both market share and profits to the newer entrants. Second, Hong Kong developers have not been able to extract from the China market profits as substantial as those from their Hong Kong-based businesses. Third, the fierce competition in China's property market is breeding an emerging group of local developers who, despite their small company scale and limited financial resources, are able to outperform many of the state-owned development companies and Hong Kong developers.

State-Owned Development Companies
Disadvantages

In an increasingly competitive market system, the difficulties faced by the state-owned property development companies originated in their corporate backgrounds and institutional structures. These companies were designated by the state as the city builders — established to take on the historical mission of implementing urban development. Many of them were run as administrative work units (*shiye danwei*) rather than as enterprises (*qiye*). They did not function autonomously, but remained a part of the bureaucratic machinery, accountable to their superior departments and ministries. Although these *shiye danwei* had the mandate to operate for profit, their corporate background dictated that they were subject to instructions issued from above, and they invariably had to shoulder certain administrative functions. Often required by local government authorities to implement particular social projects or infrastructure development, or to take on sponsorships of various sorts, these development companies found it very challenging to keep cost reduction and profit maximization as their primary corporate objectives.

Achieving the policy goal of severing the link between these developers and the state machinery was slow and difficult. Many government departments were reluctant to relinquish their leverage on property and housing production. Some state-owned developers wanted government protection and were thus unwilling to stand on their own feet. These development companies operated in accordance with bureaucratic instructions rather than in response to market signals. With the backing of the state banks, some developers simply ignored market conditions. For example, their determination to make winning bids at land auctions resulted in unrealistically high land prices that distorted the land markets and deterred other, rational investors.

Soft budgets explain why property production was carried out even when vacancy rates were high. To maintain the book value of their assets, companies declined to cut prices and thereby boost property sales. Fulfillment of production targets, rather than profit levels, was sometimes the primary criterion for staff performance appraisals. Furthermore, some developers focused on high-profit, high-risk and up-market properties such as offices, commercial centers and luxury housing. This strategy simply disregarded the lack of market demand for such properties in the cities.

Advantages

These problems notwithstanding, state-owned development companies made huge profits from property production during the 1980s and early 1990s, largely because of the uniquely immature market conditions and government subsidies. Developed space was in extremely short supply at that time; the market was, basically, a seller's market. Work units were both the major "wholesale" buyers of completed housing products and the primary distributors of those products to their employees at subsidized prices. There was no direct relationship between the purchasing power of work units and affordability for the end users. Housing demand was extremely inelastic because housing allocation was not fully marketized — the ability of work units to purchase housing depended on direct capital injections from the state.

Moreover, many projects were developed on administratively allocated land, further reducing development costs to the state-owned developers. To increase housing production, many local governments encouraged the sale of such land for profit-making property ventures, offering favorable policy treatment in the imposition of land premiums upon redevelopment.[23] Many state-owned developers

---

23 The leasing of administratively allocated land requires compliance with the following conditions: (1) current users have obtained the land use certificates from the government and are the legal owners/occupiers of the subject site and property; (2) existing users have signed a valid sale and transfer document with the buyers; (3) the buyers pay the land premiums to the government for the transfer of the land use rights; and (4) the buyers have completed the sale agreements with the government (Shi 1998, 92).

with ample land assets could thus reap enormous profits simply from engaging in land speculation, rather than from actually developing property. Although regulations allowed local governments to take back land that remained idle and undeveloped for a given period of time, this policy has only very recently been enforced.[24] All these distortions in the land and housing markets sustained both high housing prices and high profits for the state-owned developers, giving them the ability to expand their development scale and operations.

Another force that supported the early growth of these developers, according to Che (2000, 146), was related to the struggle between the interests of the central government and those of the localities. Initially, local governments used property development as a means to fund urban development. Later on, many local government departments rushed to set up property development companies as subsidiary operating branches, so as to evade tax submission to the central government. Revenue and income from land and property development became part of the real and financial assets of these companies. Indeed, property development became the cash cow of the government bureaucracy and the income from it was deemed extra-budgetary revenue.

· Because local governments also wished to extract funds from these companies, they tended to support their profiteering operations. This support might be in the form of favorable policies or direct intervention that resulted in market distortion and unfair competition. For instance, various administrative obstacles might be imposed to discourage development companies originating in other Chinese provinces from entering into the local market. To nurture their own companies, local governments might agree to speed up land allocation, sell land at extremely low land premiums, grant land administratively (with no land charge) or approve unreasonable requests.

Most of the land parcels were allocated to these developers through negotiation rather than tender or auction. According to a survey of land sales of 269 parcels between 1987 and 1990 in 21 major Chinese cities, more than 95 percent of the parcels were sold through negotiation, while auction sales constituted 1 percent. According to a study by the China Academy of Social Sciences published in 1994, the average land sale premium was approximately 1,768 yuan per square meter through auction, 1,554 yuan per square meter through tender and only 92 yuan per square meter through negotiation (Luo 1999, 79–80). These low land use premiums encouraged developers to hoard huge amounts of urban land. Land premiums

---

24 According to the regulations, the local governments can impose, on developers, a penalty fee (*tudi xianzhifei*) of no more than 20 percent of the land premium if project construction does not commence within the first year of land leasing. If the land remains idle after two years of leasing, the governments can take back the land without compensation to the developers. However, the regulations also stipulate that waivers could be granted if the construction delays are caused by uncontrollable forces, predevelopment works or government procedures (Liu et al. 1995, 91–92).

comprised only a small portion of the total revenues to the local government, making it difficult to fund urban development through the leasing of land.

Current Status

With the growing maturity of the Chinese property market and the reduction in government support, the competitive advantage of state-owned developers is on the wane. Many cities have abolished the allocation of development land by negotiation; developers now have to secure land through open, competitive means. Land premiums on development sites can now better reflect market value. Elimination of welfare housing allocation has strengthened the role of individual buyers as the key purchasers in the housing market, with the result that housing prices must now be linked with affordability. The growing number of private developers has expanded consumer choice. Under the macroeconomic austerity policy, the tightening of bank credit by the central government since 1993 (to cool down the rapidly inflating economy) further worked to harden the budget constraints of state-owned developers.[25] However, corporate torpidity, as a result of the public-sector institutional structure and mentality, has constrained these companies from reacting positively to the changing competitive environment, thereby contributing to the decline in their market dominance.

Hong Kong Development Companies

Many Hong Kong developers are capital-rich, experienced in land development and well connected with senior Chinese government officials.[26] However, despite their financial and business capabilities and their political connections, they have not achieved the level of profitability from their mainland China projects that they have from projects in their home territory. The explanation may lie in the failure of these developers to adapt their business strategies and practices to the mainland context. The attempt to transplant to the mainland market the approach that worked so well in Hong Kong was ill-conceived. Hong Kong developers assumed that mainland Chinese communities would share the Hong Kong fondness for real estate and landed property. The euphoric growth of the property market in Hong Kong before 1997 reinforced their conviction that, thanks to this deep-rooted Chinese cultural attribute, real estate prices would never fall. The idea that the "Hong Kong property miracle" would be replicated on mainland soil as China's economy took off became unquestioned dogma. Thus, Hong Kong developers did not question the appropriateness of their "strategy transplant."

---

25 To alleviate the funding constraints in the mid-1990s, the first real estate company in socialist China, the Beijing Urban Construction Company, resolved to expand its income sources through the sale of completed properties to individuals and external investors as well as to work units, and the sale of serviced land to other investors.

26 The arguments here are drawn from Tang and Liu (2001).

That strategy made land acquisition a top priority. With land costs in China so low, decisions about land purchases on the mainland were made perhaps less prudently than would have been the case for more expensive purchases in Hong Kong. Developers acquired huge amounts of land, hoping that it would eventually appreciate in value. This approach failed for several reasons.

First, local Chinese authorities were never frugal in the supply of land; as a consequence, land prices often did not appreciate at expected rates.[27] Second, continued improvements in urban transportation infrastructure (roads, highways and railways) vastly increased the availability of competing sites, thereby reducing the price differential between core and peripheral development locations. The "scarcity" of urban land was more perception than fact. Third, unlike in Hong Kong, capital gains from land value appreciation were subject to various forms of government taxation in China; consequently, land speculation for foreign-based investors incurred high transaction costs.[28]

Generally speaking, Hong Kong developers did not trust the value of market research and detailed feasibility studies, because this was not the way they made money at home. Many Hong Kong developers entered the China market based upon gut feeling and herd instincts. Predevelopment analysis of the mainland environment was totally inadequate. The China property market has been extremely price sensitive and highly competitive: in Guangzhou, for example, there are now more than 300 private housing development projects on the market. Hong Kong developers also underestimated the fierceness of local competition, failing to understand thoroughly the local markets and to respond to market changes.

Further, most Hong Kong developers did not assign their best and most trustworthy management staff to their China offices, because mainland projects accounted for only a small portion of developers' overall portfolios before 1997. This approach slowed the decision-making process considerably, because many decisions had to be referred back to headquarters in Hong Kong. Without administrative fiat, Hong Kong managers in offices in China have had difficulty commanding the respect and confidence of local governments and their local partners. The cooperation of these two stakeholders is paramount in resolving problems in complex development

---

27 The designation of special economic development zones (SEDZs) *(jingji kaifaqu)* illustrates vividly the oversupply of land by local governments. Between the State Council's approval of this concept in 1986 and the mid-1990s, more than 1,400 SEDZs comprising some 800 square kilometers were established in various provinces and cities. Only about one-fifth of the land area of those SEDZs was actually developed and utilized. This caused the central government to retire the designation of nearly 1,000 SEDZs (Zhang 1995, 40–41).

28 The tax rates for capital gains from land transactions vary across cities. For example, in Zhuhai rates ranged between 20 percent and 80 percent of the gain. Huizhou's rates were between 40 percent and 70 percent. For Guangzhou and Shenzhen, rates ranged between 15 percent and 50 percent, and between 40 percent and 100 percent, respectively (Qiu and Shi 1993, 96). Property developers were charged with numerous fees and taxes. In Guangzhou, development levies could comprise between 30 and 40 percent of total development costs (Luo 1999, 79). Another survey indicated that government taxes and administrative fees constituted 24 percent, 18 percent and 16 percent of the property prices in Guangzhou, Beijing and Shanghai, respectively (Bianweihui 1997, 54).

processes. The failure to recruit mainland staff to fill top management positions impedes efficient communication within offices in China, weakens the quality of their management and increases office overhead costs. This situation may also explain why projects of Hong Kong developers have often been plagued by considerably higher costs than have those of their mainland counterparts.

In mainland China, foreign developers have to form joint ventures with local enterprises in undertaking land development projects. Most Hong Kong developers have paid inadequate attention to the importance and repercussions of identifying the right local partners (Liu 1998). It is not unusual for Hong Kong developers to rush hastily into relationships with Chinese counterparts based on the naïve priority of capturing prime development sites. It often turns out that the synergy of the two parties is just as important to project success as site characteristics.

Good local partners are valuable business companions: they can help interpret local policies sensibly and can negotiate with local authorities to achieve substantial cost savings. Land premiums can often be negotiated down, and payments can sometimes be divided and phased. In Guangzhou, for instance, assessment of the land premium for a particular site is based on various adjustments to the benchmark land premiums.[29] These adjustments, which can be quite arbitrary and subjective, may lead to huge variations in payable land premiums, ranging from -20 percent to +90 percent of benchmark levels for commercial land, and from -65 percent to +60 percent for housing land (Zhou et al. 1992, 112–113). Without local partners to help them through these minefields, foreign-based developers have to meet all the stated (that is, official) requirements and the resultant higher costs make it difficult for them to compete in the local market.

Because Hong Kong developers are land-oriented rather than development-oriented, they have failed to pay enough attention to project management and construction efficiency. On the mainland, this approach is problematic because land costs constitute a relatively small portion of development costs, compared with construction costs. As a result, construction delays and cost overruns are the two leading reasons for project failure.[30] In most cases, Hong Kong developers have maintained good social connections (*guanxi*) with top leaders — mayors, for

---

29 In Guangzhou, the formula for assessment of the payable land premium is as follows:

  Payable land premium = benchmark land premium x (1 + locational index + site prosperity index + transport accessibility index + municipal service index + population density index + special factor 1) x plot ratio index x site orientation index x lease period index x special factor 2 (Zhou et al. 1992, 111)

30 Another reason is that the construction industry in China is monopolized by the state-owned contractor companies, which are under direct supervision of the Construction Commission. In other words, these companies do not necessarily owe total allegiance to the developers. To comply with the instructions of the Construction Commission, they can "legally" revise the construction costs in their favor from time to time. The building cost quotations are not binding, and there are no cost ceilings imposed on the property development projects. Negotiation between developers and contractors in determining tender prices is a common practice. All these factors have created enormous difficulties for developers in controlling overall project construction costs.

example — of city governments. Even so, that guanxi has to be supplemented by tangible business accomplishments and project outcomes. Project delays and trouble-making during the course of development are bound to jeopardize social ties. Furthermore, the increasing fragmentation of local government control in mainland China implies that guanxi with the top echelon of the bureaucracy is no longer enough; good guanxi must be maintained at all levels. Government bureaucracy can create obstacles throughout the land development process and lead to the ultimate project failure.[31]

Emergence of Successful Mainland Developers

At present, the property development industry in China is pluralistic and competitive. The existing market structure is subject to transformation, however, as the market becomes increasingly mature and urban land supply and bank lending become increasingly regularized. To avoid the predicaments of oversupply, like those of the late 1990s, many local governments are determined to step up their controls on land supply. In Guangzhou, for instance, between September 1997 and December 1999, the government took back, in nine phases, about 250 parcels of land with a total area of some 3.5 square kilometers. The government also announced that, from 1 August 1998 onward, all business-related land would be allocated through tender or auction, all piecemeal allocation of urban sites abandoned, and the conversion of administratively allocated land for other business uses restricted.

Severe competition is expected to weed out the weaker and less-efficient developers. Successful local mainland developers are emerging, although many describe the current circumstances of market competition as a "warlord era." Market concentration is likely to increase with increasing mergers and acquisitions. In light of the high property vacancy rate in many key Chinese cities, efficient Chinese developers have to focus on both product-price competition and development-cost control. Acquisition of prime sites and cultivation of good guanxi with public

---

31 Many government authorities are involved in monitoring property development in China. First and foremost, proposed development projects must be approved and registered (*lixiang*) with the State Planning Commission (*guojia jihua weiyuanhui*), which examines the investment scale and the economic and social impacts on the city. Because this commission is not primarily interested in the physical aspects of development, its approval may generate difficulties for the technical departments. The conflicts between the construction and land administration departments are noteworthy. In Chinese cities, implementation of property development is under the dual control of the Construction Commission (*jianshi weiyuanhui*) and the State Land Administration Bureau (*guotuju*). This administrative structure is an outcome of historical legacy. The predecessor of the Construction Commission, the National Construction and Engineering Bureau (*guojia jiangong zongju*), was set up in 1979 with responsibility for urban housing construction and management. It was restructured in 1987 as the Ministry of Construction. On the other hand, the State Land Administration Bureau was set up in 1986 by the State Council to assume responsibility for urban land management, allocation and disposal. Its primary mission was to halt the massive conversion of agricultural land for urban uses at that time (Chen 1993). Such division of responsibility between construction and land administration was based on an outmoded concept in separating property (*fangdichan*) into buildings (*fangchan*) and land (*dichan*). Their overlapping yet independent authorities constitute a major obstacle for many developers. To address this problem, Guangzhou, for instance, has sought to combine the two authorities into a Housing Management and Land Administration Bureau.

authorities are no longer adequate bases of successful competition. Developers have to embrace an all-fronts business strategy that considers a whole range of issues such as property marketing, building technology, property management and product image.

At present, these developers are invariably privately operated, nonstate companies. Generally, they employ small staffs, which reduces overhead; office bosses are more decisive and authoritative; and their local teams work hard to achieve promotions and other benefits. The business objective is clear: maximizing investment return. To achieve this end, their management style is flexible and dynamic. Fierce market competition compels these developers to collect firsthand market information through frequent site visits and local liaisons; this better positions them to respond to market changes. By closely monitoring the market environment, they can adjust construction programs and marketing strategies as necessary.

Successful developers have to be capable developer-contractors, rather than just land speculators. Based on clever sourcing and procurement of local supplies, they are able to undercut other competitors by producing properties of comparable quality but at much lower cost. Compared with foreign-based investors, these developers are well versed in local culture and market preferences; hence, they can target particular market segments effectively. They are well acquainted with the gray areas of development control regulations in mainland China, and endeavor to lobby local authorities to interpret them to their advantage.

Conclusions

In mainland China, property developers were designated as the city builders — established in the early 1980s as the agents of local governments for implementing comprehensive urban development programs and master plans. At the outset, most property development companies were state-owned enterprises whose corporate mission was to make use of land and property development opportunities to resolve the deficiency in municipal development funds, to provide needed urban infrastructure and to expand housing production. A combination of favorable government support and unique market circumstances sustained the rapid expansion of these state-owned developers, providing them lucrative investment returns. Ample profits attracted an influx of foreign-based investors, mostly from Hong Kong, and spurred the emergence of local private development capital. The mushrooming of property development companies has increased the supply of urban floor space and achieved dramatic improvement in city landscapes within a short period of time. Further, it has intensified market competition and has inevitably caused the restructuring of the real estate industry in mainland China.

This chapter has identified three distinct categories of property developers: state-owned developers, Hong Kong-based developers and local private developers. Table 5 summarizes the key characteristics linking corporate background and strategy

TABLE 5

Comparison of Different Types of Property Developers in Mainland China

Types of Property Developers

	State-Owned Companies	Hong Kong Developers	Nonstate-Owned Companies
Major Ownership	State	Private	Collective Private
Financial Capacity	Soft budget constraints	Hard budget constraints Strong financial capability	Hard budget constraints Weak financial capability
Competitive Advantage	Access to cheap land Government policy support	Finance Experience Political connection	Market sensitivity Flexible management Profit orientation Staff commitment
Weakness	Bureaucracy Government intervention Overstaffing Slow decisions Production orientation	Lack of understanding of local market Slow decisions Poor staff commitment High overhead costs Poor construction management	Small scale operations High leverage Speculative and project based
Performance and Prospects	Large-scale production Loss of market share Loss of profit margin	Highly unsatisfactory returns Inability to expand market share	High fatality rate Gains in market share Variable profitability

SOURCE: Constructed by authors

with competitive performance. According to Bao (1995, 8), China's transition from a centrally planned economy to a socialist market economy would be expected to cause five concurrent paradigm shifts in terms of organizational management:

- from implementing state directives to responding to market changes;
- from following the master plans to self-management;
- from relying on government funding ("iron rice bowls") to self-financing;
- from state monopoly to multiple forms of ownership; and
- from separate empire building to consolidated market competition.

Against this background, this study argues that the state-owned developers have largely fulfilled their historical missions as city builders, housing suppliers and infrastructure providers. They are now losing market share to the more competitive private developers, who are more efficient and sensitive to market needs. In an increasingly open economy the fittest survive, leading to growing market concentration. On the other hand, the experience of Hong Kong developers on the mainland demonstrates that financial strength does not necessarily guarantee project success. Although China's entry into the World Trade Organization is expected to attract more foreign capital, successful property development remains a local business. Thus, local mainland property developers who can survive the current market onslaughts will be able to grow further by attracting foreign capital. Despite the inexorable rise in cross-border capital and business activities, globalization of the property development process has not yet taken root in the Chinese soil.

Acknowledgments

We acknowledge the support of Z. W. Li, H. C. He and Kristy Pan of Pearl River-Hang Cheong Consultants in providing assistance to this study.

References

Asian Wall Street Journal. 1992. China property lures Hong Kong firms — Manufacturers exploit contacts to gain foothold in high-stakes market. 23 July.

Ball, M. 1994. The 1980s property boom. *Environment and Planning A* 26:671–695.

———. 1996 *Housing and construction: A troubled relationship.* Bristol, UK: JRF Policy Press.

Bao, Zonghua, ed. 1995. *Management decision making of property enterprises.* Beijing: China Urban Press.

Bi, Baode. 1994. *China's property market study.* Beijing: People's University Press.

Bianweihui, Nianjian, ed. 1997. *China real estate yearbook.* Beijing: State Planning Press.

Bramley, G., W. Bartlett, and C. Lambert. 1995. *Planning, the market and private house-building.* London: UCL Press.

Carroll, B. W. 1988. Market concentration in a geographically segmented market: House-building in Ontario, 1978–1984. *Canadian Public Policy — Analyse de Politiques* 3:295–306.

Cartier, Carolyn. 2001. "Zone fever," the arable land debate, and real estate speculation: China's evolving land use regime and its geographical contradictions. *Journal of Contemporary China* 10(28):445–469.

Chan, R. C. K., and C. Gu. 1996. Forms of metropolitan development in Guangzhou municipal city. In *Economic and social development in South China,* S. MacPherson and J. Y. S. Cheng, eds., 281–305. Cheltenham, UK: Edward Elgar.

Che, Jianghong. 2000. *Study of institutional setup of real estate market.* Shanghai: Shanghai Academy of Social Sciences Press.

Chen, Xiao-ping. 1993. *Handbook of China's real estate management.* Beijing: China University of Politics and Laws Press.

China INFOBANK. 2001. China statistical digest [summarized]. http://www.china infobank.com.

China Yahoo Finance. 2000. Publicly listed China company database. http:/cn.biz.yahoo. com/p/.

Coakley, J. 1994. The integration of property and financial markets. *Environment and Planning A* 26:697–713.

Ding, Leiyun. 1999. *Real estate development.* Beijing: China Construction Press.

E-finet.com. 2001. *Hong Kong publicly listed company information 2001.* 2 vols. Hong Kong: Lee Yuan Publisher.

Fainstein, S. S. 1994. *The city builders: Property, politics, and planning in London and New York.* Oxford, UK: Blackwell.

Feagin, J. R. 1982. Urban real estate speculation in the United States: Implications for social science and urban planning. *International Journal of Urban and Regional Research* 6(1):35–60.

———. 1983. *The urban real estate game.* Englewood Cliffs, NJ: Prentice-Hall.

———. 1998. *The new urban paradigm: Critical perspectives on the city.* Lanham, MD: Rowman & Littlefield Publishers.

Fisher, J. C. 1962. Planning the city of socialist man. *Journal of the American Institute of Planners* 28:251–265.

Gaubatz, P. R. 1995. Urban transformation in post-Mao China: Impacts of the reform era on China's urban form. In *Urban spaces in contemporary China: The potential for autonomy and community in post-Mao China,* D. S. Davis, R. Kraus, B. Naughton, and E. J. Perry, eds., 28–60. Washington, DC: Woodrow Wilson Center Press; New York: Cambridge University Press.

GD-HK Information Daily. 2001. Several Guangzhou developers are applying for public listing. 29 April.

Goldberg, M. A. 1985. *The Chinese connection: Getting plugged in to Pacific Rim real estate, trade, and capital markets.* Vancouver, BC: University of British Columbia Press.

———. 1993. Physical and economic transformation of Pacific Asia. In *Pacific Asia in the 21st century: Geographical and development perspectives,* Y.-m. Yeung, ed., 25–46. Hong Kong: Chinese University Press.

Gottdiener, M. 1977. *Planned sprawl: Private and public interests in suburbia.* Beverly Hills, CA: Sage Publications, Inc.

Gottdiener, M., C. C. Collins, and D. R. Dickens. 1999. *Las Vegas: The social production of an all-American city.* Malden, MA: Blackwell.

Haila, A. 1999a. City building in the East and West: United States, Europe, Hong Kong and Singapore. *Cities* 16(4):259–267.

———. 1999b. Why is Shanghai building a giant speculative property bubble? *International Journal of Urban and Regional Research* 23(3):583–588.

———. 2000. Real estate in global cities: Singapore and Hong Kong as property states. *Urban Studies* 37(12):2241–2256.

Harvey, D. 1989. From managerialism to entrepreneurialism: The transformation in urban governance in late capitalism. *Geografiska annaler* 71B:3–17.

Healey, P. 1991. Urban regeneration and the development industry. *Regional Studies* 25(2):97–110.

———. 1994. Urban policy and property development: The institutional relations of real-estate development in an old industrial region. *Environment and Planning A*: 26(2):177–198.

Healey, P., and R. Nabarro, eds. 1990. *Land and property development in a changing context.* Aldershot, UK: Gower.

Healey, P., S. Davoudi, M. O'Toole, S. Tavsandoglu, and D. Usher, eds. 1992. *Rebuilding the city: Property-led urban regeneration.* London: E & FN Spon.

Jefferson, G. H., and T. G. Rawski. 1994. Enterprise reform in Chinese industry. *Journal of Economic Perspective* 8(2):47–70.

King, R. J. 1988. Urban design in capitalist society. *Society and Space* 6:445–474.

Knox, P. L. 1991. The restless urban landscape: Economic and sociocultural change and the transformation of metropolitan Washington, DC. *Annals of the Association of American Geographers* 81(2):181–209.

Leitner, H. 1990. Cities in pursuit of economic growth: The local state as entrepreneur. *Political Geography Quarterly* 9:146–170.

Li, Peng. 1986. Closing Speech of the National Meeting on Urban Construction, 30 November. Reprinted in Proceedings of National Meetings on Urban Construction, 1988:20–36. Beijing: China Environmental Sciences Press.

Liu, S.-c. 1998. Letters to the editor: Entering China. *Harvard Business Review* (Jan.-Feb.):192.

Liu, Shenyou, Qilong Wang, and Shijiang Zhou. 1995. *Real estate management*. Shanghai: Shanghai People's Press.

Lo, C. P. 1987. Socialist ideology and urban strategies in China. *Urban Geography* 8(5): 440–458.

———. 1994. Economic reforms and socialist city structure: A case study of Guangzhou, China. *Urban Geography* 1994(15):128–149.

Lo, C. P., C. W. Pannell, and R. Welch. 1977. Land use changes and city planning in Shenyang and Canton. *The Geographical Review* 67(3):268–283.

Logan, John R. 1993. Cycles and trends in the globalisation of real estate. In *The restless urban landscape*, P. L. Knox, ed., 35–54. Englewood Cliffs, NJ: Prentice-Hall.

Logan, John R., and H. L. Molotch. 1987. *Urban fortunes: The political economy of place*. Berkeley, CA: University of California Press.

Luo, Longchang. 1999. *Macro-management of real estate industry*. Beijing: Economic Management Press.

Mera, Koichi, and Bertrand Renaud, eds. 2000. *Asia's financial crisis and the role of real estate*. New York: M. E. Sharpe.

Mitchell, Katharyne, and Kris Olds. 2000. Chinese business networks and the globalization of property markets in the Pacific Rim. In *Globalization of Chinese business firms*, H. W. C. Yeung and K. Olds, eds., 195–219. London: Macmillan.

Molotch, H. L. 1976. The city as a growth machine: Toward a political economy of place. *American Journal of Sociology* 82(2):309–332.

———. 1993. The political economy of growth machines. *Journal of Urban Affairs* 15(1):29–53.

Nicol, C., and A. Hooper. 1999. Contemporary change and the housebuilding industry: Concentration and standardization in production. *Housing Studies* 14(1):57–76.

Peiser, R. 1990. Who plans America? Planners or developers? *Journal of the American Planning Association* 56(4):496–503.

Perkins, D. 1994. Completing China's move to the market. *Journal of Economic Perspectives* 8(2):23–46.

Qiu, Chuangying, and Jinling Shi. 1993. *Handbook of property investment in Pearl River Delta Region*. Guangzhou: Guangzhou People's Press.

Ross, M. C., and K. T. Rosen. 1992. The great China land rush. *The China Business Review* 19(6):51–52.

Rydin, Y. 1984. The struggle for housing land: A case of confused interests. *Policy and Politics* 12(4):431–446.

Shen, Hui. 2000. *Theory and practice of real estate laws*. Shanghai: Tongji University Press.

Shi, Haijun. 1998. *Comprehensive real estate development*. 2nd ed. Dalian: Dalian University of Science and Engineering Press.

State Statistical Bureau. 1998. *China statistical yearbook.* Beijing: China Statistical Publishing House.

———. 1999. *China statistical yearbook.* Beijing: China Statistical Publishing House.

Sum, N.-l. 1999. Asian "crisis" and "Greater China": The bursting of the "property bubble" and its impact on urban regimes. Paper presented at Conference on the Future of Chinese Cities: A Research Agenda for the 21st Century, 28–31 July, Shanghai, China.

Tang, B.-s., and S.-c. Liu. 2001. Curses of arrogance: Why have Hong Kong developers been outperformed by local competitors in mainland China? Paper presented at RC21 Conference of International Sociological Association Research Committee on Urban and Regional Development, 15–17 June, Amsterdam, Holland.

Thrift, N. 1986. The internationalisation of producer services and the integration of the Pacific Basin property market. In *Multinationals and the restructuring of the world economy,* M. Taylor and N. J. Thrift, eds., 142–192. London; Dover, NH: Croom Helm.

———. 1987. The fixers: The urban geography of international commercial capital. In *Global restructuring and territorial development,* J. Henderson and M. Castells, eds., 203–233. London: Sage.

Tse, Raymond Y.-c. 2000. China: A real estate boom in a protected transition economy. In *Asia's financial crisis and the role of real estate,* Koichi Mera and Bertrand Renaud, eds., 159–182. New York: M. E. Sharpe.

Wang, Xianjin. 1995. *Implementation and development of land-use reforms in China.* Hong Kong Association for the Advancement of Real Estate and Construction Technology. Symposium on real estate, 9–16. Beijing: China People's University Press.

Weiss, M. A. 1987. *The rise of the community builders: The American real estate industry and urban land planning.* New York: Columbia University Press.

World Bank. 1990. *China: Between plan and market.* Washington, DC: World Bank.

———. 1993. *China: Urban land management in an emerging market economy.* Washington, DC: World Bank.

———. 1999. *World development indicators.* Washington, DC: World Bank.

———. 2000. Country data: China at a glance. 30 August. http://www.worldbank.org /data/countrydata/countrydata.html.

Wu, F. 1995a. Changes in the urban spatial structure of a Chinese city in the midst of economic reforms: A case study of Guangzhou. Ph.D. diss., University of Hong Kong.

———. 1995b. Urban processes in the face of China's transition to a socialist market economy. *Environment and Planning C: Government and Policy* 13(2):159–177.

———. 1997. Urban restructuring in China's emerging market economy: Towards a framework for analysis. *International Journal of Urban and Regional Research* 21(4):640–663.

———. 1998a. Polycentric urban development and land-use change in a transitional economy: The case of Guangzhou. *Environment and Planning A* 30(8):1077–1100.

———. 1998b. The new structure of building provision and the transformation of the urban landscape in metropolitan Guangzhou, PRC. *Urban Studies* 35(2):259–283.

———. 1999a. Real estate development and the transformation of urban space in China's transitional economy, with special reference to Shanghai. Paper presented at Conference on the Future of Chinese Cities: A Research Agenda for the 21st Century, 28–31 July, Shanghai, China.

———. 1999b. The "game" of landed-property production and capital circulation in China's transitional market, with reference to Shanghai. *Environment and Planning A* 31(10):1757–1771.

Wu, F., and A. G. O. Yeh. 1999. Urban spatial structure in a transitional economy: The case of Guangzhou, China. *Journal of the American Planning Association* 65(4):377–394.

Xu, X. 1985. Guangzhou: China's southern gateway. In *Chinese cities: The growth of the metropolis since 1949,* V. F. S. Sit, ed., 167–187. Oxford, UK; New York: Oxford University Press.

Xu, J. 1999. The changing role of land use planning in the land development process in Chinese cities: The case of Guangzhou. Paper presented at Conference on the Future of Chinese Cities: A Research Agenda for the 21st Century, 28–31 July, Shanghai, China.

Yang, Qing, and Xiaohai He. 1998. *Real estate development and management.* Chengdu: Southwest University of Financial Policy Press.

Ye, Rutang. 1986. Ministerial Speech in the National Meeting on Urban Construction. Ministry of Urban and Rural Construction and Environmental Protection, 25 November. Reprinted in Proceedings of National Meetings on Urban Construction, 1988:20–36. Beijing: China Environmental Sciences Press.

Yeh, A. G. O., and F. Wu. 1996. The new land development process and urban development in Chinese cities. *International Journal of Urban and Regional Research* 20(2): 330–353.

———. 1999. The transformation of the urban planning system in China from a centrally planned to a transitional economy. *Progress in Planning* 51(3):167–252.

Yusuf, S., and W. Wu. 1997. *The dynamics of urban growth in three Chinese cities.* Oxford, UK; New York: Oxford University Press.

Zhang, Qingyun, and Meilin Zhang. 1993. *Real estate management practices.* Beijing: Economic Management Press.

Zhang, Suiqiang. 1995. *China's real estate investment inside-out.* Hong Kong: Mingbao Newspaper Press.

Zhang, Yuanduan. 1991. *Handbook of China's real estate.* Harbin: Heilongjiang Science and Technology Press.

Zhao, Zhuowen, and Liuqing Chen. 2000. *Guangzhou real estate review 2000.* Guangzhou: Guangzhou Provincial Map Publication Press.

Zhongguo Jingyingbao. 2001. Public listing of development companies should maximize strengths and eliminate weaknesses. 29 April.

Zhou, Zhiping, Zhangxi Chen, and Zijie Zou. 1992. *A thorough review of China's real estate industry.* Hong Kong: Joint Publishing (HK) Co. Ltd.

Zhu, J. 1999a. The formation of a market-oriented local property development industry in transitional China: A Shenzhen case study. *Environment and Planning A* 31(10): 1839–1856.

———. 1999b. Local growth coalition: The context and implications of China's gradualist urban land reforms. *International Journal of Urban and Regional Research* 23(3):534–548.

Chapter 10

Socialism, Market Reform and Neighborhood Inequality in Urban China

JOHN R. LOGAN

The current market reforms in China have markedly improved the standard of living for many Chinese. At the same time, there is evidence of growing inequality in many dimensions of urban life — new patterns of advantage and disadvantage that affect the way people understand their own situations. Income inequality is perhaps the most evident, because cash income played a relatively small role in quality of life during the socialist era. Today, people have more money, more commodities are allocated to people at market prices and there are much greater disparities between rich and poor (Bian and Logan 1996).

It is in this overall context of commodification that changes are now taking place in the stratification of urban neighborhoods. Szelenyi (1996, 287) has made the excellent point that socialism produced distinctive urban patterns, not necessarily according to the designs of socialist planners, but due broadly to "the consequences of the abolition of private property, of the monopoly of state ownership of the means of production, and of the redistributive, centrally planned character of the economic system." These patterns included under-urbanization (relative to capitalist systems at the same industrial level), low levels of spatial differentiation, unusually low density in central areas and few signs of socially marginal groups. Old neighborhoods were allowed to deteriorate, while new construction was focused in high-density developments in peripheral zones.

It is natural, then, to wonder whether market reform will result in new spatial forms: perhaps more rapid urbanization, greater spatial differentiation, restructuring of core urban zones or new concentrations of marginal social groups. Data are still insufficient for an analysis of the trends in spatial structure of the new Chinese city, and perhaps it is even too early for recent changes to show their full impact. This study reviews certain features of spatial inequality in the city of Tianjin relatively

early in the reform period (1988–1993), and formulates questions about the development process that will affect the future direction and consequences of change.
The following premises inform the analysis.

- Neighborhood inequalities at the start of the 1990s were, in part, an inheritance from the presocialist era, and more precisely, in the coastal cities, were
  a legacy of foreign enclaves that divided Chinese cities. These inequalities
  were reproduced after 1949 as Chinese of higher social standing and political
  authority occupied the former foreign zones.

- Inequalities also derived from decisions by municipal authorities about the
  location of infrastructure and service investment. There is the potential, in a
  socialist system, for such allocations to be driven by the hierarchy of
  influence and authority, with significant repercussions for the quality of life
  in different neighborhoods.

- The emerging neighborhood pattern of the reform era will be, to some extent,
  a function of market forces. Especially evident may be disparities in ability to
  purchase or rent housing, efforts by real estate developers and speculators to
  profit from redevelopment activities, and the impact of newly unleashed
  migration to cities. But these market forces continue to operate in a bureaucratic context, and the direction and magnitude of their influence are affected
  by the decisions made by government agencies and work units.

The empirical analysis is based on the case of Tianjin, and uses census information from 1990, a survey of subdistrict leaders in 1993 by the Tianjin Academy of
Social Science, and 1988 health statistics from a World Bank study of environmental health in the city (Bertaud and Young 1991). Patterns almost certainly vary widely
across the country, but the results for this city are generally in line with what has
been observed elsewhere. This case study is used not to draw specific conclusions
for all of urban China, but rather to provide a starting point for future research.

Social Status Segregation

A fundamental trait of the built environment is its persistent quality. Many urban
neighborhoods retain their character — as areas of large homes for the affluent or
high-density apartments for the working class, as mixed industrial/residential zones
or as purely residential areas — for a century or more. Even the composition of a
neighborhood's residents has a persistent quality, because those who leave tend to
be replaced by others similar to them.

For this reason, a high degree of continuity in the urban mosaic, even in revolutionary periods, ought not be surprising. Specifically, the People's Republic of China
inherited a deeply entrenched pattern of social and spatial differentiation in 1950, and
strong traces of the pre-revolutionary pattern could still be found in the 1990s.

Figure 1 shows schematically the social status configuration of the city in 1990. The indicator is the proportion of each subdistrict's population with post-secondary education. In a Western setting, it would be assumed that education is a proxy for income, and that housing costs are the mechanism by which people are segregated by income. In the Chinese case, however, income was a minor factor; more important were position and influence, and education is intended to capture these characteristics.

The oldest parts of the city, at the north end of the Nan Kai District and including most of the Hong Qiao District in the northwest, and much of He Bei and

FIGURE 1
Tianjin: Proportion of Population with Post-Secondary Education
by Subdistrict, 1990

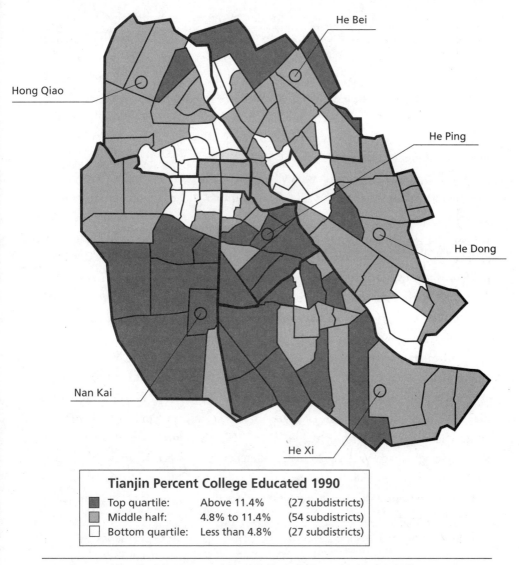

Tianjin Percent College Educated 1990

■	Top quartile:	Above 11.4%	(27 subdistricts)
▨	Middle half:	4.8% to 11.4%	(54 subdistricts)
☐	Bottom quartile:	Less than 4.8%	(27 subdistricts)

SOURCE: Constructed by author from 1990 census data provided by the Tianjin Municipal Statistical Office

He Dong along the east, are clearly low-status neighborhoods. In the oldest sections, people still lived along narrow alleys, often without running water and reliant on public toilets and baths (though such neighborhoods have been targets of urban renewal in subsequent years). Most residences in these sections are not the same houses of a century before, but are structures that reproduce the dimensions and facilities of homes from that period. Farther out from the center are zones of working-class apartment buildings constructed after 1950.

The He Ping District near the center of the city — the former foreign zone of Tianjin — figures among the highest-status neighborhoods. The apartment buildings and single-family houses in this area have generally been subdivided since 1950. But the neighborhood retains a prestigious reputation, and some original structures are now the offices of venerable institutions or foreign companies, or homes of high-ranking officials.

There are also high-status areas with more recent roots. Relatively new wealthy areas extend southward from He Ping into the Nan Kai and He Xi districts. Though not shown on the map, a new subdistrict is being developed in the southwest as a zone of high-cost (that is, market-priced) housing of excellent quality. Chinese geographers have identified the emergent social segregation of affluent households — those capable of purchasing luxury housing in gentrified neighborhoods within cities or prestigious suburban developments — as a key source of urban inequality (Gu and Liu 2002).

Another phenomenon, which only began to emerge in Tianjin by 1990, is massive migration from the countryside. China's urban "floating population" reached 80–100 million by 1995 (Chan 1996); Chen and Parish (1996) estimate it to have ranged from 10 percent of the population in Harbin to 30 percent in Guangzhou at that time. Most migrants cannot legally live in cities due to China's restrictive residential registration system (hukou). They are concentrated primarily in the urban fringe, where they are able to rent private housing from peasants in outlying towns and villages, though new mechanisms exist whereby more affluent migrants can maintain residence rights in the city proper (Wu 2002).

Some migrants live in urban villages — former villages that have been enveloped by urban development but retain their official rural status. Gu and Liu (2002) count as many as 100 such enclaves in Beijing; Fan and Taubmann (2002) document as many as 15 around Shanghai. In many of these cases, settlements have a strong ethnic character, concentrating migrants from a specific province or district. Names like Zhejiang Village or Anhui Village, referencing the place of origin, are widely used despite having no official status. Hence, in urban China as in market societies throughout the world, large-scale migration results in new patterns of social inequality and spatial segregation.

These observations can be summarized in a measure of residential segregation — the commonly used index of dissimilarity (D). The value of this index ranges from 0 to 100 and indicates the proportion of members of one group that would have to be relocated to areas in which they are under-represented in order to achieve an even distribution across areas. Based on differences across subdistricts in the distribution of people with post-secondary education and those with less education, D has a value of .40 in Tianjin. This represents about the same degree of segregation of college-educated and non-college-educated people as is the case in New York and Los Angeles (across comparable spatial units). Given that these U.S. metropolitan regions are well known for their entrenched spatial inequalities, based largely on class inequalities and racial/ethnic divisions, it is remarkable that a Chinese city, where neither of these factors was central to residential patterns in the early 1990s, nevertheless had the same outcome.

Inequalities in Public Infrastructure

Another aspect of neighborhood quality is the availability of public services and infrastructure, which can reinforce the status of advantaged neighborhoods or raise the status of less-privileged ones.

Following up on a pilot study of neighborhood inequality in Tianjin (Logan and Bian 1993), the 1993 subdistrict survey provided information on many aspects of public infrastructure at the subdistrict level. An index composed of four key indicators was used.

(1) **Public school facilities.** The municipal school system in 1993 was organized hierarchically, so that some schools were considered "leading" schools (run by the municipal government rather than by the subdistrict) and benefited from better facilities and more qualified teaching staff. But only some subdistricts were favored in this way. The indicator, which ranges from 0 to 4, represents the number of elementary schools, middle schools and high schools in the subdistrict that are managed at the city level.

(2) **Preschool facilities.** Though some kind of childcare facility was generally available in all subdistricts, another indicator is the number of nurseries and kindergartens in the area managed at the city level; the indicator ranges from 0 to 8.

(3) **Parks and gardens.** Another indicator is the quality of the physical environment, as reflected in the number of public parks and street gardens in the subdistrict. This indicator ranges from 0 to 14.

(4) **Piped gas.** Finally, in a city where people historically relied on coal burners for heat and cooking, the availability of piped gas in some zones but not in others is a significant indicator of neighborhood quality both in terms of convenience and air quality. The indicator is the percentage of housing units with piped gas, ranging from 0 to 99 percent.

TABLE 1

Correlations Among Indicators of Public Services to Subdistricts, 1993

	Leading Schools	Preschools	Parks
(1) Leading schools			
(2) City-run preschools	0.40**		
(3) Parks and gardens	0.18	0.04**	
(4) Piped gas	0.06	0.23*	0.40**

* statistically significant at the .05 level; ** statistically significant at the .01 level

SOURCE: Data compiled by author

It is quite natural to find some variation in all of these indicators. What is more interesting is the systematic geographic overlap among them. Location of city-level schools is not much related to availability of piped gas (r = .06) or parks/gardens (.18), but the correlations among all other pairs of indicators are between .23 and .40 and are statistically significant (see Table 1). This pattern suggests that the various types of service inequalities are cumulative — that a neighborhood poorly served in one dimension is likely to be poorly served in another. In fact, creating a scale of city services (by adding together the standardized scores on each of the four indicators) yields an index with a statistically significant reliability coefficient of .59.

These neighborhood disparities in Tianjin are mapped in Figure 2. There is a fairly clear distance gradient, with the least-served areas near the city center, including the more central subdistricts in the Hong Qiao, He Bei, and He Dong Districts. The best-served areas are found in Nan Kai and parts of the He Ping and He Xi Districts, in the southern part of the city. There is noticeable overlap with the education demographic of these zones: the majority of high-status subdistricts in the south also are in the top quartile of public services, and the majority of low-status subdistricts in the older central areas are in the bottom quartile of services. In fact, the correlation between education and public services is a very substantial .68, suggesting that the neighborhood with the more highly educated population nearly always enjoys higher-quality collective resources (see Table 2).

TABLE 2

Correlations Among Education, Public Services, Institutional Authority and Public Health, 1993

	College Education	Services	Authority
Public services scale	.60**		
Institutional authority scale	.52**	.45**	
Tuberculosis rate	-.40**	-.24*	-.24*

* statistically significant at the .05 level; ** statistically significant at the .01 level

SOURCE: Education data from 1990 census, provided by the Tianjin Municipal Statistical Office; public services and institutional authority data compiled by author; tuberculosis data from Bertaud and Young (1991)

FIGURE 2
Tianjin: Neighborhood Quality in Terms of Public Services by Subdistrict, 1993

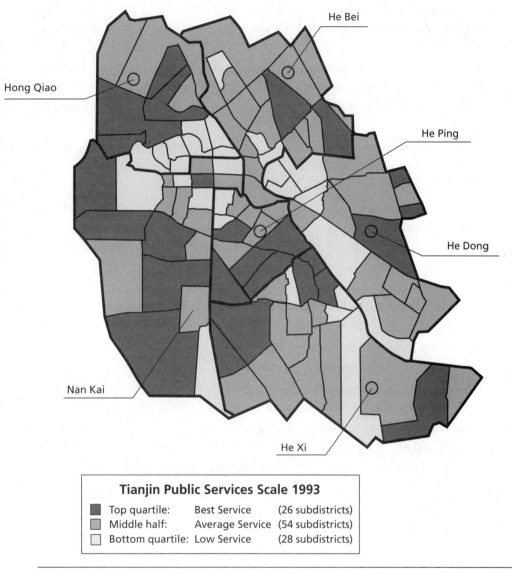

Tianjin Public Services Scale 1993		
Top quartile:	Best Service	(26 subdistricts)
Middle half:	Average Service	(54 subdistricts)
Bottom quartile:	Low Service	(28 subdistricts)

SOURCE: Data compiled by author

Neighborhood Quality and Authority in the Socialist System

What accounts for the fact that some parts of the city seem to be systematically favored over others, even at a point in time (the early 1990s) when market reform was only recently underway? Are there features of Chinese socialism that could help to account for the pattern?

In their approach to the same question as it applies to income inequality, sociologists have employed the theoretical distinction between a redistributive system based on authority (characteristic of the socialist period), and a market system based on financial resources. There are, of course, disagreements about the extent to which market forces have been unleashed in the current period. But there is broad consensus that income inequality was previously closely associated with the ranking of people in the established hierarchy of work units, government offices and political standing. Much research has demonstrated that party members had privileged access to better jobs and higher incomes, and that people employed by higher-ranked work units also earned higher wages (Zhou 2000; Bian and Logan 1996). Similar results have been reported for access to housing (Walder 1992; Logan, Bian, and Bian 1999).

Is the provision of neighborhood public services similarly correlated with the authority and political influence of the neighborhood? There are some useful potential indicators of whether a subdistrict has "strong connections" (guanxi) in municipal government.

(1) **Development zones.** Some subdistricts had been designated as foreign investment development zones, slated to attract new resources from outside the country during the 1990s. The access to foreign currency that such subdistricts would gain was a highly prized resource.

(2) **High-status office locations.** Some subdistricts were the locations of administrative offices for institutions with very high levels of political authority, such as the municipal party committee, municipal government or the Standing Committee of the People's Congress of Tianjin.

(3) **High-status housing compounds.** Equally relevant may be whether the same institutions had their housing compounds within the subdistrict.

(4) **Municipal bureau housing compounds.** There are many forms of municipal public housing, but being the location of housing for employees at the municipal bureau level — that is, of the highest rank — is distinctive.

The majority (79 percent) of Tianjin's subdistricts had none of these potential sources or indicators of influence in 1993. Only one had as many as three; the remainder (21 percent) had one or two. An institutional influence scale — comprising these four indicators, equally weighted — has a reliability coefficient of .50. Figure 2 shows how the more-privileged zones are distributed around the city.

The pattern is already familiar. These areas fall almost entirely within the He Ping, Nan Kai, and He Xi Districts south of the city center. Again this result can be summarized in correlation coefficients. The correlation between institutional influence and public services is .45; between institutional influence and educational composition it is even higher, at .52 (see Table 2).

Living and Dying in the City

One final step in analyzing the geography of opportunity is an evaluation of the relationship between these inequalities and more direct indicators of residents'

FIGURE 3

Tianjin: Neighborhood Health Represented by Tuberculosis Incidence, 1986–1988

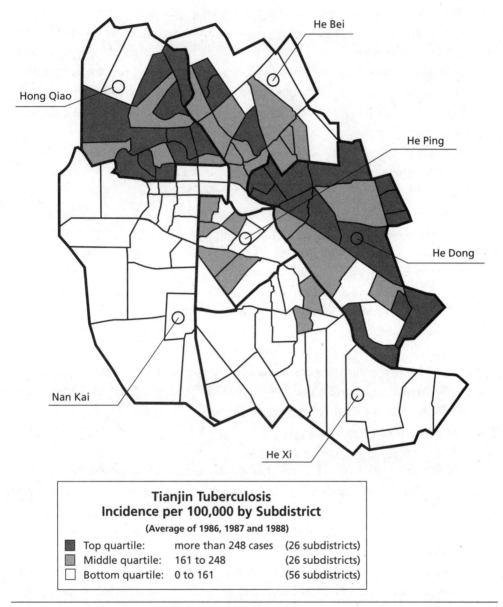

Hong Qiao

He Bei

He Ping

He Dong

Nan Kai

He Xi

**Tianjin Tuberculosis
Incidence per 100,000 by Subdistrict**
(Average of 1986, 1987 and 1988)

■	Top quartile:	more than 248 cases	(26 subdistricts)
▨	Middle quartile:	161 to 248	(26 subdistricts)
□	Bottom quartile:	0 to 161	(56 subdistricts)

SOURCE: Constructed by author using data from Bertaud and Young (1991)

quality of life. The "hierarchy of place" can have many repercussions for the people tied to particular locations, especially in the quality of public education for their children, personal safety at home and on the street, access to jobs and healthfulness of their living environment. Data on this last dimension — specifically, the incidence of tuberculosis (the three-year average for 1986–1988) — are presented in Figure 3.

The authors of the study from which these health data are drawn argue (in their explanation of the importance of this topic) that "in prosperous cities of East Asia, the variance in the distribution of environmental quality is a better indicator of poverty than variations in cash income" (Bertaud and Young 1991, 8). They describe tuberculosis, in particular, as a barometer of social welfare in the developing world, given its association with overcrowding, inadequate sunlight, substandard ventilation and poor hygiene. Before 1949 tuberculosis was one of the leading causes of death in China, and it is still the leading cause of death due to infectious disease. Preventive services and control measures such as chemotherapy and chemoprophylaxis were previously provided at no cost at tuberculosis control stations. At the completion of this study in 1991 they were available on a fee-for-service basis, making affordability an issue for those infected with the disease.

Subdistrict data are provided as rates per 100,000 people for the years 1986–1988; the three-year average is used here. One important limitation is that these data do not reflect Tianjin's temporary population, estimated by the authors at one million or more at that time (compared with the registered urban population of about 3.5 million). Inequalities, therefore, are presumably understated.

Results are summarized in Figure 3, showing "the dramatic environmental inequity that exists in an otherwise prosperous and well-managed city" (Bertaud and Young 1991, 2). Not only tuberculosis, but also cancer and infant mortality, tend to be higher in the northwestern and eastern parts of the city — in the Hong Qiao, He Bei, and He Dong districts. Health risks are possibly related to industrial air pollution or unhealthful workplace conditions for those employed in and living near those areas. By contrast, most of the Nan Kai, He Ping, and He Xi districts have below-average rates of tuberculosis.

Once again, the map is familiar. The overlap among all four main indicators of relative advantage or disadvantage described here is summarized in the correlations in Table 2. Incidence of tuberculosis is most closely associated with residents' educational level ($r = - .40$). But correlations with both level of public services and institutional authority are statistically significant and moderately high (both are $- .24$).

This is the key empirical finding of this study: not only are there various kinds of inequalities among neighborhoods, but these disparities turn out to be closely linked to one another. This pattern holds for a point early in the reform period — well before efforts to introduce commodity housing, and when massive urban redevelopment efforts had only just begun (and were temporarily stalled from 1989–1990). Neighborhood inequality in urban China, at least in Tianjin, can be described in terms of the same multidimensional stratification of places that occurs in market societies — except that it has been produced under socialism. The outcome is a familiar one, but the process that has created it is less so.

Neighborhood Quality, Social Status and Political Influence

What are the sources of this urban stratification? In most Western market societies, the manner in which the housing market segregates more affluent, college-educated people from others is easily understood. New housing is built to varying standards and prices, geared to different social groups. Older housing loses value if it becomes less desirable, and so is passed down the class ladder when more affluent people find better opportunities elsewhere.

In addition, there are evident mechanisms through which higher-status residents are more capable of protecting their neighborhoods — by using their informal contacts with public officials when possible, and resorting to collective political action when necessary. In a representative democratic system, some voices speak more loudly than do others. Hence, once an area's social standing has become established through market mechanisms, it tends to be perpetuated through political influence.

This process extends, of course, to demands for excellent schools and other services. In the U.S. metropolis, high-status residents typically do not pay higher taxes to gain better services. The more common approach is to shelter themselves from the service needs of other groups by drawing jurisdictional boundaries around their suburbs and school districts, ensuring that their resources will be taxed only for their own benefit. Though there are also some redistributive mechanisms of public financing, these are recognized as halfway measures. More consequentially, the concepts of home rule and local control are deployed as ideological supports for this system, and proposals for stronger redistributive policies are attacked for promoting class war. Cumulative patterns of advantage and disadvantage in the U.S. city are common, overlaying class segregation with public-service disparities.

In comparison with these processes that are familiar to researchers in the U.S., what are the processes through which the stratification of places in Tianjin is created and maintained? One process found in most cities around the world is historical continuity: some of today's "best" and "worst" neighborhoods were already recognized as such in the early twentieth century. Detailed historical research, perhaps based on hukou registration, would be needed to document the population changes that took place after 1950 in Tianjin. Certainly the desirable sections in the older part of the city became more densely settled as large housing units were subdivided, and it is unlikely that the new tenants settled themselves randomly.

But even in a city where people had few opportunities to move (and those in better areas had little incentive to do so), there continued to be some reshuffling of population around the city in subsequent years. The earthquake suffered by Tianjin in 1976 required considerable reconstruction and reassignment of residents. New residential zones were built up, especially after 1978, and the methods of housing allocation (through work units and the municipal housing office) remained unchanged up to the time of our subdistrict survey. This fact identifies another topic for research: how higher- and lower-status people were allocated to different parts of the city. If, as past research has shown, party membership, occupational level and work-unit rank all affected the size and quality of the housing people were allocated through this system, did similar factors also affect the location of that housing?

Research on these topics may elucidate how the residential segregation between higher- and lower-status people was maintained and reproduced under socialism. The role of public infrastructure is another factor in this analysis.

Infrastructure Decisions Under Socialism

In dealing with infrastructure, it is useful to ask how obvious disparities were interpreted by the public officials who were responsible for investment decisions. In light of the strong official commitment to egalitarian norms, a uniform standard applied to all subdistricts might have been expected. However, the hierarchy — from ordinary schools or preschools supported by district governments to leading schools managed by the municipality — is perfectly consistent with the bureaucratic structure of both government and work units. Under Chinese socialism, institutions and individuals with higher bureaucratic rank were legitimately afforded higher priority for many sorts of resources.

Routine patterns of decision making contributed to some inequalities. For example, the relative absence of parks and gardens outside historically affluent zones is due, in part, to the fact that these facilities were viewed by official policy with some suspicion during the socialist era, and few new investments were made in them after 1950. Some long-standing inequalities persisted because insufficient funds were available to implement long-term plans that could equalize conditions — such as the overdue, citywide, piped-gas network. Bertaud and Young (1991) comment, with respect to health services, that it was routine for analyses of needs and plans for future investments to be based on global indicators rather than on neighborhood variations, so that the issue of deficits in particular neighborhoods was not considered in the planning process.

What else may help explain the particular spatial pattern that clustered public facilities in higher-status residential zones? If public officials were responding to the desires of the residents, how were those desires expressed and acted upon? One hypothesis is that, within the range of their discretion, officials responded to back-channel pressures, or anticipated those pressures, or made choices that best served their own neighborhoods.

Such abuse of bureaucratic discretion was reinforced by the influence of key institutions. It is not surprising that those institutions with the greatest discretion would select the most desirable locations for their offices and housing compounds, or that subdistricts containing these institutions would be well placed to compete for public resources. By the 1980s it was clear to local officials that political reforms would increase the autonomy of district and subdistrict governments, while giving them greater responsibility for raising the revenues needed to maintain services. For a subdistrict at that time, designation as a foreign investment zone was perhaps as tangible a victory as landing a leading school would have been in the previous decade. The hierarchy of subdistricts that had developed by the time of our 1993 study was not only a legacy of the pre-revolutionary period, but also, and perhaps more significant, a product of allocation processes and decision making under socialism.

Looking to the Future: Impacts of Market Reform

This analysis would be merely an exercise in urban history, except that interpretation of recent history so often is the best guide to anticipating the future. What is the future of neighborhood inequality in urban China? The standard hypothesis is that introduction of a real estate market, as a mechanism of determining the use of urban space, will sharply increase inequalities. In particular, two powerful trends would be expected to exacerbate these inequalities in the near future: urban renewal and suburbanization (Gaubatz 1999; Lin 1999; Wu and Yeh 1999; Zhu 2000).

The urban renewal trend is a potent force, tapping the economic value of central locations through redevelopment of inner-city areas. It has the potential to displace working class populations from areas where they have been concentrated, much like urban renewal in the U.S. did during the 1950–1970 period. Structural changes in the real estate industry now make it possible for private investors and a wide range of Chinese institutions to speculate in city-center projects, including both office complexes and high-priced commodity apartment buildings. Many long-time residents already have been relocated to new developments on the fringes of cities. But many new buildings remain unoccupied, suggesting that demand may have been overestimated. If the middle class grows more slowly than predicted, or if it does not buy into commodity housing in the inner city, eventually these empty structures will need to be converted to other uses — presumably, to meet the housing needs of less-affluent urbanites.

Because China has little experience with bankruptcy in the real estate sector, how it may respond to such a contraction in the market is not obvious. Will it allow the real estate market to experience cycles of growth and depression, with the concomitant oscillations of property values, as is common in the U.S.? Or, alternatively, will China follow the Japanese (or Hong Kong) example of manipulating public policy in the interest of current investors (by protecting them from having to acknowledge the loss in value of their real estate portfolios)? Given these unknowns, it is not yet clear whether inner cities will experience the widespread gentrification that appeared to be underway in the 1990s, or whether a countertrend of conversion of high-quality housing to lower-rent occupancy will emerge.

A second powerful trend is the expansion of suburban zones (Zhou and Ma 2000). The overall expansion of metropolitan economies is the principal driver of decentralization, though another important factor is the growth-promoting activities of outlying districts and county governments. The process of competition between jurisdictions — all eager to reap the potential rewards of economic growth within their borders — leads to high levels of public investment in infrastructure. Consequently, the low cost of building on the periphery can be exploited without losing too much in access to transportation and utilities.

What is less clear is whether the new suburban zones will be able to support the school, health care and transportation infrastructure needed for their burgeoning residential populations. Overbuilding in the suburbs could have consequences different from overbuilding in the central city. In these suburban zones, the system for providing essential services must be built almost entirely anew, creating the potential for large numbers of people generating private solutions for collective problems.

Will living on the edge of the city become synonymous with a higher quality of life and services, as was certainly true in the early years of residential suburbanization in the U.S.? That is, will the current inequalities within the city be compounded by a suburban wall around it? Or will suburban China catch up quickly to the emergent reality of the U.S. suburbs, in which many exurban communities are becoming the new ghettos of the metropolis? The answers depend largely on the ability of planners to link more closely the rate of development with the creation of livable neighborhoods.

Another trend that has drawn much attention is the explosive growth of migration. Because current institutional arrangements so strongly restrict the residential options of the floating population, it now settles predominantly in villages within suburban counties, with smaller enclaves within the city limits (Ma and Biao 1998). Researchers have identified the convergence of interests between migrants needing shelter, and village residents and public officials looking to profit from higher rents and tax revenues drawn from the migrant population. The substantial component of suburban growth due to migration suggests that the most likely future is one of a highly differentiated suburban ring in which migrant enclaves are interspersed with, but clearly separated from, residential zones intended for the urban working class or more-affluent people.

Yet, public policy can significantly affect this future. Easing of restrictions on where the floating population can live — more effectively, erasing the legal distinctions between the rights and prerogatives of people with urban hukous and those without — would likely stimulate significant shifts in migrants' locational patterns.

During 2001 authorities in many towns and smaller cities initiated reforms in the hukou system, and it appeared that the central government might take similar action. Wherever housing is oldest and least desirable (and this is potentially as likely to be found in city neighborhoods as in the suburbs), there is the potential for development of migrant zones.

Just as some aspects of class segregation and disparity in public infrastructure were inherited by the socialist city from the prior capitalist and neocolonial ones, so also is there a legacy of socialist patterns for the reform period. Results of urban restructuring in the new century must be interpreted carefully, so as not to conflate the persistence of an established pattern with what is truly a function of new market forces. And of course, there must be points at which the two merge to create unexpected outcomes.

These shifts must be seen as developments from within the system, rather than as massive transformations of the system. New forces unleashed by the market will be coupled with old interests and methods. What will be most persistent is the constellation of social status, political influence and public service quality that has marked Chinese cities through the last century, regardless of the political or economic regime. The locations of the most favored and most disadvantaged neighborhoods may shift, and so may the processes that create and reproduce them. But the same kinds of spatial disparities that we see today will very likely be visible 10 years from now, and will continue to demand our attention.

References

Bertaud, Alain, and Mary Young. 1991. *Geographical pattern of environmental health in Tianjin, China: The development of an environmental health database.* Working paper #13. New York: World Bank, Urban Development Division.

Bian, Yanjie, and John R. Logan. 1996. Market transition and the persistence of power: The changing stratification system in urban China. *American Sociological Review* 61: 739–758.

Chan, Kam Wing. 1996. Internal migration in China: An introductory overview. *Chinese Environment and Development* 7:3–13.

Chen, Xiangming, and William Parish. 1996. Urbanization in China: Reassessing an evolving model. In *The urban transformation of the developing world*, Josef Gugler, ed., 61–90. Oxford, UK; New York: Oxford University Press.

Fan, Jie, and Wolfgang Taubmann. 2002. Migrant enclaves in large Chinese cities. In *The new Chinese city: Globalization and market reform*, John R. Logan, ed., 183–197. London: Blackwell.

Gaubatz, Piper. 1999. China's urban transformation: patterns and processes of morphological change in Beijing, Shanghai and Guangzhou. *Urban Studies* 36:1495–1521.

Gu, Chaolin, and Haiyong Liu. 2002. Social polarization and segregation in Beijing. In *The new Chinese city: Globalization and market reform*, John R. Logan, ed., 183–197. London: Blackwell.

Lin, G. C. S. 1999. State policy and spatial restructuring in post-reform China, 1978–1995. *International Journal of Urban and Regional Research* 23(4):670–696.

Logan, John R., and Yanjie Bian. 1993. Inequalities in access to community resources in a Chinese city. *Social Forces* 72(Dec.):555–576.

Logan, John R., Yanjie Bian, and Fuqin Bian. 1999. Housing inequality in urban China in the 1990s. *International Journal of Urban and Regional Research* 23(March):7–25.

Ma, Laurence J. C., and Xiang Biao. 1998. Native place, migration and the emergence of peasant enclaves in Beijing. *The China Quarterly* 155(Sept.):546–581.

Szelenyi, Ivan. 1996. Cities under socialism — And after. In *Cities after socialism: Urban and regional change and conflict in post-socialist societies*, Gregory Andrusz, Michael Harloe, and Ivan Szelenyi, eds., 286–317. Cambridge, MA: Blackwell Publishers.

Walder, Andrew G. 1992. Property rights and stratification in socialist redistributive economies. *American Sociological Review* 57:524–539.

Wu, Fulong, and A. G. O. Yeh. 1999. Urban spatial structure in a transitional economy: The case of Guangzhou, China. *Journal of the American Planning Association* 65:377–394.

Wu, Weiping. 2002. Temporary migrants in Shanghai: Housing and settlement patterns. In *The new Chinese city: Globalization and market reform*, John R. Logan, ed., 212–226. London: Blackwell.

Zhou, Xueguang. 2000. Economic transformation and income inequality in urban China: Evidence from panel data. *American Journal of Sociology* 105:1135–1174.

Zhou, Yixing, and Laurence J. C. Ma. 2000. Economic restructuring and suburbanization in China. *Urban Geography* 21:205–236.

Zhu, Jieming. 2000. Urban physical development in transition to market: The case of China as a transitional economy. *Urban Affairs Review* 36:178–196.

Conclusion

CHENGRI DING AND YAN SONG

As China's land and housing markets have emerged to serve the needs of the country's developing socialist market economy, the study of those markets has become a focus of attention both within the country and overseas. The initial impetus for this book was the advancement of knowledge about the current state of China's land and housing markets, remaining problems in their operation and impacts, and potential development trends. A subsequent motivation, based on understanding those remaining, unresolved issues, has been to investigate possible solutions. Though the country's land and housing policy reforms have taken shape and scored initial successes, its land and housing markets are still in an early stage of development — one that will last for quite a long time. During this period there are, and will be, many problems whose solutions will challenge scholars, practitioners and policy makers.

China's land market already exhibits great vitality and potential strength. Prior to reform nearly all land was owned by collectives or by the state, and by 1976 private property rights had virtually disappeared and land transactions had been banned. Modern land reforms began in the mid-1980s, when market structure began to be established incrementally through the sale and transfer of land use rights. Under this regime, land ownership remains with the state to minimize social and political conflicts. The emerging land market, however, provides Chinese residents and businesses with greater economic freedom. The active transaction of land use rights has facilitated the development of the real estate industry, enhanced the fiscal capacity of local governments and accelerated the advancement of market socialism.

Despite its advantages, the system has created many new challenges. Price distortion prevails in the land use rights market due to acquisition by state-owned enterprises through administrative channels rather than through the market. Government officials generally have neglected long-term plans for land leasing, casting doubt on the sustainability of the system. Finally, the government lacks the ability to capture its share of rents as they increase over time. As capital investments and location premiums rise, these losses could be substantial.

China also has made great progress in reforming its housing sector. Prior to reform it had practiced a housing allocation system befitting a planned economy. The government or working units provided housing for employees, and there was grave underinvestment in new housing construction. Since then, reforms have provided strong motivation and institutional guarantees for housing development. Through the sale of publicly owned housing and the replacement of administrative allocation of housing with home ownership, the proportion of commercial housing purchased by individuals has grown, since the 1990s, from 0 to more than 93 percent, and the average per capita living space of urban residents has increased from 7 square meters in 1978 to 21 square meters by 2001. The fundamental role of the market in the distribution of housing resources is now well established.

Despite these successes, many Chinese still live in housing deemed inadequate by Western standards, and critical financial institutions necessary for a healthy housing market remain underdeveloped. Furthermore, the rapid rise of commercial housing undermines the long-standing tradition in which access to affordable housing is an integral part of the social contract. The challenges of solving the housing problems of low- and medium-income urban residents and of enhancing social equity have become critical.

The legacy of China's socialist history is an important explanation for the persistence of these problems in the country's land and housing markets. Since 1949 the principles of central planning and state ownership have permeated political and institutional systems as well as individual conduct. Implementation of market instruments is not a part of either the institutional memory or the current aspirations of Chinese governments. These historical factors contribute to institutional constraints on, and political and cultural attitudes toward, land and housing policy reforms.

This book has sought to add an important dimension to the existing literature on land and housing policy reforms by presenting current aspects of China's land and housing markets, past determinants of the present situation and potential trends for land and housing development. The historical legacy, however, explicates the current policy reform landscape only to a point. Overcoming the imperfections in China's land and housing markets — the presence of multiple markets, the fragmentation of institutions, the irrationality of bureaucratic behaviors and the fickleness of political interference — is the key to breaking through to the next stage in the formation of more rational and mature markets. The authors represented in this book have taken the first steps toward that next stage in suggesting innovative, market-oriented mechanisms. It is important to reiterate those suggestions that offer opportunities to improve current practices in four key areas.

First, to abolish multiple land and housing markets it is imperative to phase out the involvement of administrative units in those markets. Adoption of more explicit land use planning laws and regulations can effect better management of land transactions and restraints on the excessive use of bureaucratic power. Enhancing public scrutiny of land use decisions and land transactions can further prevent corruption and other problems intrinsic to multiple land markets.

Second, while it is essential to preserve farmland in the course of rapid urbanization, there are many ongoing debates about the principle and efficacy of China's "no net loss of agricultural land" approach. New strategies — ones that take into account comparative advantages in economic development and agricultural production, and other indigenous factors — are more effective in preserving farmland, securing food resources and stimulating local economic development.

Third, though land acquisition is instrumental in ensuring land supply for urban development, there are many problems associated with current acquisition processes. Innovative land acquisition approaches represent an alternative. For example, land supply can be increased by involving affected farmers in land development projects and by redeveloping urban brownfield areas.

Fourth, the improvement of quality of life through land and housing policy reforms should not neglect the dimension of social justice. It is notable and worrying that China's current trends toward suburbanization, urban renewal and redevelopment are creating inequities in the spatial distribution of various population groups.

In all of these areas further academic research is needed to provide better theoretical grounding for practice. Two particular arenas for future work have emerged. First is the need for more effective instruments for reforming land and housing policies. For example, case studies analyzing the benefits and costs of China's current "no net loss of agricultural land" approach can greatly facilitate the ongoing debate about that strategy. Pilot projects implementing land and housing information systems can be used to monitor those markets, to provide knowledge that can ease the tension between land demand and supply, and to maintain market stability by avoiding overheated investment. Second, impact analyses are needed across a wide spectrum of sectors in China's land and housing markets. For example, how do emerging land markets shape land development patterns and the internal structure of cities? Are the markets contributing to urban sprawl? What are the effects of vigorous housing markets on all segments of the population?

In summary, China's land and housing markets — along with comprehensive economic reforms in many other sectors — are clearly moving, slowly but progressively, toward a full-fledged market system. Opportunities abound for both scholars and practitioners to engage in the ongoing debates and grapple with the challenges of China's continuing economic growth and urbanization.

Glossary

Acronyms and Initialisms

BFPR
Basic Farmland Protection Regulation

CBD
central business district

CCP
Chinese Communist Party

CERCLA
The Comprehensive Environmental Response, Compensation, and Liability Act of 1980 (U.S.)

CMLR
China Ministry of Land and Resources

CPL
City Planning Law

ETDZ
Economic and Technological Development Zones

FDI
foreign direct investment

GDP
gross domestic product

GNP
gross national product

IT
information technology

LAL
Land Administration Law

LMB
Land Management Bureau

LUR
land use rights system

MCI
multiple cropping index

NPC
National People's Congress

PRC
People's Republic of China

RMB
Renminbi, or "People's Currency"; the basic unit of Chinese currency

ROE
return on equity

SEDZ
special economic development zone

SEZ
special economic zone

SLAB
State Land Administrative Bureau

UPB
Urban Planning Bureau

General Terms

administrative allocation
the assignment of land use rights without payment for them

benchmark land premium
a reference price used to guide the setting of fees paid, by individuals
or cooperatives to government, to acquire land use rights

benchmark land use rights price system
a system developed in the early 1990s to guide the granting and transferring
of land use rights

brownfield
abandoned, idle or underused industrial and commercial real property where
expansion or redevelopment is complicated by real or perceived environmental
contamination (based on U.S. EPA definition)

carrot-and-stick approach
an approach that simultaneously offers incentives for compliance and threatens
consequences for noncompliance

Central Committee of the Chinese Communist Party
the highest authority within the Chinese Communist Party; the Central
Committee has about 300 members and nominally appoints the *politburo*
of the Communist Party of China

comprehensive urban development
development that includes unified planning, rational layout and supportive
infrastructure, all by local government

danwei
a work unit in the Chinese socioeconomic system, originally responsible
for both the production activities and the housing of its members

double-track system
the coexistence of the market system and the older, allocative system
for acquiring land use rights

dual land market
another term for the "double-track system," above

dynamic equilibrium of farmland
maintenance of a consistent amount of cultivated land through various legal
mechanisms; see "zero net loss of farmland"

floor-area ratio
the ratio of the area of a structure to the land area on which the structure is built

hidden land markets
illegal and/or unofficial commerce in land use and property rights; also known as invisible land markets

home rule
self-government or limited autonomy in internal affairs by a dependent unit

Hong Kong property miracle
euphoric growth of the property market in Hong Kong prior to 1997

housing filtering process
the process in which middle-income households assume housing previously inhabited by more affluent households that have migrated to newly constructed housing

index of dissimilarity
an assigned value that represents the proportion of members of one group that would have to be relocated to areas in which they are under-represented in order to achieve an even distribution of groups across areas

iron rice bowl
a tenure system in which a worker, once hired, is automatically granted tenure

land markets
the transaction, leasing, mortgaging or renting of land use rights

>   **primary**
>   the sale of land use rights from the state to individual or corporate users

>   **secondary**
>   the transaction, leasing or renting of land use rights (from an entity that has acquired the rights of use, or of disposal of property) to other users

multiple cropping index
the ratio between the total area sown in a year and the area of cultivated land

National Congress of the Chinese Communist Party
a political convention, held approximately once every five years, that sets up middle- and long-range socioeconomic development goals and elects members of the Central Committee of the Chinese Communist Party

National People's Congress
literally, the "Pan-Nation Congress of the People's Representatives," the highest
legislative body in the People's Republic of China; approximately 3,000 delegates
are elected by the provincial people's congresses for terms of five years

one-child policy
a national policy permitting each family to have only one child

open-door policy
a national policy that allows inflows of foreign capital, establishment of joint
ventures and foreign direct investment in China, ending the country's isolation
from world markets, particularly from the West

rice bowl
center of agricultural production that provides the bulk of the nation's food

self-build housing
informal housing not legally permitted by local governments and usually failing
to meet building standards

shortage economy
an economic condition in which potential demand exceeds supply and a rationing
system is used to allocate goods

socialist market with Chinese characteristics
the mixed system of civil law and market-economic and administrative control
mechanisms aimed at development of efficient private initiative and effective
state protection of society and the environment

spatial differentiation
the difference in the type and intensity of land use in a spatial context,
measurable by population density and capital density

spatial disequilibrium
all other things being equal, the variance (depending on housing consumption,
neighborhood amenities, transporatation costs, etc.) in level of utilities infrastructure between different locations in a city

spatial inequality
the variance of earned income with location

special economic development zones
designated areas that enjoy special treatment by economic policies (such as tax
exemptions, loan allowances, reduced tariffs on imported or exported goods, etc.)
not enjoyed by other areas

spontaneous land use conversion

the phenomenon of farmers constructing housing, without approval from local governments, to reap profits from real estate markets

State Council

the chief civilian administrative body of the People's Republic of China; its membership (of approximately 50) is chaired by the Premier and contains the heads of each governmental department and agency

urban village

a former village that has been enveloped by urban development but retains its official rural status

zero net loss of farmland

or "no net loss," mandated by the 1998 LAL; see "dynamic equilibrium of farmland," above

Currency and Equivalences

(exchange rates as of 10 January 2005)

HK$

Hong Kong dollars (HKD)

HK$1 = US$ .128
HK$1 = 1.06 RMB (yuan/CNY)

RMB

Renminbi ("People's Currency"), the basic unit of Chinese currency; also, yuan (CNY)

1 RMB (yuan/CNY) = HK$ .941
1 RMB (yuan/CNY) = US$ .121

US$

United States dollars (USD)

US$1 = 8.28 RMB (yuan/CNY)
US$1 = HK$ 7.79

Land Area and Equivalences

acre

the standard unit of area for measuring real estate in English-speaking countries

1 acre = .405 ha

1 acre = (slightly more than) 6 mu

hectare (ha)

the customary metric unit of land area; one hectare is a square hectometer, that is, the area of a square that is 100 meters on each side

1 ha = 15 mu (approximately)

1 ha = 2.471 acres

mu

the basic, traditional measure of land area in the Chinese surveying system

1 mu = .0667 (or 1/15) hectare

1 mu = .165 (or slightly less than 1/6) acre

Index

acid rain, 149–150
administrative allocation system, 40;
    amount of land in, 46 (figure); black
    market and, 46–48; definition of, 255;
    effects of, 55, 249; land acquisition
    and, 43–45; land leasing and, 218n23;
    land prices and, 47–48; land use
    restructuring and, 52; replacement of,
    250; spontaneous land use conversions
    and, 48–51; state-owned property
    developers and, 205–206, 218–220.
    See also dual land market
affiliation, theory of, 62–63
agricultural land. *See* farmland
agriculture: economic reforms introduced
    in, 201; geographic variations in,
    92–94; history of, 107; restructuring
    of, 100, 103–106, 112–113, 112n24
aiju housing, 193
air pollution, 148–149, 149n1, 152;
    environmental protection standards
    for, 154
alienation, right of, 66
Ambient Air Quality Standard (GB3095-
    1996), 154
Anhui Province, 149
aquifers, contamination of, 150
arable land, 91–92. *See also* farmland
Ash, Robert, 97n12, 111n22, 112n24,
    115n27
Asian economic crisis, 195–196, 200
Atkin, Lord, 151

banks, housing financing and, 175
Basic Farmland Protection Regulation
    (BFPR): farmland acquisition/
    conversion regulated by, 18, 146;
    negative effects of, 24–25; urban

villages created by, 23, 27
Beijing: commercial housing in, 189–190;
    housing reform in, 173; industrial
    land use patterns in, 11n1; industrial
    restructuring in, 148; land develop-
    ment costs in, 28–29; land prices
    in, 17n12, 25; revenue generation
    for infrastructure improvement
    in, 52; secondary land markets in, 76,
    76n19; 3321 Project in, 149n1; unsafe
    residential property in, 143; vacancy rates
    in, 193. *See also* Shangdi Information
    Technology Industrial Zone
Beijing Tianhong Baoye, 212
Beijing Urban Construction Co. Ltd.,
    213, 220n25
benchmark land premium, 222, 255
benchmark land use rights price system,
    16–17, 28, 29 (table), 255
Bertaud, Alain, 244
BFPR. *See* Basic Farmland Protection
    Regulation
"big leap" (political movement), 9–10
black market, 2, 46–48, 47 (figure),
    50–51, 54–55
BOT (build, operate and transfer), 51–52,
    51n1
Brown, Lester, 18, 94n11
brownfields: carrot-and-stick approach to,
    152–153; causes of, 147–151;
    definition of, 147, 255; extent of, 151;
    recommendations for, 157; recycling
    of, 142, 147, 151–152, 155–156, 251;
    remediation of, 151–152, 153–154
budget constraints, 220
building codes, 138
building oversupply, 199–200
building permits, 138

About the Lincoln Institute of Land Policy

The Lincoln Institute of Land Policy is a nonprofit, tax-exempt educational institution established in 1974 to study and teach land policy, including land economics and land taxation. The Institute is supported primarily by the Lincoln Foundation, which was established in 1947 by Cleveland industrialist John C. Lincoln. He drew inspiration from the ideas of Henry George, the nineteenth-century American political economist, social philosopher and author of the book, *Progress and Poverty*.

The Institute's goals are to integrate theory and practice to better shape land policy decisions and to share understanding about the multidisciplinary forces that influence public policy in the United States and internationally. The Institute organizes its work among three departments: valuation and taxation, planning and development, and international studies, with special programs in Latin America and China.

The Lincoln Institute seeks to improve the quality of debate and to disseminate knowledge of critical issues in land policy by bringing together scholars, policy makers, practitioners and citizens with diverse backgrounds and experience. We study, exchange insights and work toward a broader understanding of complex land and tax policies. The Institute does not take a particular point of view, but rather serves as a catalyst to facilitate analysis and discussion of these issues — to make a difference today and to help policy makers plan for tomorrow.

L Lincoln Institute of Land Policy
113 Brattle Street
Cambridge, MA 02138-3400 USA

Phone: 617-661-3016 x127 or 800-LAND-USE (800-526-3873)
Fax: 617-661-7235 or 800-LAND-944 (800-526-3944)
E-mail: *help@lincolninst.edu*
Web: *www.lincolninst.edu*